DECORATIVE TECHNIQUES

THE TIME-LIFE LIBRARY OF BOATING
HUMAN BEHAVIOR
THE ART OF SEWING
THE OLD WEST
THE EMERGENCE OF MAN
THE AMERICAN WILDERNESS
THE TIME-LIFE ENCYCLOPEDIA OF GARDENING
LIFE LIBRARY OF PHOTOGRAPHY
THIS FABULOUS CENTURY
FOODS OF THE WORLD
TIME-LIFE LIBRARY OF AMERICA
TIME-LIFE LIBRARY OF ART
GREAT AGES OF MAN
LIFE SCIENCE LIBRARY
THE LIFE HISTORY OF THE UNITED STATES
TIME READING PROGRAM
LIFE NATURE LIBRARY
LIFE WORLD LIBRARY
FAMILY LIBRARY:

    HOW THINGS WORK IN YOUR HOME
    THE TIME-LIFE BOOK OF THE FAMILY CAR
    THE TIME-LIFE FAMILY LEGAL GUIDE
    THE TIME-LIFE BOOK OF FAMILY FINANCE

TIME
LIFE
BOOKS
®

THE ART OF SEWING

DECORATIVE TECHNIQUES

BY THE EDITORS OF TIME-LIFE BOOKS

TIME-LIFE BOOKS, NEW YORK

TIME-LIFE BOOKS

FOUNDER: Henry R. Luce 1898-1967

Editor-in-Chief: Hedley Donovan
Chairman of the Board: Andrew Heiskell
President: James R. Shepley

Vice Chairman: Roy E. Larsen

MANAGING EDITOR: Jerry Korn
Assistant Managing Editors: Ezra Bowen,
David Maness, Martin Mann, A. B. C. Whipple
Planning Director: Oliver E. Allen
Art Director: Sheldon Cotler
Chief of Research: Beatrice T. Dobie
Director of Photography: Melvin L. Scott
Senior Text Editors: Diana Hirsh, William Frankel
Assistant Planning Director: Carlotta Kerwin
Assistant Art Director: Arnold C. Holeywell
Assistant Chief of Research: Myra Mangan

PUBLISHER: Joan D. Manley
General Manager: John D. McSweeney
Business Manager: John Steven Maxwell
Sales Director: Carl G. Jaeger
Promotion Director: Paul R. Stewart
Public Relations Director: Nicholas Benton

THE ART OF SEWING
EDITORIAL STAFF FOR
DECORATIVE TECHNIQUES:
Editor: Fred R. Smith
Designer: Virginia Gianakos
Assistant Designer: Elaine Zeitsoff
Text Editors: Betsy Frankel, Anne Horan,
Gerry Schremp
Chief Researcher: Wendy A. Rieder
Staff Writers: Sondra R. Albert,
Marian Gordon Goldman, Angela D. Goodman,
Susan Hillaby, Marilyn Kendig, Jill Spiller,
Sandra Streepey, Reiko Uyeshima
Research Staff: Diane Asselin, Laura James,
Mary Kay Moran, Robin Richman,
Ginger Seippel, Cinda Siler
Art Staff: Anne B. Landry (art manager),
Angela Alleyne, Penny Burnham,
Catherine Caufield, Jean Held
Editorial Assistant: Anne Gordon

EDITORIAL PRODUCTION
Production Editor: Douglas B. Graham
Assistant Production Editors:
Gennaro C. Esposito, Feliciano Madrid
Quality Director: Robert L. Young
Assistant Quality Director: James J. Cox
Associate: Serafino J. Cambareri
Copy Staff: Eleanore W. Karsten (chief),
Kathleen Beakley, Elaine Pearlmutter,
Florence Keith, Pearl Sverdlin
Picture Department: Dolores A. Littles,
Susan Hearn
Traffic: Carmen McLellan

THE CONSULTANTS:
Gretel Courtney taught for several years at the
French Fashion Academy in New York City. She
has studied patternmaking and design at the
Fashion Institute of Technology in New York and
haute couture at the French Fashion Academy.

Annette Feldman is a knitting and crocheting designer, both for clothing and interior decoration.
She is the author of several books, including *Knit,
Purl and Design; Crochet and Creative Design;*
and *Beginner's Needlecraft.*

Tracy Kendall has for many years designed sets
and costumes for commercial films and advertis-
ing. She is currently a fashion stylist.

Julian Tomchin is a textile designer who has re-
ceived the Vogue Fabric Award and a Coty
Award of the American Fashion Critics. A grad-
uate of Syracuse University's Fine Arts College,
he has been chairman of the Textile Design Department at the Shenkar College of Fashion and
Textile Technology in Tel Aviv and now teaches
at the Parsons School of Design in New York.

Valuable assistance was provided by these
departments and individuals of Time Inc.:
Editorial Production, Norman Airey; Library,
Benjamin Lightman; Picture Collection, Doris
O'Neil; Photographic Laboratory, George Karas;
TIME-LIFE News Service, Murray J. Gart;
Correspondents Ann Natanson and Deborah
Sgardello (Rome), Helga Kohl (Athens), Margot
Hapgood and Dorothy Bacon (London), Knud
Meister (Copenhagen).

CONTENTS

THE DELIGHTS
OF LAVISH
DETAIL

ear Patsy," wrote Thomas Jefferson to his schoolgirl daughter while he was American Minister to France, "In the country life of America there are many moments when a woman can have recourse to nothing but her needle for employment. In a dull company and in dull weather, for instance, it is ill manners to read, it is ill manners to leave them; no card-playing there among genteel people—that is abandoned

AN ENDURING FANCY FOR DECORATION

to blackguards. The needle is then a valuable resource."

Travel was difficult in Jefferson's day, and guests, when they came to visit, were apt to stay for a long time—reason enough to escape into needlework to relieve the tedium of boring conversations. But women also had more inspiring reasons for bending their heads over embroidery hoops, crochet work, rug-hooking frames or the plump pillows that held the paraphernalia of bobbin lace. Pride in accomplishment was one, pure joy in doing was another. And more than family need went into the bright patchwork coverlets so lovingly pieced together. For the pioneer women of the Western plains, hairpin lace and broomstick lace — produced with the aid of the homely articles for which they were named — were a means as well as an end: the product brightened the spartan surroundings while the work lifted the spirits of the doer.

Even well-to-do Victorian ladies, trapped in their crinolines and the cluttered taste of the day, delighted in their fancywork. Mornings were for utilitarian sewing, the making of shirts and underclothes. But in the afternoons gentlefolk sat in the parlor, entertaining their friends at tea, and stitched away industriously at beaded comb cases, crocheted carriage robes, needlepoint carpets, pearl-encrusted pincushions and embroidered cigar cases, faithfully following the directions printed in *Harper's Bazaar* and *Godey's Lady's Book.*

With the coming of electricity, the telephone and the motorcar, women discovered other things to do with their time, and workbaskets, embroidery hoops and beading frames went into the attic. But the skills did not die. Around the world there were women who preserved them — sometimes for pleasure, often for the livelihood they provided.

The Irish lacemaking industry, a cottage craft that involved thousands of Irish crocheters, played a major role in Ireland's recovery from the potato famine. With patterns of shamrocks and wild Irish roses, Irish lace edged the garments of no less a person than Queen Victoria, one of the lacemakers' prime supporters. Similarly, after World War II, Queen Frederika of Greece mobilized the countrywomen of her land into a cottage industry of beading, embroidery and soutache-trimming for which they had long been famous.

Encouraging rural women to revive the old techniques and apply them to modern needs and tastes is now a pattern worldwide in scope. It has reawakened interest in the time-consuming but very rewarding techniques themselves, more for adding small, special touches to personal and home accessories than for the usually tedious work of making a complete object. Young people, fascinated by examples of piecing and appliqué in big-city stores, explore the decorative effects by using the techniques to personalize everything from blue jeans to hostess dresses. The popularity of appliqué and piecework, for instance, can be traced in part to the beautiful examples produced by craftswomen still practicing ancient skills: appliqué from Panama *(page 40)*, beadwork from Europe *(page 76)*, rug hooking from America *(pages 94-95)*, smocking from America and Canada *(page 22)*, and piecework from craft groups all over North America from Alabama to Nova Scotia.

One of the best-known of these craft groups is Mountain Artisans. Founded in 1968 by a group of West Virginia women, Mountain Artisans uses piecing and quilting to decorate pillows, place mats and chair covers, as well as to make unusual hostess skirts and tennis dresses. A local artist known for her patchwork paintings provided the women with modern versions of such old patchwork favorites as Fenced Rail, Slashed Diagonal and Tumbling Blocks. To update them, she used contemporary color combinations, sometimes got her effects from contrasting textures and in one case altered a traditional pattern by changing its scale: Giant Maxigon is simply an old hexagon quilt with patches enlarged to supergraphic size.

The same goal—to find modern applications for traditional decorative techniques—inspired Nova Scotia designer Vicki Lynn Crowe to organize a similar operation. Called Suttles and Seawinds, it draws upon the talents of the wives of fishermen and farmers living around New Germany, Nova Scotia. Suttles is the local word for scraps of cloth; much of the work of Suttles and Seawinds involves patchwork. Some of the women, however, hook rugs, while others use fishermen's twine to crochet ruggedly handsome hairpin lace place mats.

When Vicki Crowe introduced her design ideas to her New Germany neighbors, they were startled. "Such bright colors," they said. In rural Nova Scotia, patchwork quilts were seen as blankets to be covered by, Crowe noted, "a Sears Roebuck chenille bedspread." They were made in pastels so the color would not show through. Today the bright quilts delight them. "This is pretty enough," they say, looking at their finished work, "to put on top of the bed."

The use of old crafts for new designs and purposes—or vice versa—has long been common practice. Although certain kinds of needlecraft are usually associated with certain finished products—piecework with bedcovers, beading with evening bags—one of the charms of decorative skills is their almost endless adaptability. In Panama and Alaska, for instance, two remote groups of artisans have at different times converted two standard techniques to suit their own ideas.

Long ago the Cuna Indians of Panama's San Blas Islands were introduced to a kind of appliqué in which layers of material are cut away—literally appliquéd in reverse. No one knows who taught the Indians the technique but it was certainly Europeans, for in pre-Columbian days the Cuna had little use for cloth or clothing. The skills may have been brought by Yankee traders or by Huguenots from France who lived there briefly. Whatever the source, reverse appliqué—as practiced by the Cuna—is a distinctively different product, drawing upon an ancient Cuna design tradition.

Since the Cuna originally wore very few clothes, they decorated themselves by painting their bodies. The tribal painters were the women, reported one 17th Century account, adding, "The colors they like and use most are red, yellow and blue, very bright and lovely," with which they made "figures of birds, beasts, men, trees or the like up and down in every part of the body." Persuaded to wear clothes, the Cuna women simply transferred their superb design sense onto cloth and decorated their garments with reverse appliqué panels in the same bright colors. They have continued the craft since, providing treasures for modern collectors and inspiration to needleworkers who adapt their technique.

Halfway around the globe, in Alaska, Eskimo women have also exploited an imported technique, applying it to a unique resource to produce perhaps the world's most exotic decorative accessories. Their material is musk-ox wool, spun from the animal's soft winter undercoat, which it sheds in spring. The Eskimos have been taught how to knit and are using musk-ox yarn to fashion scarves, stoles and tunics in a lacy openwork stitch of their own invention; it combines knitting and purling but looks like crochet. The yarn is called *qiviut;* a *qiviut* scarf can cost hundreds of dollars—a price that reflects the rarity of the material as well as the quality of the workmanship.

Though no woman can hope to add a *qiviut* scarf to her wardrobe simply by knitting it herself, she can add distinctive touches to her home or her wardrobe by using any one of the decorative techniques that brought such pleasure to her ancestors. If *qiviut* yarn is scarce, other yarns are not—nor are beads, cording, silk thread and embroidery cotton. Grandmother's scrap box—with its snippets of cloth—probably has its equivalent among the paraphernalia of contemporary home seamstresses. Putting the scraps to use—for accents rather than large-scale projects—is a way of rediscovering the charms of traditional decorative techniques without long hours of labor.

Patchwork quilts, pillows and a dazzling coverlet of animal-appliqué jigsaw blocks surround Sharon Percy Rockefeller *(left),* a sponsor of the West Virginia needlework group, Mountain Artisans. At right, Vicki

Lynn Crowe, guiding spirit of a similar Nova Scotia organization, Suttles and Seawinds, sits among an array of aprons, pillows, tote bags and quilts pieced by a traditional technique in bold modern designs.

Extra touches for home and costume

Though few women have time for the elaborate handwork projects of their grandmothers, the old techniques, used for decorative details, lend a cachet to accessories. Sometimes, as here, the nostalgia of grandmother's technique is preserved. But modern versions of traditional handwork (*following pages*) are equally fascinating.

Hairpin lace, hand-hooking, beading and Suffolk piecing decorate, respectively, an openwork place mat, a hearth rug strewn with tendriled flowers, a bead-trimmed suede vest and a ruffled pillow made of gingham.

Traditional decorative devices that produce boldly modern designs include the intricate folds of cathedral-window piecing used on a patterned pillow, and the swirling accents of passementerie braid on a sleek, head-hugging helmet. Reverse appliqué, in which successive layers of fabric are cut away and hemmed to disclose the color beneath, forms the geometric pattern of a wood-handled handbag. And accordion pleating is revived for a polka dot fabric lampshade, its permanent pleats made the modern way, with a fusible interfacing plus a coating of clear acrylic plastic laquer.

Exotic touches such as fringes and beading
make a shawl suitable for the Casbah and an
Art Nouveau bag that might have dazzled
patrons in a Toulouse-Lautrec café. Equally
unusual effects enhance a pillow's peasant-
print border and a linen napkin, which is
embroidered with a design reminiscent of one
on a Cossack's blouse and worked in a
cross-stitch that is known as counted-thread.

2
NEW WAYS WITH OLD HANDWORK

While on an expedition that stopped at Tierra del Fuego, the windy and cold southern-most tip of South America, the 19th Century naturalist Charles Darwin gave a piece of red cloth to a native whose sole protection against the bitter climate was a shield made of animal skin. Far from turning the cloth into a warm cloak, as might have been expected, the native ripped it into tiny bits, which he distrib-

TECHNIQUES THAT LEND EMBELLISHMENT

uted among his equally scantily clad companions to wear as ornaments.

To the Fuegians, as to many others, decoration has been more important than warmth in clothing or serviceability in the home. And intricate techniques for embellishing clothes, furnishings and accessories have been devised ever since men and women learned to knot and weave yarns and make a needle from a piece of bone.

The decoration may come from adding to

a basically simple garment to give it character. Both beads *(page 46)* and fringe *(page 54),* for instance, have wide and varied uses when applied to blue jeans or evening gowns; either decoration can give a look of workaday carelessness to the one or understated elegance to the other. The effect depends on whether you use beads as tough as nail studs or gemlike bits of glitter, and whether you use shredded denim or rich silken cord. Appliqué is an equally old technique, frequently used on sturdy fabrics. An interesting variation is shadow appliqué *(page 45),* using gossamer fabrics that allow the light to shine through. Shadow appliqué is especially effective on articles that billow in the breeze or shift with movement, such as scarves and curtains.

Most such decoration is ornamental and plays no role in the garment's structure. One exception is smocking, used on dresses, blouses and hats as well as pillows and lampshades *(pages 22 and 127).* It makes a design into fabric by gathering it—usually with embroidery. Smocking has the effect of changing the fabric, strengthening it and giving it a degree of elasticity. At the same time, smocking helps shape the garment it decorates.

Smocking's delicate appearance—which has made it so congenial to dainty baby dresses—belies its sturdy nature; and indeed, smocking has an earthy and utilitarian origin. It seems to have been used first on the 17th Century English farm laborer's smock frock—a voluminous, shirtlike garment that was worn with a pair of breeches. The smocking, which was done in panels, went from a neck yoke almost to the waist and gathered the sleeves just above the cuff. It served the practical purpose of containing the fullness of the garment where it had to be close fitting so it would not get in the wearer's way as he bent over the soil. The smocking also had sufficient give to permit freedom of movement for the laborer when he wielded hoe or pitchfork.

Every smocking method is worked by stitching over a grid of dots that is marked on the fabric, drawing one dot to another. In English smocking the fabric is gathered with thread in vertical rows of pleats before the design is worked. And American smocking is a variation in which the decorative stitches themselves provide the gathering. Still another variation is Canadian or lattice smocking, which does not make use of embroidery: stitches that are hidden on the underside gather the fabric in deep interlaced pleats, and the pleats themselves form the decoration for the article.

The attractiveness of smocking is exploited in a number of traditional designs *(pages 23-31).* The cable or outline stitch, which is worked in straight lines across the fabric, holds the gathers tightly and is often used at the top and bottom of an otherwise more intricate design to give it definition. The wave stitch zigzags up and down across several rows of dots and gives the smocking more elasticity than the outline stitch. These stitches, which are used in a number of combinations, form decorative patterns that have made this humbly born embellishment one of the most appealing and elegant of decorations.

Artful shaping with smocking

The ancient art of smocking is one technique that was—and occasionally still is—decorative and utilitarian. Its gathers make fabric elastic so it can be shaped without seams. Both virtues are used in this ruffle-brimmed hat and pillow (inset), made from dotted swiss and Canadian smocking. Dual purposes are also served by American smocking, taken from English smocking, in which embroidery forms a design.

CANADIAN SMOCKING

A PREPARING THE FABRIC

1. Measure the width of the pattern piece or project section you plan to smock. Then multiply by three and add 2 inches for seam allowances to determine the fabric width you need.

2. Cut out a rectangle of your fabric. Use the measurement determined in Step 1 for the crosswise dimension; for the length, add 2 inches to the measurement called for by your project instructions.

3. Straighten the edges of the rectangle and, if necessary, straighten the fabric grains (Appendix).

4. Place the fabric wrong side up on a flat surface.

5. Use a pencil and an L-shaped square to draw a grid of dots evenly spaced from 1/2 to 1 inch apart, starting an inch inside the edges of the rectangle and covering the fabric area you plan to smock. Make an odd number of dots along crosswise threads for the horizontal rows and an even number of dots along lengthwise threads for the vertical rows of the grid.

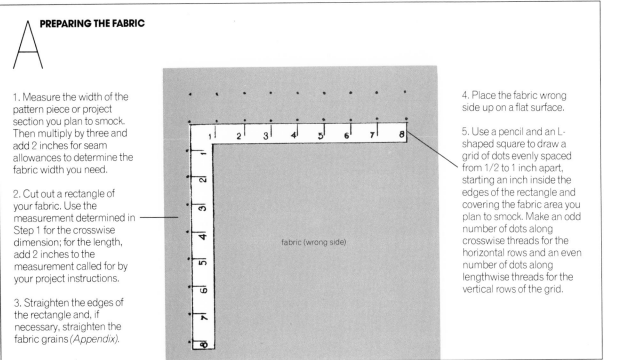

fabric (wrong side)

B STARTING THE SMOCKING

6. Thread a wide-eyed needle with heavy-duty thread and double-knot the thread end. Insert the needle into the fabric from the wrong side and make a tiny stitch under the second dot of the second vertical row. Pull the thread taut.

7. Pointing the needle to the left and holding it horizontally, make a tiny stitch underneath the first dot to the left in the row above the preceding stitch.

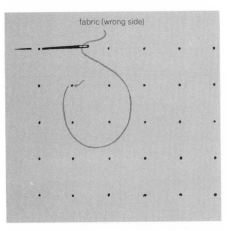

fabric (wrong side)

8. Pull the thread taut, joining the two dots. Make a tiny stitch through the two dots, leaving a small thread loop.

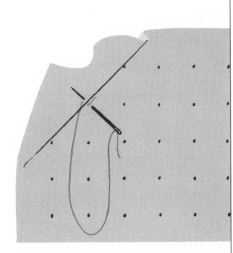

9. Insert the needle through the loop, knotting the stitch.

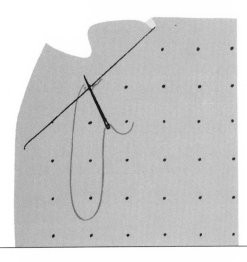

10. Pointing the needle to the left, and holding it horizontally, make a tiny stitch underneath the dot directly below the preceding stitch. Pull the thread just taut enough to lie flat against the fabric.

11. Make a second tiny stitch underneath the dot, leaving a small loop, then repeat Step 9 to knot the stitch.

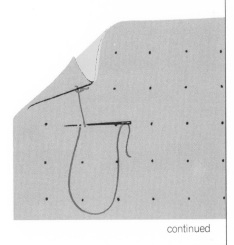

MAKING THE FIRST VERTICAL ROW OF SMOCKING

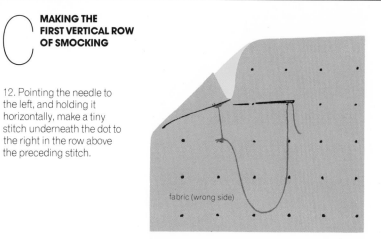

12. Pointing the needle to the left, and holding it horizontally, make a tiny stitch underneath the dot to the right in the row above the preceding stitch.

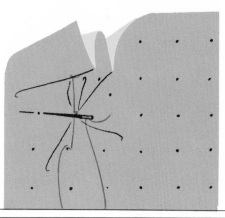

fabric (wrong side)

13. Pull the thread taut, joining the two dots stitched in Steps 10 and 12. Make a tiny stitch through the two dots, leaving a small loop, and knot the stitch.

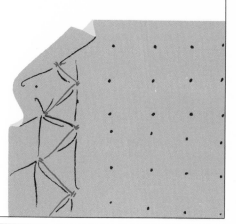

14. Pointing the needle to the left, and holding it horizontally, make a tiny stitch underneath the dot directly below the preceding stitch. Keep the thread flat against the fabric. Make another tiny stitch underneath the dot and knot.

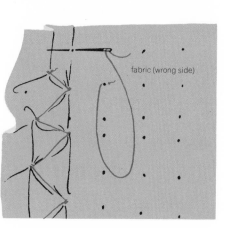

15. Repeat Steps 7-14 as many times as necessary to complete the row, ending the final sequence with Step 9. Cut the thread.

FINISHING THE SMOCKING PATTERN

16. Using a knotted thread, make a tiny stitch underneath the second dot in the adjacent vertical row to the right of the preceding row.

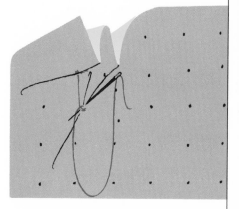

fabric (wrong side)

17. Repeat Steps 7-15 to complete the row of smocking.

18. Complete the remaining rows by following Steps 16 and 17.

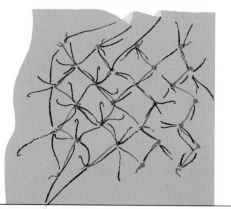

19. Pin the finished smocking to an ironing board. Holding the iron about 1/2 inch above the fabric, steam it for about 20 seconds. Do not touch the pleats directly with the iron.

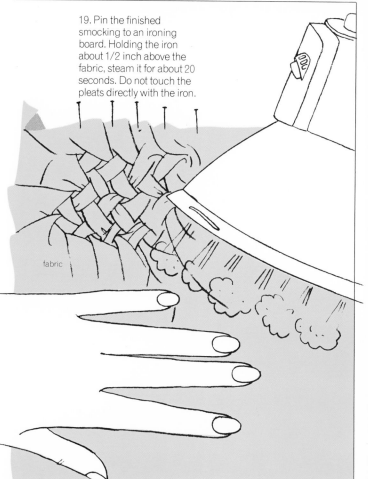

fabric

A PREPARING THE FABRIC

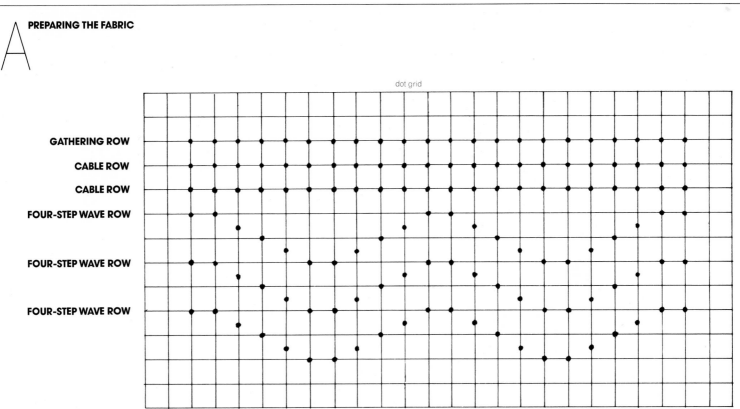

dot grid

GATHERING ROW

CABLE ROW

CABLE ROW

FOUR-STEP WAVE ROW

FOUR-STEP WAVE ROW

FOUR-STEP WAVE ROW

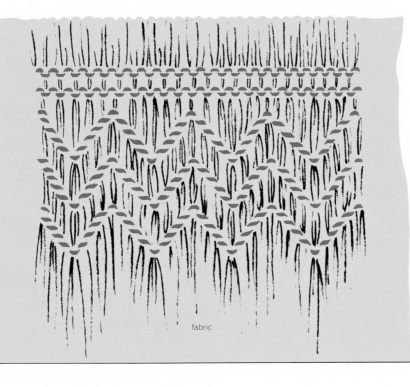

fabric

1. Cut out your fabric, following the directions for Canadian smocking *(page 23, Box A, Steps 1 and 2).* Then straighten the fabric edges and fabric grains *(Appendix).*

2. To make pattern one of American smocking *(left),* first trace the dots and all four outside lines of the grid *(above)* onto tissue paper, using a ruler if necessary to keep the rows of dots straight.

continued

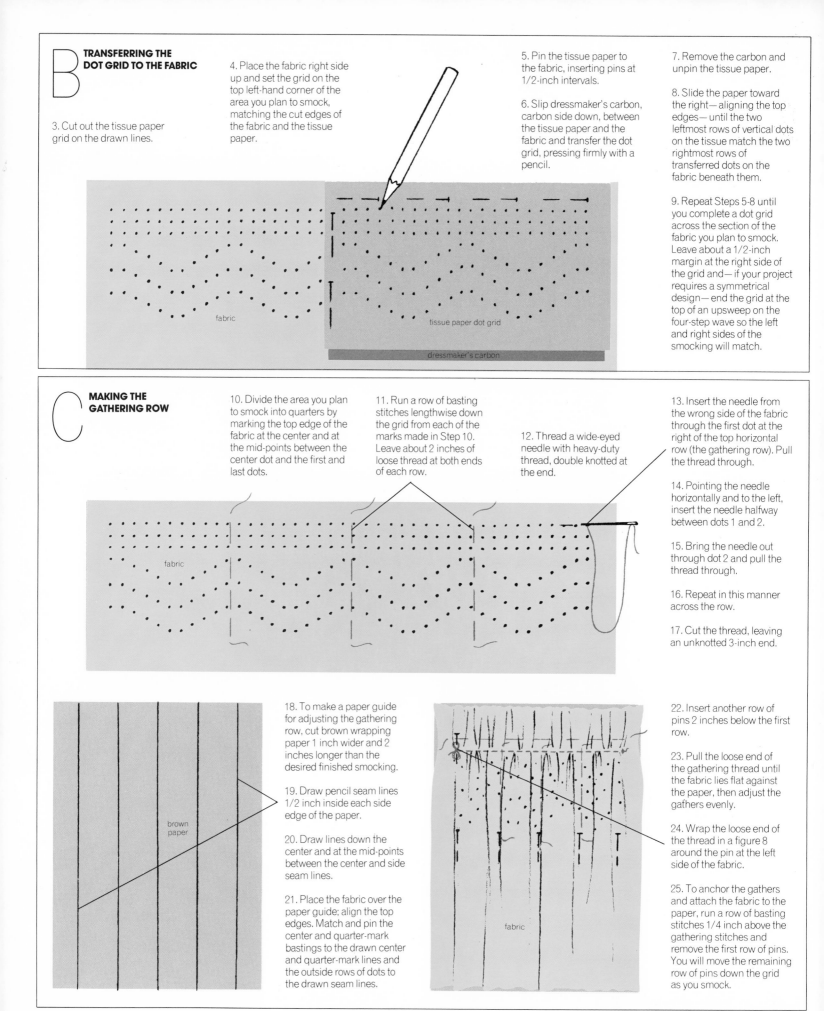

B TRANSFERRING THE DOT GRID TO THE FABRIC

3. Cut out the tissue paper grid on the drawn lines.

4. Place the fabric right side up and set the grid on the top left-hand corner of the area you plan to smock, matching the cut edges of the fabric and the tissue paper.

5. Pin the tissue paper to the fabric, inserting pins at 1/2-inch intervals.

6. Slip dressmaker's carbon, carbon side down, between the tissue paper and the fabric and transfer the dot grid, pressing firmly with a pencil.

7. Remove the carbon and unpin the tissue paper.

8. Slide the paper toward the right—aligning the top edges—until the two leftmost rows of vertical dots on the tissue match the two rightmost rows of transferred dots on the fabric beneath them.

9. Repeat Steps 5-8 until you complete a dot grid across the section of the fabric you plan to smock. Leave about a 1/2-inch margin at the right side of the grid and—if your project requires a symmetrical design—end the grid at the top of an upsweep on the four-step wave so the left and right sides of the smocking will match.

fabric

tissue paper dot grid

dressmaker's carbon

C MAKING THE GATHERING ROW

10. Divide the area you plan to smock into quarters by marking the top edge of the fabric at the center and at the mid-points between the center dot and the first and last dots.

11. Run a row of basting stitches lengthwise down the grid from each of the marks made in Step 10. Leave about 2 inches of loose thread at both ends of each row.

12. Thread a wide-eyed needle with heavy-duty thread, double knotted at the end.

13. Insert the needle from the wrong side of the fabric through the first dot at the right of the top horizontal row (the gathering row). Pull the thread through.

14. Pointing the needle horizontally and to the left, insert the needle halfway between dots 1 and 2.

15. Bring the needle out through dot 2 and pull the thread through.

16. Repeat in this manner across the row.

17. Cut the thread, leaving an unknotted 3-inch end.

fabric

18. To make a paper guide for adjusting the gathering row, cut brown wrapping paper 1 inch wider and 2 inches longer than the desired finished smocking.

19. Draw pencil seam lines 1/2 inch inside each side edge of the paper.

20. Draw lines down the center and at the mid-points between the center and side seam lines.

21. Place the fabric over the paper guide; align the top edges. Match and pin the center and quarter-mark bastings to the drawn center and quarter-mark lines and the outside rows of dots to the drawn seam lines.

brown paper

22. Insert another row of pins 2 inches below the first row.

23. Pull the loose end of the gathering thread until the fabric lies flat against the paper, then adjust the gathers evenly.

24. Wrap the loose end of the thread in a figure 8 around the pin at the left side of the fabric.

25. To anchor the gathers and attach the fabric to the paper, run a row of basting stitches 1/4 inch above the gathering stitches and remove the first row of pins. You will move the remaining row of pins down the grid as you smock.

fabric

MAKING THE CABLE ROWS

26. Spread out the top left-hand corner of the grid so you can see the pencil dots on the fabric. To clarify the stitches demonstrated in the step-by-step illustrations beginning with Step 28, the first group of dots is numbered and shown against a flat surface. Do not write numbers on your fabric.

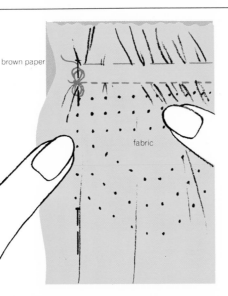

brown paper

fabric

27. Thread an embroidery needle with Size 3 or 5 pearl cotton or six-strand embroidery thread and knot the end.

28. Insert the needle into the fabric from the wrong side to the left of dot 2, the second dot from the left-hand side of the grid. Pull the thread through.

29. Pointing the needle to the left and holding it horizontally, insert the needle into the fabric, halfway between dots 2 and 1. Then bring the needle out through dot 1.

30. Pull the thread through.

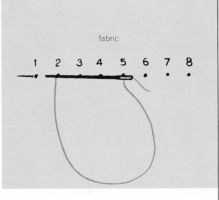

fabric

31. Insert the needle into the fabric, halfway between dots 2 and 3, keeping the thread above the needle as shown.

32. Bring the needle out through dot 2.

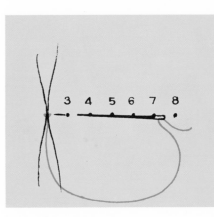

33. Pull the thread through and down toward the bottom of the grid.

34. Insert the needle into the fabric, halfway between the next pair of adjacent dots. Keep the thread below the needle as shown.

35. Bring the needle out through the left-hand dot of the pair.

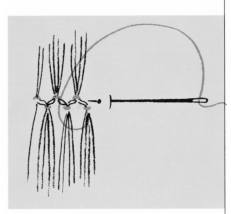

36. Pull the thread through and up toward the top of the fabric.

37. Repeat across the row, inserting the needle halfway between each successive pair of adjacent dots and bring it out through the left-hand dot of the pair. Be sure to alternate keeping the thread above or below the needle and pulling the thread down or up with every other stitch.

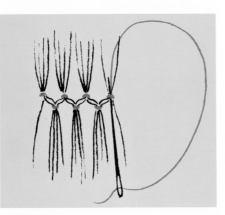

38. Pointing the needle to the left and holding it horizontally, insert the needle into the fabric, just to the right of the last dot at the right-hand side of the grid.

39. Bring the needle up through the dot. Be sure to keep the thread above or below the needle, depending on the stitch used on the row.

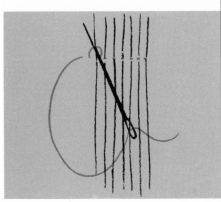

40. Insert the needle between the last two pleats on the left. Push the needle through to the wrong side of the fabric and pull the thread through.

41. Turn the fabric to the wrong side.

42. Insert the needle through the first pleat on the left. Pull the thread through, leaving a small loop.

43. Insert the needle into the loop and pull the loop tight to knot the thread. Cut off the excess thread.

44. Repeat Steps 27-43 to make the second cable row.

continued

45. Thread an embroidery needle with Size 3 or 5 pearl cotton or six-strand embroidery thread and knot the end. Insert the needle into the fabric from the wrong side just to the left of dot 2. Pull the thread through.

46. Pointing the needle to the left and holding it horizontally, insert the needle halfway between dots 2 and 1. Bring the needle up through dot 1.

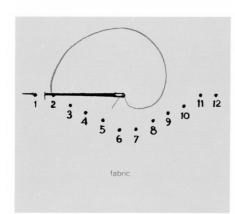

fabric

47. Insert the needle through the fabric halfway between dots 2 and 3, but on the same horizontal level as dot 2. Keep the thread above the needle as shown.

48. Bring the needle out through dot 2.

49. Pull the thread through and down toward the bottom of the grid.

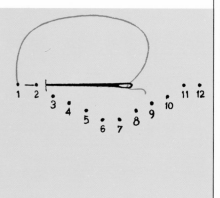

50. Pick up dots 3, 4 and 5 similarly by following the instructions in Steps 47-49 for the second dot.

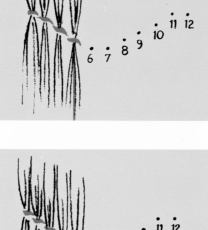

51. Insert the needle through the fabric halfway between dots 6 and 7. Keep the thread above the needle as shown.

52. Bring the needle out through dot 6. Then pull the thread through and down toward the bottom of the fabric.

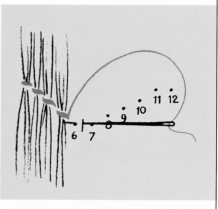

53. Insert the needle through the fabric halfway between dots 7 and 8, but on the same horizontal level as dot 7. Keep the thread below the needle as shown.

54. Bring the needle out through dot 7. Then pull the thread through and up toward the top of the fabric.

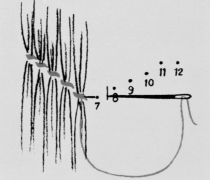

55. Pick up dots 8, 9 and 10 similarly by following the instructions in Steps 53 and 54.

56. Insert the needle through the fabric halfway between dots 11 and 12. Keep the thread below the needle as shown.

57. Bring the needle out through dot 11. Then pull the thread through and up toward the top of the fabric.

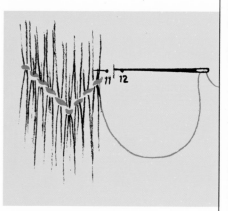

58. Repeat across the row, following the instructions in Steps 47-57 for each pair of adjacent dots.

59. End the four-step wave row by following the instructions for the cable row *(page 27, Box D, Steps 38-43)*.

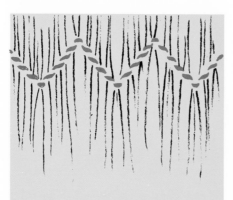

60. Repeat Steps 45-59 for the second and third four-step wave rows. Move down the pins inserted in Step 22 an inch or so if needed.

61. Remove the pins as well as the basting stitches made in Step 11 and the gathering row made in Steps 13-17.

62. Steam the smocking, following the instructions for Canadian smocking *(page 24, Box D, Step 19)*.

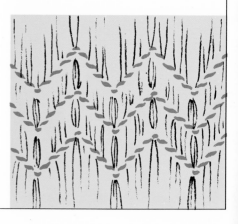

A PREPARING THE FABRIC

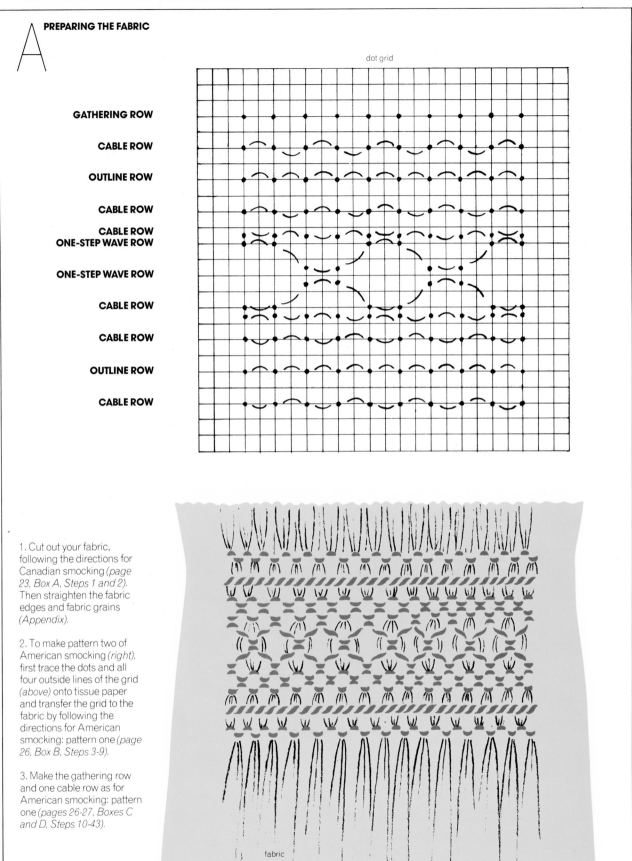

dot grid

GATHERING ROW

CABLE ROW

OUTLINE ROW

CABLE ROW

CABLE ROW
ONE-STEP WAVE ROW

ONE-STEP WAVE ROW

CABLE ROW

CABLE ROW

OUTLINE ROW

CABLE ROW

fabric

1. Cut out your fabric, following the directions for Canadian smocking (*page 23, Box A, Steps 1 and 2*). Then straighten the fabric edges and fabric grains (*Appendix*).

2. To make pattern two of American smocking (*right*), first trace the dots and all four outside lines of the grid (*above*) onto tissue paper and transfer the grid to the fabric by following the directions for American smocking: pattern one (*page 26, Box B, Steps 3-9*).

3. Make the gathering row and one cable row as for American smocking: pattern one (*pages 26-27, Boxes C and D, Steps 10-43*).

continued

B MAKING THE OUTLINE ROW

4. Thread an embroidery needle with Size 3 or 5 pearl cotton or six-strand embroidery thread; knot one end.

5. Insert the needle into the fabric from the wrong side, just to the left of dot 2 — the second dot from the left-hand side of the grid. Pull the thread through.

6. Point the needle to the left and hold it horizontally; insert it halfway between dots 2 and 1.

7. Bring the needle out through dot 1 and pull the thread through.

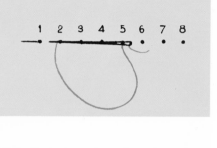

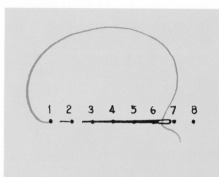

8. Pointing the needle to the left and holding it horizontally, insert the needle through the fabric halfway between the next dots, 2 and 3. Keep the thread above the needle as shown.

9. Bring the needle out through dot 2.

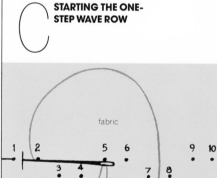

10. Pull the thread through and down toward the bottom of the fabric.

11. Repeat across the row, inserting the needle midway between pairs of adjacent dots and bringing it out through the left-hand dot of each pair. Be sure to keep the thread above the needle and pull the thread down after each stitch.

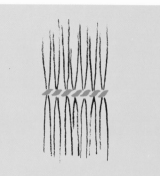

12. To end the row, follow the instructions for the cable row (page 27, Box D, Steps 38-43).

13. Make the second and third cable rows as the first; on the third, reverse the thread position and the direction you pull it after each stitch.

14. Move the pins holding the fabric to the paper down an inch.

C STARTING THE ONE-STEP WAVE ROW

15. Thread an embroidery needle with Size 3 or 5 pearl cotton thread or six-strand embroidery thread; knot one end.

16. Insert the needle into the fabric from the wrong side, just to the left of dot 2. Pull the thread through.

17. Pointing the needle to the left and holding it horizontally, insert the needle halfway between dots 2 and 1.

18. Bring the needle up through dot 1 and pull the thread through.

19. Insert the needle through the fabric, halfway between dots 2 and 3, but on the same horizontal level as dot 2. Keep the thread above the needle as shown.

20. Bring the needle out through dot 2.

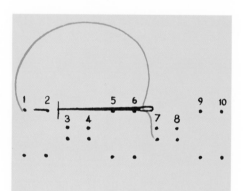

21. Pull the thread through and down toward the bottom of the fabric.

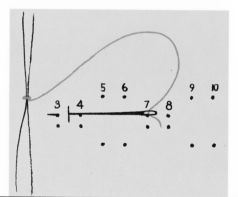

22. Insert the needle through the fabric halfway between dots 3 and 4. Keep the thread above the needle as shown.

23. Bring the needle out through dot 3, pulling the thread through and downward.

D | COMPLETING THE ONE-STEP WAVE ROW

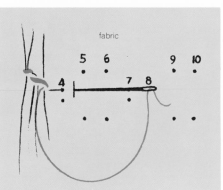

24. Insert the needle through the fabric, halfway between dots 4 and 5, but on the same horizontal level as dot 4. Keep the thread below the needle.

25. Bring the needle out through dot 4.

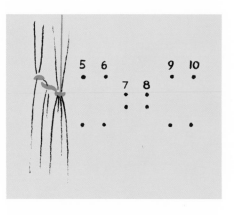

26. Pull the thread through and up toward the top of the fabric.

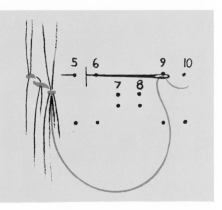

27. Insert the needle through the fabric halfway between dots 5 and 6. Keep the thread below the needle.

28. Bring the needle out through dot 5, then pull the thread through and upward.

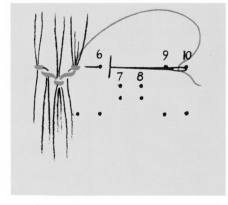

29. Insert the needle through the fabric halfway between dots 6 and 7, but on the same horizontal level as dot 6. Keep the thread above the needle.

30. Bring the needle out through dot 6, then pull the thread through and downward.

31. Repeat across the row, following the instructions in Steps 22-30 for each pair of adjacent dots.

32. End the row, following the instructions for the cable row *(page 27, Box D, Steps 38-43)*.

E | FINISHING THE SMOCKING

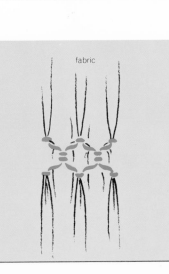

33. To make the second one-step wave row, repeat Steps 15-32, but reverse the position in which you keep the thread and the direction in which you pull it after each stitch.

34. Make the fourth cable row identical to the first *(Step 3)*, the second outline row identical to the first *(Steps 4-12)*, the fifth cable row identical to the third *(Step 13)* and the sixth identical to the first. Move the pins holding the fabric to the paper down the grid if needed.

35. Remove the pins, the basting stitches and the gathering row.

36. Steam the smocking, following the instructions for Canadian smocking *(page 24, Box D, Step 19)*.

Mosaics made from patchworks

Folded into miniature envelopes, the network of patches in the vest and place mat here began as myriad scraps of fabric, each one seamed and shaped so none of its raw edges show. The envelopes were then tacked together, providing their own lining and requiring no further finishing. Two other types of dimensional patchwork—Suffolk-work and cathedral-window *(pages 35-38)*—can be used the same way to make decorative accessories.

Because none of these patchwork fabrics can be gathered successfully or seamed except along their edges, only very simple shapes can be made from them. For instructions on adapting commercial patterns to patchwork fabrics, see page 39.

ENVELOPE PATCHWORK

A | MAKING THE PATTERN

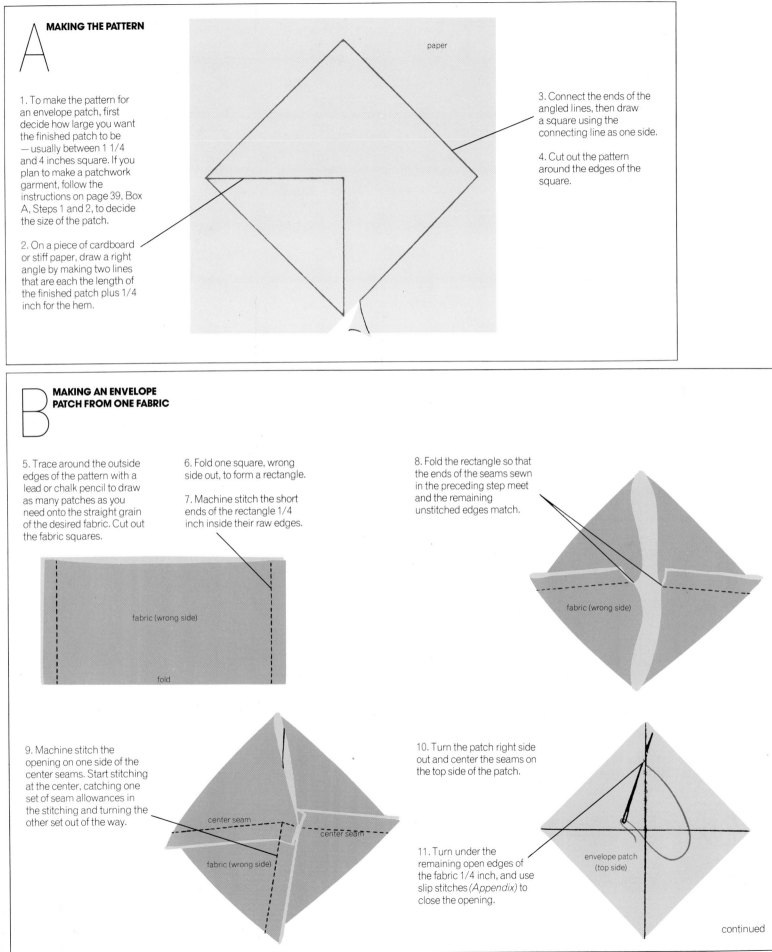

1. To make the pattern for an envelope patch, first decide how large you want the finished patch to be — usually between 1 1/4 and 4 inches square. If you plan to make a patchwork garment, follow the instructions on page 39, Box A, Steps 1 and 2, to decide the size of the patch.

2. On a piece of cardboard or stiff paper, draw a right angle by making two lines that are each the length of the finished patch plus 1/4 inch for the hem.

paper

3. Connect the ends of the angled lines, then draw a square using the connecting line as one side.

4. Cut out the pattern around the edges of the square.

B | MAKING AN ENVELOPE PATCH FROM ONE FABRIC

5. Trace around the outside edges of the pattern with a lead or chalk pencil to draw as many patches as you need onto the straight grain of the desired fabric. Cut out the fabric squares.

6. Fold one square, wrong side out, to form a rectangle.

7. Machine stitch the short ends of the rectangle 1/4 inch inside their raw edges.

8. Fold the rectangle so that the ends of the seams sewn in the preceding step meet and the remaining unstitched edges match.

fabric (wrong side)

fold

fabric (wrong side)

9. Machine stitch the opening on one side of the center seams. Start stitching at the center, catching one set of seam allowances in the stitching and turning the other set out of the way.

center seam

center seam

fabric (wrong side)

10. Turn the patch right side out and center the seams on the top side of the patch.

11. Turn under the remaining open edges of the fabric 1/4 inch, and use slip stitches (Appendix) to close the opening.

envelope patch (top side)

continued

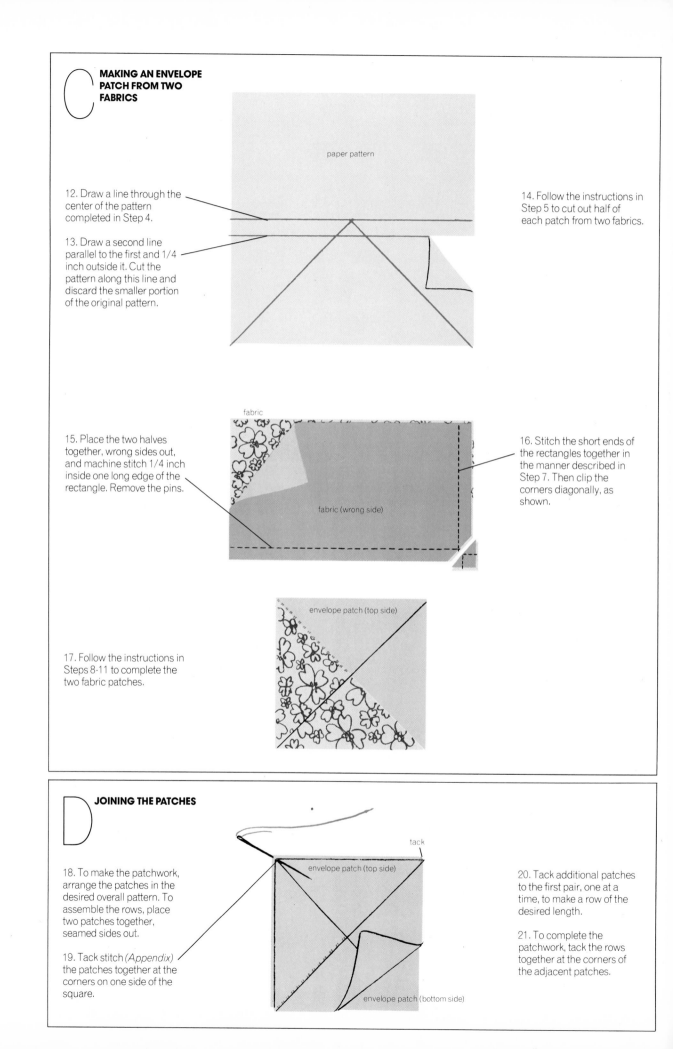

C MAKING AN ENVELOPE PATCH FROM TWO FABRICS

paper pattern

12. Draw a line through the center of the pattern completed in Step 4.

13. Draw a second line parallel to the first and 1/4 inch outside it. Cut the pattern along this line and discard the smaller portion of the original pattern.

14. Follow the instructions in Step 5 to cut out half of each patch from two fabrics.

fabric

15. Place the two halves together, wrong sides out, and machine stitch 1/4 inch inside one long edge of the rectangle. Remove the pins.

fabric (wrong side)

16. Stitch the short ends of the rectangles together in the manner described in Step 7. Then clip the corners diagonally, as shown.

17. Follow the instructions in Steps 8-11 to complete the two fabric patches.

envelope patch (top side)

D JOINING THE PATCHES

tack

18. To make the patchwork, arrange the patches in the desired overall pattern. To assemble the rows, place two patches together, seamed sides out.

19. Tack stitch (Appendix) the patches together at the corners on one side of the square.

envelope patch (top side)

envelope patch (bottom side)

20. Tack additional patches to the first pair, one at a time, to make a row of the desired length.

21. To complete the patchwork, tack the rows together at the corners of the adjacent patches.

CATHEDRAL WINDOW PATCHWORK

A MAKING A BACKGROUND PATCH

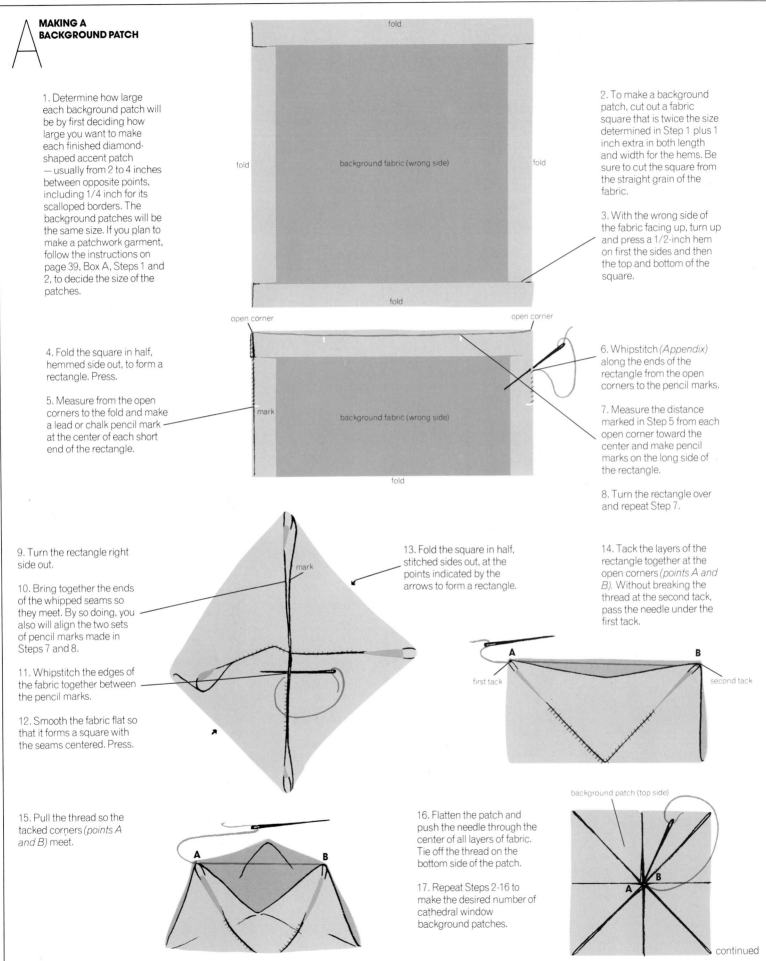

1. Determine how large each background patch will be by first deciding how large you want to make each finished diamond-shaped accent patch — usually from 2 to 4 inches between opposite points, including 1/4 inch for its scalloped borders. The background patches will be the same size. If you plan to make a patchwork garment, follow the instructions on page 39, Box A, Steps 1 and 2, to decide the size of the patches.

2. To make a background patch, cut out a fabric square that is twice the size determined in Step 1 plus 1 inch extra in both length and width for the hems. Be sure to cut the square from the straight grain of the fabric.

3. With the wrong side of the fabric facing up, turn up and press a 1/2-inch hem on first the sides and then the top and bottom of the square.

4. Fold the square in half, hemmed side out, to form a rectangle. Press.

5. Measure from the open corners to the fold and make a lead or chalk pencil mark at the center of each short end of the rectangle.

6. Whipstitch (*Appendix*) along the ends of the rectangle from the open corners to the pencil marks.

7. Measure the distance marked in Step 5 from each open corner toward the center and make pencil marks on the long side of the rectangle.

8. Turn the rectangle over and repeat Step 7.

9. Turn the rectangle right side out.

10. Bring together the ends of the whipped seams so they meet. By so doing, you also will align the two sets of pencil marks made in Steps 7 and 8.

11. Whipstitch the edges of the fabric together between the pencil marks.

12. Smooth the fabric flat so that it forms a square with the seams centered. Press.

13. Fold the square in half, stitched sides out, at the points indicated by the arrows to form a rectangle.

14. Tack the layers of the rectangle together at the open corners (*points A and B*). Without breaking the thread at the second tack, pass the needle under the first tack.

15. Pull the thread so the tacked corners (*points A and B*) meet.

16. Flatten the patch and push the needle through the center of all layers of fabric. Tie off the thread on the bottom side of the patch.

17. Repeat Steps 2-16 to make the desired number of cathedral window background patches.

continued

B | JOINING BACKGROUND PATCHES

18. Place two background patches together, bottom sides out.

19. Whipstitch the patches together along one edge.

20. Whipstitch additional patches to the first pair, one at a time, to make a row of the desired length. Then whipstitch the rows together until the entire background is complete.

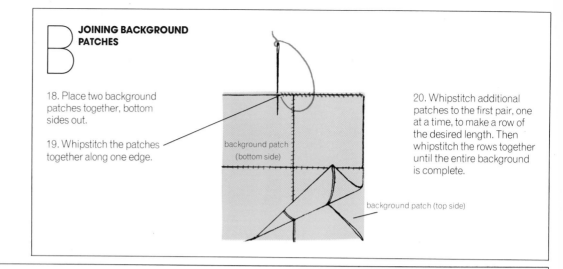

background patch (bottom side)

background patch (top side)

C | ADDING THE ACCENT PATCHES

accent patch

background patch

21. To make a cathedral window accent patch, cut a square 1/4 inch smaller than a finished background patch from the straight grain of the fabric.

22. Place the accent patch square on the seam between two background patches, set at an angle so it forms a diamond. Pin.

23. Fold the adjacent edge of background fabric over one raw edge of the accent patch and shape the background patch fabric into a scallop 1/4 inch deep at the center and tapering to nothing at the points of the diamond. Pin. Repeat on the remaining edges of the accent patches.

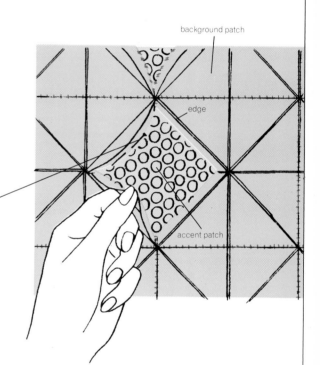

background patch

edge

accent patch

24. Slip stitch (Appendix) the scalloped border in place, removing the pins as you go. At the points, stitch the adjacent edges of the border together.

25. Repeat Steps 21-24 to cover each seam between the background patches with accent patches.

26. If desired, you can scallop the half diamonds around the completed patchwork by turning over the edges and slip-stitching them to resemble the accent patch borders.

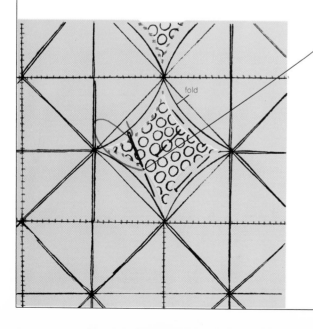

fold

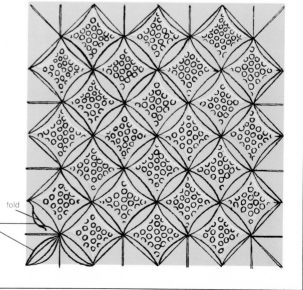

fold

SUFFOLK WORK

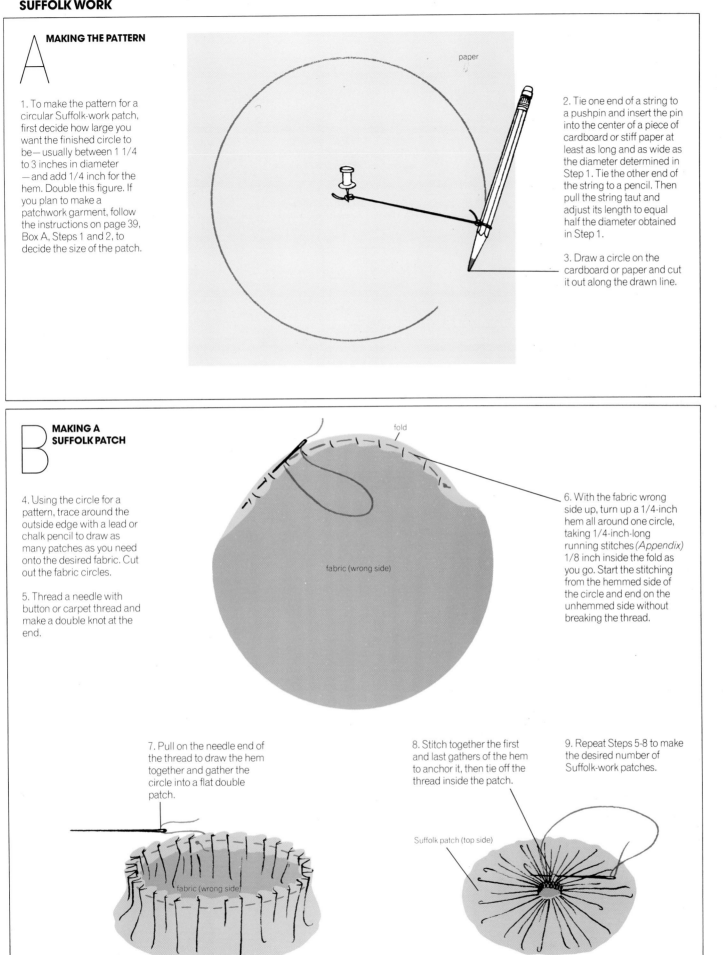

A ▸ MAKING THE PATTERN

1. To make the pattern for a circular Suffolk-work patch, first decide how large you want the finished circle to be—usually between 1 1/4 to 3 inches in diameter—and add 1/4 inch for the hem. Double this figure. If you plan to make a patchwork garment, follow the instructions on page 39, Box A, Steps 1 and 2, to decide the size of the patch.

2. Tie one end of a string to a pushpin and insert the pin into the center of a piece of cardboard or stiff paper at least as long and as wide as the diameter determined in Step 1. Tie the other end of the string to a pencil. Then pull the string taut and adjust its length to equal half the diameter obtained in Step 1.

3. Draw a circle on the cardboard or paper and cut it out along the drawn line.

paper

B ▸ MAKING A SUFFOLK PATCH

4. Using the circle for a pattern, trace around the outside edge with a lead or chalk pencil to draw as many patches as you need onto the desired fabric. Cut out the fabric circles.

5. Thread a needle with button or carpet thread and make a double knot at the end.

6. With the fabric wrong side up, turn up a 1/4-inch hem all around one circle, taking 1/4-inch-long running stitches (Appendix) 1/8 inch inside the fold as you go. Start the stitching from the hemmed side of the circle and end on the unhemmed side without breaking the thread.

fold

fabric (wrong side)

7. Pull on the needle end of the thread to draw the hem together and gather the circle into a flat double patch.

fabric (wrong side)

8. Stitch together the first and last gathers of the hem to anchor it, then tie off the thread inside the patch.

Suffolk patch (top side)

9. Repeat Steps 5-8 to make the desired number of Suffolk-work patches.

continued

C JOINING PATCHES INTO ROWS

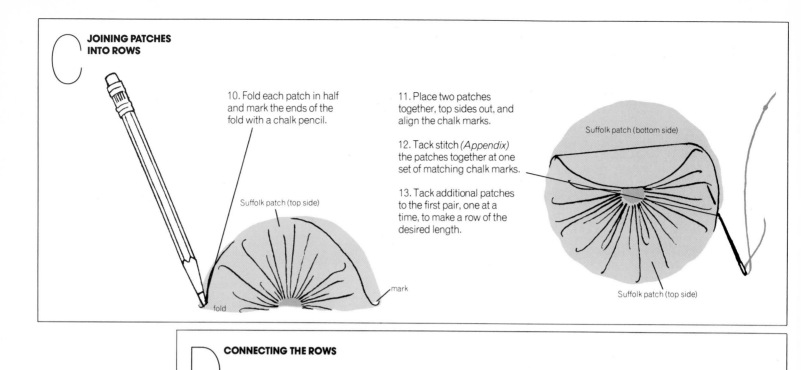

10. Fold each patch in half and mark the ends of the fold with a chalk pencil.

11. Place two patches together, top sides out, and align the chalk marks.

12. Tack stitch *(Appendix)* the patches together at one set of matching chalk marks.

13. Tack additional patches to the first pair, one at a time, to make a row of the desired length.

Suffolk patch (top side)

Suffolk patch (bottom side)

Suffolk patch (top side)

fold

mark

D CONNECTING THE ROWS

14. To make even rows of connecting patches, match the bottom center of each patch on one row with the top center of each patch on the adjacent row. Tack the rows together where the patches meet.

15. To make half-drop rows with staggered side edges, fit the upper edges of each patch in one row into the spaces between the bottom edges of each patch in the adjacent row. Tack the rows together where the patches meet.

MAKING A PATTERN FOR A FOLDED PATCHWORK GARMENT

A DETERMINING THE SIZE OF THE PATCH

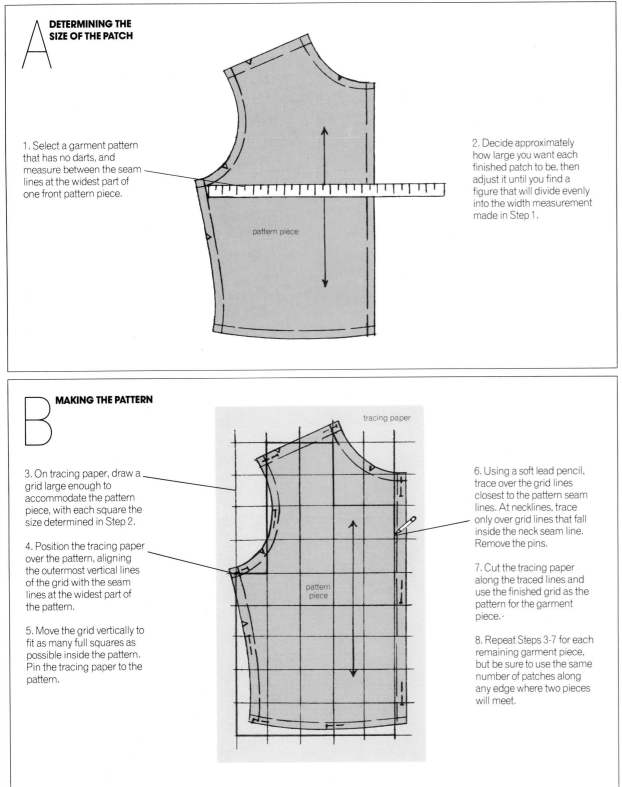

1. Select a garment pattern that has no darts, and measure between the seam lines at the widest part of one front pattern piece.

2. Decide approximately how large you want each finished patch to be, then adjust it until you find a figure that will divide evenly into the width measurement made in Step 1.

B MAKING THE PATTERN

3. On tracing paper, draw a grid large enough to accommodate the pattern piece, with each square the size determined in Step 2.

4. Position the tracing paper over the pattern, aligning the outermost vertical lines of the grid with the seam lines at the widest part of the pattern.

5. Move the grid vertically to fit as many full squares as possible inside the pattern. Pin the tracing paper to the pattern.

6. Using a soft lead pencil, trace over the grid lines closest to the pattern seam lines. At necklines, trace only over grid lines that fall inside the neck seam line. Remove the pins.

7. Cut the tracing paper along the traced lines and use the finished grid as the pattern for the garment piece. ·

8. Repeat Steps 3-7 for each remaining garment piece, but be sure to use the same number of patches along any edge where two pieces will meet.

Designing with colorful cutouts

Appliqué is collage with fabric—designs or pictures are formed by applying cutout shapes of fabric on top of a fabric surface. Shadow appliqué uses tissue-thin fabric cutouts to build up a spectrum of see-through color changes. Reverse appliqué is a decorative variation of the build-up process. Layers of fabric are stitched together; the design is then revealed by the process of cutting through the successive multicolored layers, as in the apron and chair seat pictured here.

REVERSE APPLIQUÉ

A | MAKING THE DESIGN

1. Sketch the outside lines of the large motifs you wish to use for the appliqué onto paper or transfer them onto paper *(Appendix)*. Be sure that adjacent lines are at least 1/2 inch apart.

2. To create a frame of fabric around the motifs, draw a border of the desired size and shape outside the design. Cut off the paper around the border.

B | PREPARING THE FABRIC FOR THE APPLIQUÉ

3. To determine how many layers of fabric you can use, draw one appliqué motif on scrap paper and sketch in different numbers of layers of various widths. You will need at least three or four layers of solid-colored, broadcloth-weight cotton to give the effect of depth, but you may use as many as six or seven.

4. Cut as many layers of fabric as you need, leaving 5/8 inch for seam allowances around the outside edges of the design pattern.

5. Place the fabric layers wrong side down on a flat surface, arranging them in the sequence you desire. Usually the lightest, or weakest, color is on the bottom in the finished work, and the darkest, or strongest, color is on the top. This sequence prevents the cutaway and turned-under edges from showing through as shadows.

C | MARKING THE DESIGN ON THE FABRIC

6. Lift off the top layer of fabric and transfer the drawn design to it with dressmaker's carbon and a tracing wheel. Remove the paper and the carbon.

D | SECURING THE FABRIC LAYERS

7. Press each fabric section, then rearrange the sections in sequence, matching the raw edges. Pin the sections together.

8. Make sure all of the layers are smooth, then baste 1/4 inch inside the edges through all layers of fabric. Remove the pins.

9. Baste around the outline of the design, sewing 1/4 inch outside the tracing wheel markings.

10. Baste 1/4 inch from the tracing wheel markings along any interior areas of the design where the top layer of fabric will remain — in this case, the spokes radiating from the center of the hexagon.

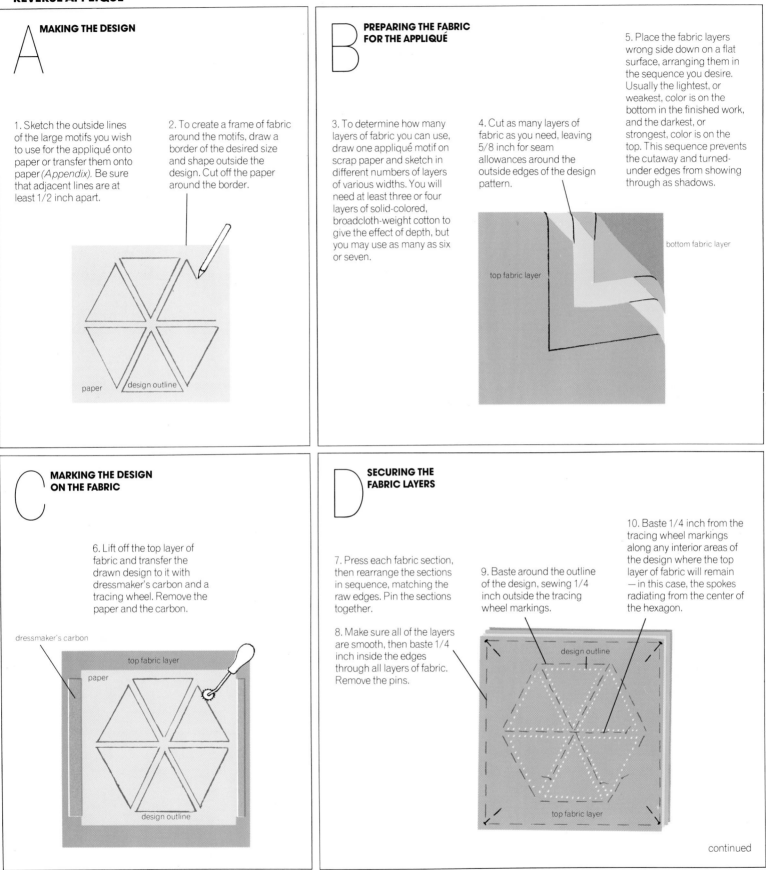

continued

11. To draw the cutting lines for one motif of the design, first make a mark 1/4 inch inside the design lines at each corner or angle of the motif, using a pencil or chalk—whichever shows up better on your fabric.

12. Using a ruler, draw lines to connect the marks made in the preceding step.

13. Repeat Steps 11 and 12 to draw cutting lines on all other motifs of the designs.

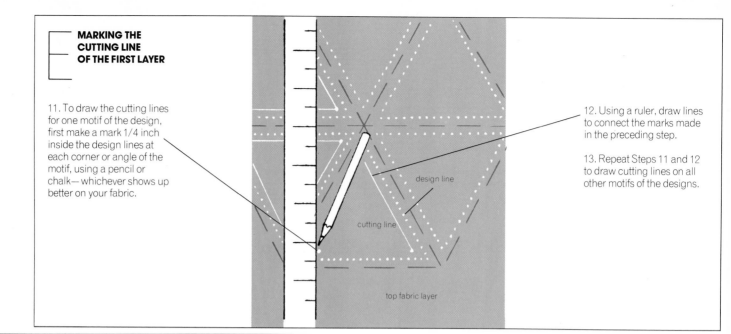

design line

cutting line

top fabric layer

CUTTING AWAY THE FIRST FABRIC LAYER

14. Working on one motif only, pinch the top layer of fabric between your fingers at the center of the motif. Roll the fabric with your fingers and pull it away from the underneath layers. Check carefully to see that all underneath layers are free.

15. Use sharp-pointed embroidery scissors to make a 1/4-inch clip into the top layer where it is pulled away from the fabric underneath.

16. Insert the scissors into the clip and—making sure you are cutting only the top layer of fabric—cut up to one of the cutting lines drawn in Steps 11 and 12.

17. Carefully cut away the design motif from the top layer of fabric along each cutting line.

18. Remove the fabric you have cut away to reveal the second layer underneath.

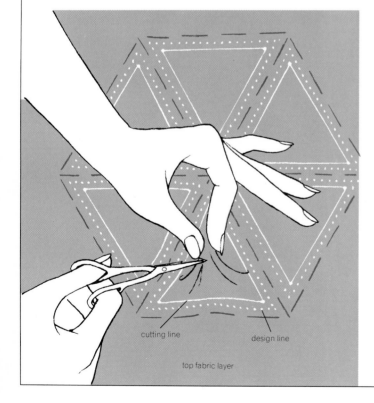

cutting line   design line

top fabric layer

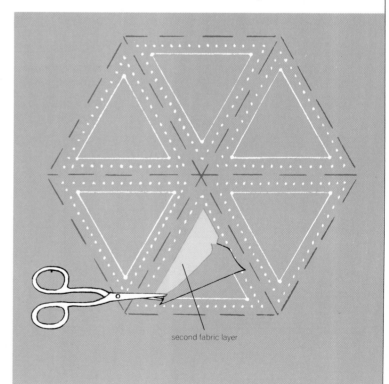

second fabric layer

G | CLIPPING AND TURNING UNDER THE FIRST LAYER

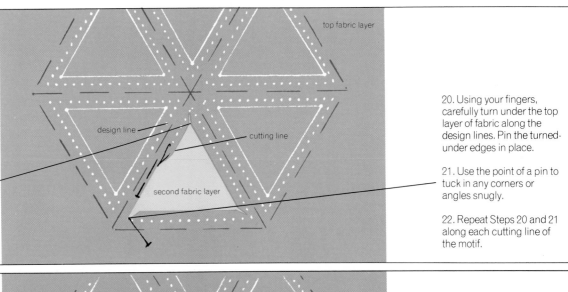

19. Clip into any corners or angles of the motif to within 1/16 inch of the design line. If you have chosen a curved design, make tiny V-shaped notches along any convex curves and clip into the fabric along any concave curves, cutting to within 1/16 inch of the design lines.

20. Using your fingers, carefully turn under the top layer of fabric along the design lines. Pin the turned-under edges in place.

21. Use the point of a pin to tuck in any corners or angles snugly.

22. Repeat Steps 20 and 21 along each cutting line of the motif.

H | STITCHING THE FIRST LAYER

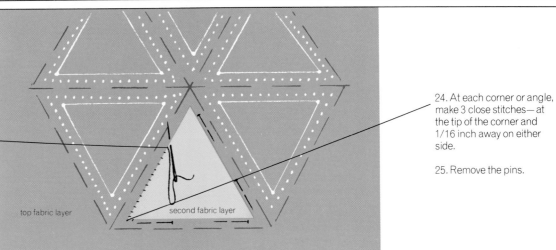

23. Secure the turned-under edges of the first layer by making tiny hemming stitches *(Appendix)* about 1/4 inch apart. For a decorative effect, use contrasting color thread, or matching thread if you wish the stitches to be invisible.

24. At each corner or angle, make 3 close stitches—at the tip of the corner and 1/16 inch away on either side.

25. Remove the pins.

WORKING THE SECOND LAYER OF FABRIC

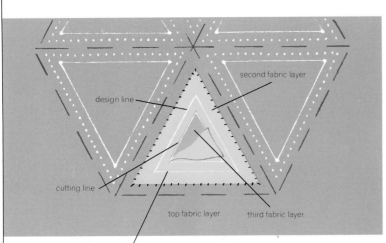

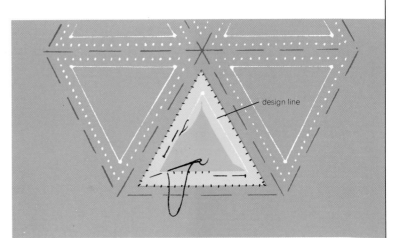

26. Determine how wide you wish the band of color to be on the second layer. Then draw a new design line on the second layer the desired distance in from the stitched edge of the first layer.

27. Repeat Steps 11 and 12 to draw the cutting lines for this layer and Steps 14-18 to trim away the second layer, exposing the third layer underneath.

28. Repeat Steps 19-25 to clip, turn under and stitch down the free edges of the second layer of fabric. Be sure to carefully tuck in each corner with the tip of a pin and to make the 3 close stitches at each corner to hold it firmly in place.

continued

29. If you are using three layers of fabric, skip to Step 31.

30. If you are using more than three layers of fabric, repeat Steps 26-28 on each of the successive layers until you have exposed the bottom fabric of the appliqué.

31. Repeat Steps 14-28 on each of the remaining individual motifs within the overall appliqué design.

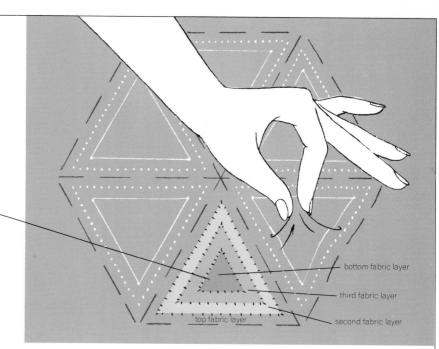

bottom fabric layer

third fabric layer

top fabric layer

second fabric layer

32. Remove the bastings around the design outline made in Steps 9 and 10, but leave in the bastings around the outside edges of the border made in Step 8 until you have assembled the appliqué with other parts of the project.

33. Press the finished appliqué on the wrong side of the fabric.

SHADOW APPLIQUÉ

A MAKING AND TRACING THE DESIGN

1. Sketch the design you wish to use onto paper or transfer it onto paper (*Appendix*).

2. Using a lightweight, transparent fabric such as organza or chiffon, cut a piece large enough to accommodate the design.

3. Place the fabric over the design and tape it in place.

4. Using a soft lead pencil, carefully trace the outline of the design onto the fabric. Remove the fabric from the paper.

5. Cut out the design carefully along the outline.

6. Repeat Steps 2-5 for each fabric you plan to use. You may want to experiment by overlapping different colors in various ways to see what effects you can create before you choose your final colors.

B ARRANGING THE MOTIFS

7. Again using lightweight, transparent fabric, this time in white or a very light color, cut out a background of the size and shape required for your project.

8. Arrange the design motifs on the background fabric as desired.

C APPLIQUÉING THE MOTIFS

9. When all of the motifs have been arranged to your satisfaction, use silk pins to secure them in place.

10. Baste 1/4 inch inside the perimeter of each group of motifs—and the edges of any solitary one—to hold them to the background fabric. Remove the pins.

11. Using an embroidery needle and matching or contrasting colored thread, attach the motifs with tiny buttonhole stitches (*Appendix*) spaced 1/8 inch apart.

12. Make buttonhole stitches directly over the overlaps of each motif to keep the edges from fraying and to clearly define the outline of each motif.

13. Remove the bastings.

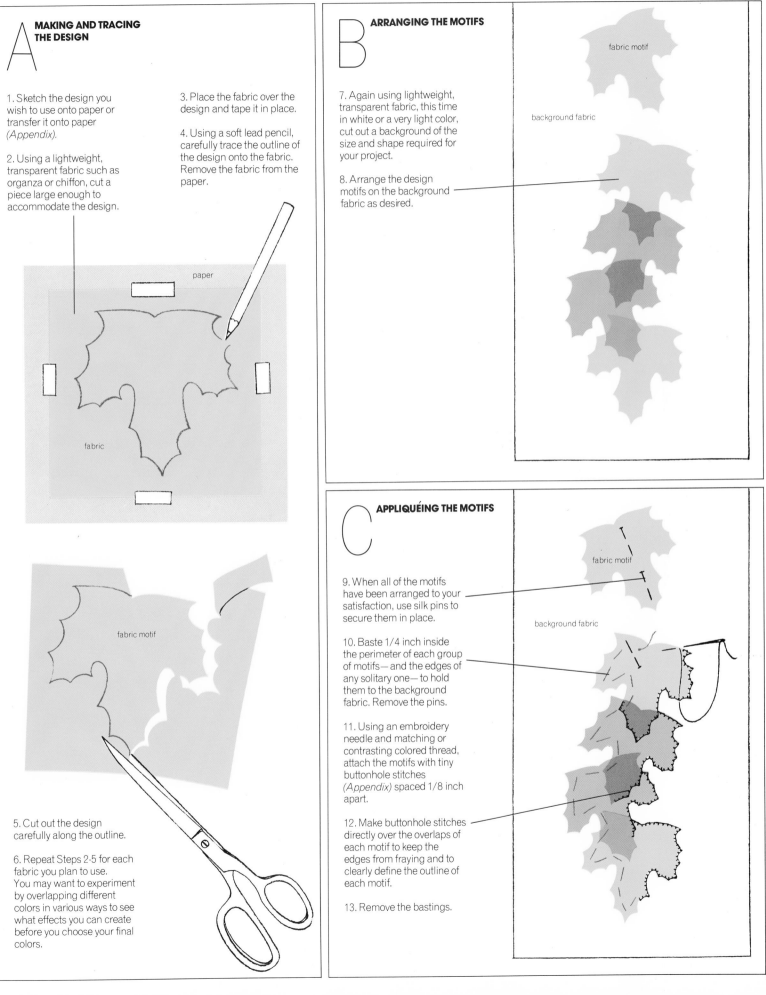

A sparkling display from beading

Beadwork, a popular pastime at the turn of the century, took endless patience and used a hook scarcely bigger around than a darning needle. Today, the same technique—used on this bolero jacket and napkin ring—can be worked with a tiny crochet hook on a net fabric backing.

In other techniques for beading, strings of beads are formed into a design with needle and thread, then fastened to the project with a couching stitch, as on the vest on page 12. In addition, beads can be anchored directly to the project—as completed designs, or one or two at a time—using the lace knot *(page 52).*

BEADING ON A FRAME

A PREPARING THE FABRIC

1A. If you are using a beading hook, arrange the pattern pieces for your project on the wrong side of the fabric, leaving a rectangle of fabric with margins at least 1 inch wide outside the edges of each piece you plan to bead. Pin the pattern pieces to the fabric.

2A. Using dressmaker's carbon and a tracing wheel, transfer all the pattern markings to the wrong side of the fabric. Also transfer the cutting lines for each piece you plan to bead. Remove the patterns.

3A. Cut out a rectangle around each piece you plan to bead, leaving fabric margins 1 inch wide outside the cutting lines. Measure the dimensions of each rectangle.

4A. Follow your pattern or project instructions to cut out the other sections of the project.

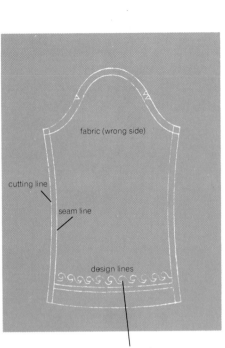

fabric (wrong side)

cutting line

seam line

design lines

5A. Draw the outline of your design on paper, then transfer the design to the wrong side of the fabric with dressmaker's carbon and a pencil. Make sure the design lines do not cross seam lines.

1B. If you are using a Size 14 crochet hook for beading, cut out and mark the pattern pieces for your project, following your pattern or project instructions.

2B. Draw the outline of the design you have chosen for your beading on paper.

3B. To make the pattern for the net fabric backing, draw a rectangle around the design, leaving margins at least 1 inch wide outside the design area.

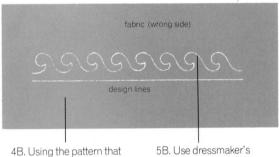

fabric (wrong side)

design lines

4B. Using the pattern that you made in the preceding step, cut out a rectangular piece of net fabric with holes smaller than the beads you plan to use.

5B. Use dressmaker's carbon and a pencil to transfer the design onto the net fabric. Then cut out the fabric backing.

B MAKING THE BEADING FRAME

6. Use four 1-by-2-inch furring strips to make a beading frame. Cut two strips at least 4 inches longer than the long sides of the fabric rectangle and two strips at least 4 inches longer than the short sides.

7. Wrap 3-inch-wide twill tape (Glossary) around one long edge of each strip; staple the tape in place.

8. Put the strips in a rectangle, the short sides overlapping the long ones at the corners, the taped edges facing together. Secure the strips at the corners with C clamps.

9. Hammer a 2-inch finishing nail into the frame midway along one edge to hold a spool of threaded beads.

10. Place the fabric wrong side up on top of the frame and pin the edges of the fabric to the tapes. Then adjust the size of the frame until the fabric is stretched taut but is still rectangular in shape.

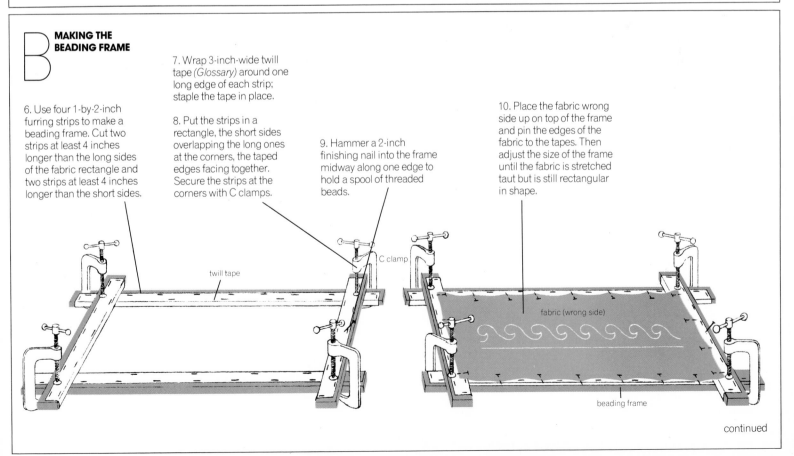

twill tape

C clamp

fabric (wrong side)

beading frame

continued

C PREPARING THE BEADS

11. To determine approximately how many beads you will need, first lay string along the lines of the design. Cut off the string needed to trace the design and measure its length in inches. Then divide that figure by the width of one bead.

12. If you are using single beads, first unwind a length of beeswax-coated thread of a matching or neutral color from its spool and—without cutting it—thread it through a slender beading needle. Then string the beads onto the thread. Skip to Step 16.

13. If you are using already-strung beads, restring them onto beeswax-coated thread of a matching or neutral color. To do this, first unwind a length of coated thread and—without cutting it—tie a loose knot at the end.

14. Insert the end of the thread on which the beads are strung through the loop of the knot and tighten the knot around the thread.

15. Carefully slide the beads over the knot and along the beeswax-coated thread to the spool. Do not restring more than two strands at a time.

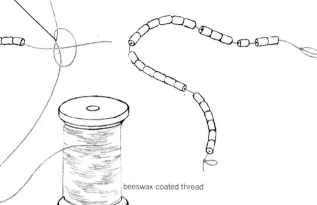
prestrung beads

beeswax-coated thread

D ANCHORING THE THREAD

16. Place the beading frame over two sawhorses or chairs so you can work from underneath the fabric. Place the spool of beads on the nail at the edge of the beading frame.

17. With your right hand, push the tip of a beading hook or a Size 14 steel crochet hook down through the fabric (shown in cross section) at the right-hand end of the design line.

18. With your left hand, bring the beaded thread around the edge of the frame and underneath the fabric. Loop it over the hook 2 inches from the end.

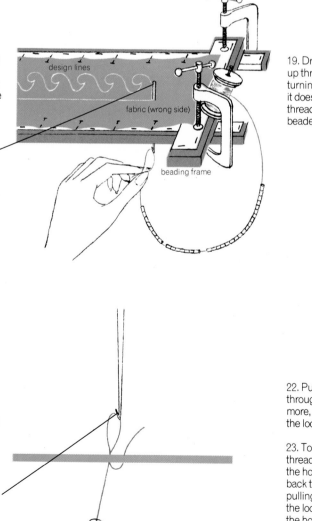
design lines
fabric (wrong side)
beading frame

19. Draw the tip of the hook up through the fabric, turning the hook slightly so it doesn't catch on fabric threads. Pull the end of the beaded thread through.

20. Push the hook down through the fabric again, slightly to the left of the point from which the thread last emerged, and loop the thread underneath the fabric over the tip of the hook.

21. Draw the hook back up, pulling a small loop of thread through the fabric.

22. Push the hook down through the fabric once more, slightly to the right of the loop made in Step 21.

23. To anchor the end of the thread, loop the thread over the hook and draw the hook back through the fabric, pulling a small loop through the loop that is already on the hook.

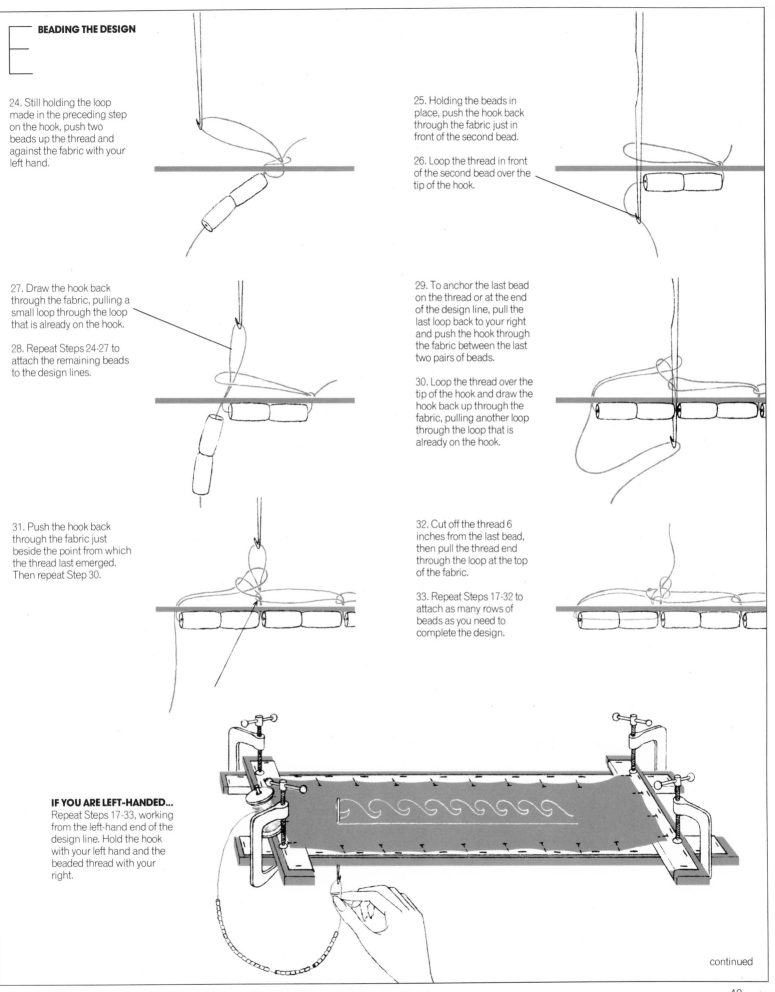

24. Still holding the loop made in the preceding step on the hook, push two beads up the thread and against the fabric with your left hand.

25. Holding the beads in place, push the hook back through the fabric just in front of the second bead.

26. Loop the thread in front of the second bead over the tip of the hook.

27. Draw the hook back through the fabric, pulling a small loop through the loop that is already on the hook.

28. Repeat Steps 24-27 to attach the remaining beads to the design lines.

29. To anchor the last bead on the thread or at the end of the design line, pull the last loop back to your right and push the hook through the fabric between the last two pairs of beads.

30. Loop the thread over the tip of the hook and draw the hook back up through the fabric, pulling another loop through the loop that is already on the hook.

31. Push the hook back through the fabric just beside the point from which the thread last emerged. Then repeat Step 30.

32. Cut off the thread 6 inches from the last bead, then pull the thread end through the loop at the top of the fabric.

33. Repeat Steps 17-32 to attach as many rows of beads as you need to complete the design.

IF YOU ARE LEFT-HANDED...
Repeat Steps 17-33, working from the left-hand end of the design line. Hold the hook with your left hand and the beaded thread with your right.

continued

FINISHING THE PROJECT

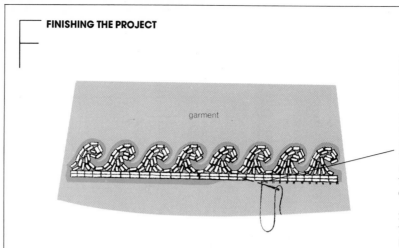

garment

34A. If you used a beading hook, cut out the beaded project section on the cutting lines.

34B. If you used a crochet hook, cut the net 1/4 inch outside the beading. Then turn under the raw edges and slip stitch (*Appendix*) the beading to the right side of the project section.

35. Assemble the project, following your pattern or project instructions.

ATTACHING BEADED EDGING WITH A COUCHING STITCH

A STRINGING THE BEADS

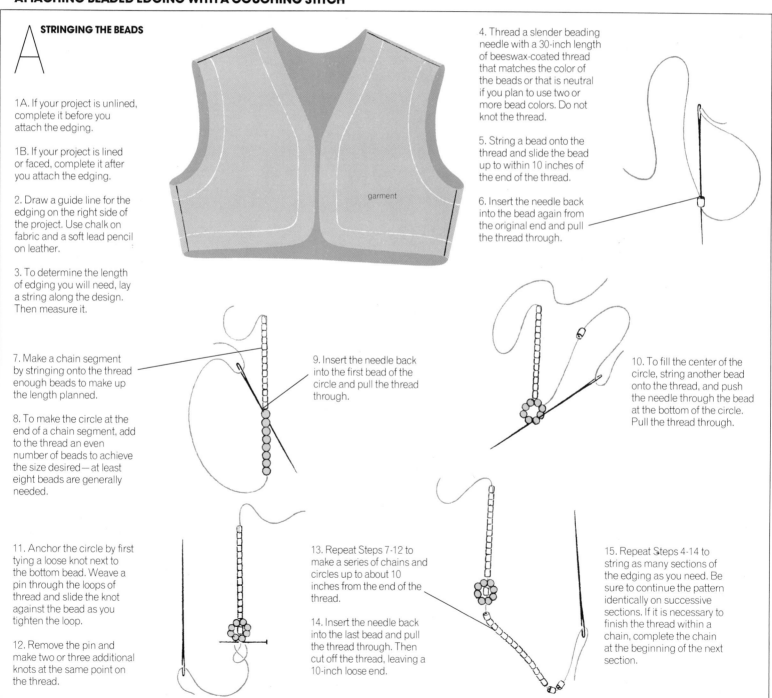

1A. If your project is unlined, complete it before you attach the edging.

1B. If your project is lined or faced, complete it after you attach the edging.

2. Draw a guide line for the edging on the right side of the project. Use chalk on fabric and a soft lead pencil on leather.

3. To determine the length of edging you will need, lay a string along the design. Then measure it.

7. Make a chain segment by stringing onto the thread enough beads to make up the length planned.

8. To make the circle at the end of a chain segment, add to the thread an even number of beads to achieve the size desired—at least eight beads are generally needed.

11. Anchor the circle by first tying a loose knot next to the bottom bead. Weave a pin through the loops of thread and slide the knot against the bead as you tighten the loop.

12. Remove the pin and make two or three additional knots at the same point on the thread.

garment

4. Thread a slender beading needle with a 30-inch length of beeswax-coated thread that matches the color of the beads or that is neutral if you plan to use two or more bead colors. Do not knot the thread.

5. String a bead onto the thread and slide the bead up to within 10 inches of the end of the thread.

6. Insert the needle back into the bead again from the original end and pull the thread through.

9. Insert the needle back into the first bead of the circle and pull the thread through.

10. To fill the center of the circle, string another bead onto the thread, and push the needle through the bead at the bottom of the circle. Pull the thread through.

13. Repeat Steps 7-12 to make a series of chains and circles up to about 10 inches from the end of the thread.

14. Insert the needle back into the last bead and pull the thread through. Then cut off the thread, leaving a 10-inch loose end.

15. Repeat Steps 4-14 to string as many sections of the edging as you need. Be sure to continue the pattern identically on successive sections. If it is necessary to finish the thread within a chain, complete the chain at the beginning of the next section.

50

B ATTACHING BEADS ON FABRIC WITH A COUCHING STITCH

16. Thread the beading needle with the loose strand remaining at the starting point of the edging (Step 5). Then push the needle through to the wrong side of the fabric at the beginning of the guide line that you drew in Step 2.

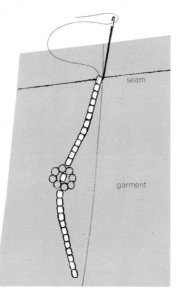

17. Anchor the thread with a fastening stitch (Appendix). Cut off the excess thread.

18. Thread the beading needle with a new 18-inch length of the beeswax-coated thread.

19. Make a tiny fastening stitch on the wrong side of the project fabric just to the right of the stitch made in Step 17. Bring the needle through the fabric just to the right of the edging.

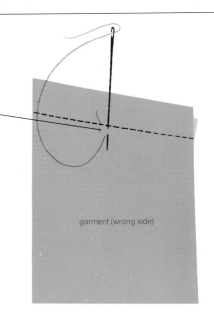

20. Holding the edging in place with your left thumb, insert the needle just to the left of the edging directly opposite the point from which the thread last emerged.

21. Slant the needle downward and push the tip out between the fourth and fifth beads just to the right of the chain. Pull the thread through.

22. Repeat Steps 20 and 21 all along the chain.

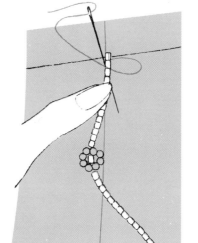

23. At the circle, anchor the outside beads on each side with separate stitches.

24. Repeat Steps 20-23 until you reach the end of the edging or edging segment.

25. Secure the end of the thread by making a fastening stitch on the wrong side of the fabric, then repeat Steps 16 and 17 to anchor the end of the edging.

26. Repeat Steps 16-25 with each remaining segment of edging.

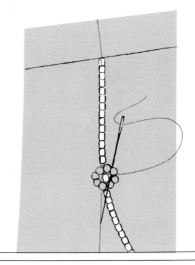

C STITCHING BEADS ON LEATHER

27. Thread a slender leather needle with the loose strand left in Step 5. Then anchor the edging at the beginning of the design guide line with a tiny fastening stitch (Appendix). Slide the needle through the leather without piercing the wrong side.

28. Cut the thread next to the stitch.

29. Thread the leather needle with a new 18-inch length of beeswax-coated thread.

30. Make a tiny fastening stitch just to the right of the stitch made in Step 27.

31. Attach the edging to the leather along the design guide line by repeating Steps 20-26, Box B. Be sure to slide the needle carefully through the layers of the leather so the stitches will not show on the wrong side.

IF YOU ARE LEFT-HANDED...
Follow Steps 16-31 but hold the chain with your right thumb and make each stitch by first bringing the needle up just to the left of the chain and then inserting the needle just to the right of the chain.

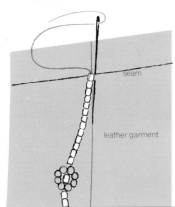

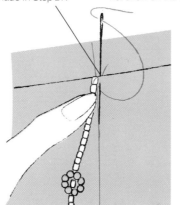

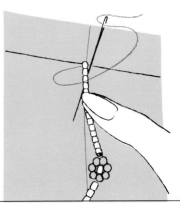

ATTACHING SINGLE BEADS WITH A LACE KNOT

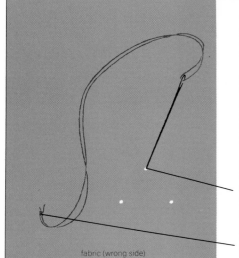

fabric (wrong side)

fabric

1. Determine the position for each bead; mark each point on the wrong side of the fabric with a tiny chalk dot.

2. Thread a beading needle with an 18-inch length of nylon or beeswax-coated thread that matches the bead color. Pull the ends even for a double strand.

3A. If you are using nylon thread, secure the ends with a fastening stitch at a chalk mark on the wrong side of the fabric.

3B. If you are using beeswax-coated thread, knot the ends of the threads.

4. Bring the needle up from the wrong side of the fabric at one of the chalk marks. Then thread one or two beads onto the needle and pull the thread through.

5. Insert the needle back into the fabric close to the point from which the thread first emerged. Pull the thread through so that it is taut enough for the bead to lie flat against the fabric with its holes parallel to the surface, but not so taut that the fabric puckers.

6. Turn the fabric wrong side up.

7. Make a tiny fastening stitch, picking up a few threads of the fabric with the needle. Pull the thread partially through the fabric, leaving a small loop.

fabric (wrong side)

8. Insert the needle through the loop formed in the preceding step. Pull the thread partially through the loop, leaving a second small loop.

9. Pull the fastening stitch tight without tightening the second loop.

10. Insert the needle through the second loop and pull the thread through to tighten the knot.

11A. If you are attaching a cluster of beads, insert the needle up through the fabric at the next chalk dot and repeat Steps 4-10 to attach the next bead.

11B. If you are attaching a single bead, clip the thread next to the knot.

BEADING A RECTANGULAR APPLIQUÉ FOR LEATHER

A PREPARING THE APPLIQUÉ

1A. For small beads, thread a slender beading needle with a nylon or beeswax-coated thread that is the same color as the beads and at least 30 inches long. Do not knot the thread.

1B. For large beads, thread buttonhole twist or embroidery floss that is at least 30 inches long through a needle that slips easily through the hole in the bead. Do not knot the thread.

2. Slip the needle through a bead and slide it to within 5 inches of the end of the thread.

3. To anchor the bead, slide the needle through the bead again in the same direction and pull the thread through.

4. String an even number of beads into the thread to make a row of the length desired for the finished rectangle.

5. To start the second row, first string an additional bead onto the thread.

6. Insert the needle from right to left back into the second bead from the right-hand end of the first row.

7. Pull the thread through and string another bead onto the thread.

8. Continuing to work from right to left, insert the needle through the fourth bead from the right-hand end of the first row.

9. Adjust the beads of the new row so that the first one lies above the first bead at the right-hand end of the first row and the second one lies above the third bead on the first row.

first bead, second row

first row

10. Repeat Steps 7 and 8 to complete the second row, inserting the needle into every other bead on the first row. Insert the needle into the bead on the left-hand end to complete the row.

11. Pivot the appliqué 180°. For the fourth row, repeat Steps 6-10, but insert the needle through the beads on the third row, working from right to left.

12. Continue to add beads by repeating Steps 6-11 until the appliqué is the desired size or until you reach the end of the thread.

13. To finish the appliqué, insert the needle back through the last bead to anchor it. Cut the thread 5 inches beyond the bead.

IF YOU ARE LEFT-HANDED...
Repeat Steps 1-13, but work from left to right.

B ATTACHING THE APPLIQUÉ

14. Thread a slender beading needle with beeswax-coated thread the color of the fabric. Anchor the thread with a fastening stitch (Glossary) on the wrong side of the leather at one corner of the appliqué.

15. Bring the needle up from the wrong side of the leather and pull it through.

16. Insert the needle through the corner bead and pull the thread through.

17. Push the needle down to the wrong side of the leather again and anchor the bead with a lace knot, following the instructions on page 52, Steps 6-10.

18. Working along the bottom edge of the rectangle, bring the needle up from the wrong side again beside the fourth or fifth bead. Repeat Step 17 to anchor that bead.

19. Repeat Step 18 at three- or four-bead intervals all around the appliqué. Be sure to anchor the other three corner beads.

20. To secure the loose thread ends at the beginning and end of the appliqué, thread them through the needle and insert the needle down to the wrong side of the leather just beside the end bead. Anchor the thread with a fastening stitch on the wrong side and cut the thread next to the stitch.

appliqué

leather

Silken braids and fringe

Strands of silken thread and coils of passementerie braid are the basis of some of the most decorative and versatile trims. The strands, when attached to the edge of an evening shawl or table cover, as here, can be knotted or interwoven to form a luxuriant fringe. The same methods work with yarn or strips of leather. Passementerie braid, tubular in construction, coils smoothly into loops and arabesques to be applied as a decorative accent to garments like the vest on page 69.

FRINGE WITH A WOVEN TOP

A PREPARING THE GARMENT

1. Measure the edge you plan to fringe and figure out how many separate clusters of fringe—spaced 3/8 inch to 1/2 inch apart—the edge can hold. To weave the top, you must have an even number of evenly spaced clusters.

2. Use a dressmaker's awl or a sharp knitting needle to punch holes along the garment edge at the interval determined in Step 1. Place the holes just inside a rolled hem, but 1/4 inch inside a folded edge.

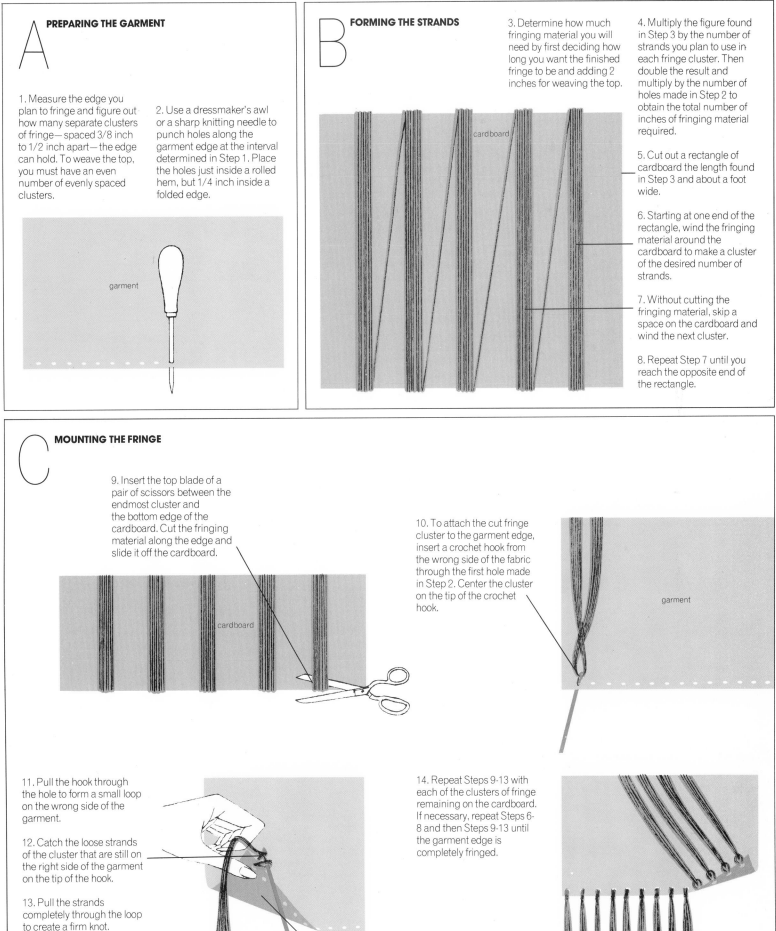

garment

B FORMING THE STRANDS

3. Determine how much fringing material you will need by first deciding how long you want the finished fringe to be and adding 2 inches for weaving the top.

4. Multiply the figure found in Step 3 by the number of strands you plan to use in each fringe cluster. Then double the result and multiply by the number of holes made in Step 2 to obtain the total number of inches of fringing material required.

5. Cut out a rectangle of cardboard the length found in Step 3 and about a foot wide.

6. Starting at one end of the rectangle, wind the fringing material around the cardboard to make a cluster of the desired number of strands.

7. Without cutting the fringing material, skip a space on the cardboard and wind the next cluster.

8. Repeat Step 7 until you reach the opposite end of the rectangle.

cardboard

C MOUNTING THE FRINGE

9. Insert the top blade of a pair of scissors between the endmost cluster and the bottom edge of the cardboard. Cut the fringing material along the edge and slide it off the cardboard.

cardboard

10. To attach the cut fringe cluster to the garment edge, insert a crochet hook from the wrong side of the fabric through the first hole made in Step 2. Center the cluster on the tip of the crochet hook.

garment

11. Pull the hook through the hole to form a small loop on the wrong side of the garment.

12. Catch the loose strands of the cluster that are still on the right side of the garment on the tip of the hook.

13. Pull the strands completely through the loop to create a firm knot.

garment (wrong side)

14. Repeat Steps 9-13 with each of the clusters of fringe remaining on the cardboard. If necessary, repeat Steps 6-8 and then Steps 9-13 until the garment edge is completely fringed.

continued

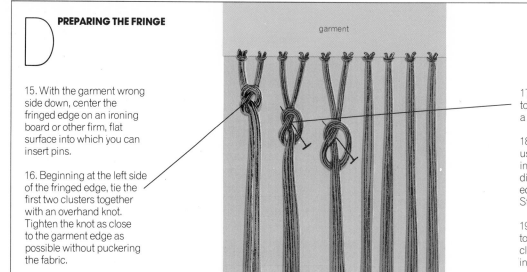

D ▸ PREPARING THE FRINGE

15. With the garment wrong side down, center the fringed edge on an ironing board or other firm, flat surface into which you can insert pins.

16. Beginning at the left side of the fringed edge, tie the first two clusters together with an overhand knot. Tighten the knot as close to the garment edge as possible without puckering the fabric.

17. Tie the next two clusters together loosely, then insert a straight pin into the knot.

18. As you tighten the knot, use the pin to slide the knot into position at the same distance from the garment edge as the knot tied in Step 16. Remove the pin.

19. Repeat Steps 17 and 18 to knot pairs of fringe clusters across about 10 inches of the garment edge.

E ▸ WEAVING THE FRINGE

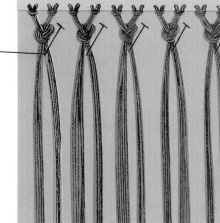

20. Divide each knotted unit in half below the knot and insert a pin to keep the segments separated.

21. To create the first row of weaving, start at the left side of the fringe clusters and pass the right half of the first fringe (*shown here in blue*) over the left half of the second fringe about 1/2 inch below the mounting knot. Insert a pin below the point where the segments meet.

22. Pass the right half of the second fringe over the left half of the third fringe and insert a pin. Then continue across the row, weaving and pinning pairs of adjacent segments.

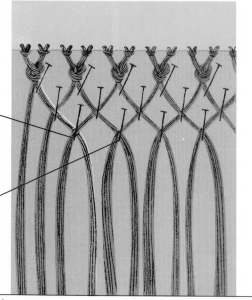

23. To weave the second row, first pick up the original right half of the first fringe —which is now the third segment from the left side —and pass it under the adjacent or fourth segment about an inch below the mounting knot. Insert a pin below the point where the segments meet.

24. Pick up the fifth segment from the left edge, pass it under the sixth segment and insert a pin. Continue across the row, weaving and pinning pairs of adjacent segments.

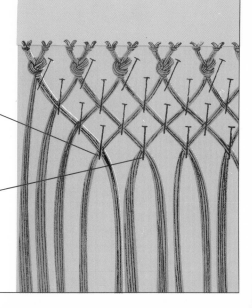

25. To weave the third row, first pick up the original right half of the first fringe —which is now the fourth segment from the left side —and pass it over the adjacent or fifth segment about 1 1/2 inches below the mounting knot. Insert a pin below the point where the segments meet.

26. Pick up the sixth segment from the left edge, pass it over the seventh segment, and insert a pin. Continue across the row, weaving and pinning pairs of adjacent segments.

FINISHING THE FRINGE

27. To finish the woven top of the fringe, first pick up the original right half of the first fringe—which is now the fifth segment from the left side—and tie it to the sixth segment with an overhand knot positioned 2 or 3 inches below the mounting knot.

28. Knot the seventh segment to the eighth, inserting a pin as in Steps 17 and 18 to position the knot; repeat across the row.

29. If your garment edge is wider than 10 inches, repeat Steps 17 and 18 plus Steps 20-28 for each 10-inch width.

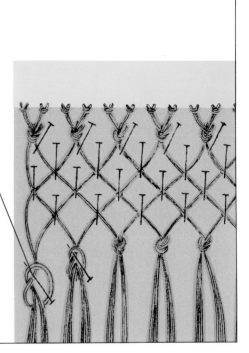

garment

30. To weave the four segments that remain untied at each side of the fringe, pick up the first segment on the left side. Pass the first segment under the second segment and over the third segment, then tie it to the fourth segment 2 or 3 inches below the mounting knot, inserting a pin to make it even with the others.

31. Tie together the two remaining untied segments at the left edge of the garment, inserting a pin to position it.

32. To finish the right edge, turn the garment wrong side up; repeat Steps 30 and 31.

33. Trim the ends of the fringe evenly to the desired length with sharp scissors.

PULLED FRINGE WITH A KNOTTED TOP

A PREPARING THE FRINGE AND THE GARMENT

1. To determine how much fringing material you will need, measure in inches the garment edge you want to fringe; multiply by two to find how many fringe clusters you will have.

2. Decide how long you want the finished fringe to be and add 4 inches for knotting. Multiply by four —the number of strands in each cluster.

3. Multiply the figure found in Step 1 by that found in Step 2 for the total inches of fringing material required.

4. Insert silk pin markers at 6-inch intervals along the garment edge you plan to fringe so you can work one short section at a time.

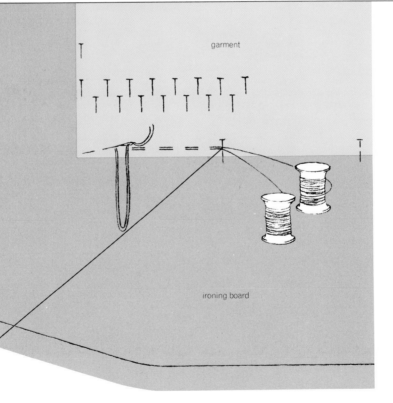

garment

ironing board

5. With the garment wrong side down, use silk pins to secure the leftmost 6-inch section of the edge to an ironing board or other firm, flat working surface.

6. Using two spools of fringing material, thread a needle with one strand from each spool. If your fringing material is on one large spool, wind half of it off onto a second spool or a bobbin so you can use two strands simultaneously.

7. Without breaking off or tying the strands, push the needle down through the right corner of the section to be worked, 1/4 inch inside the garment's finished edge. Make 1/2-inch running stitches (*Appendix*) across the edge.

continued

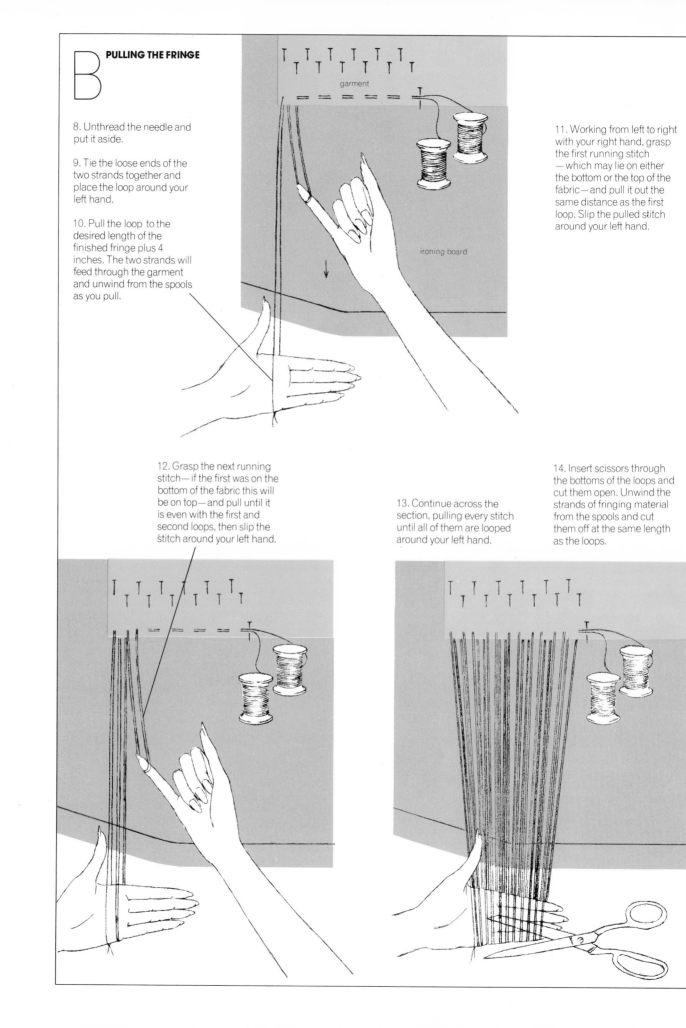

B   PULLING THE FRINGE

8. Unthread the needle and put it aside.

9. Tie the loose ends of the two strands together and place the loop around your left hand.

10. Pull the loop to the desired length of the finished fringe plus 4 inches. The two strands will feed through the garment and unwind from the spools as you pull.

11. Working from left to right with your right hand, grasp the first running stitch —which may lie on either the bottom or the top of the fabric—and pull it out the same distance as the first loop. Slip the pulled stitch around your left hand.

12. Grasp the next running stitch—if the first was on the bottom of the fabric this will be on top—and pull until it is even with the first and second loops, then slip the stitch around your left hand.

13. Continue across the section, pulling every stitch until all of them are looped around your left hand.

14. Insert scissors through the bottoms of the loops and cut them open. Unwind the strands of fringing material from the spools and cut them off at the same length as the loops.

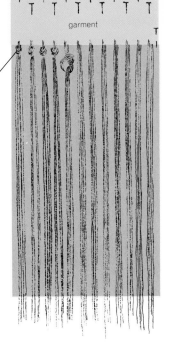

garment

15. Working from left to right, pull the ends of each pair of double strands to even them, and tie each pair together in an overhand knot as close to the edge of the garment as possible without puckering the fabric.

16. To create the second row of knots, start by tying an overhand knot about 1/2 inch below the garment edge with half the strands from the leftmost cluster and half the strands from the adjacent cluster.

17. Continue across the row from left to right, knotting adjacent halves of clusters and keeping the row of knots even by inserting a pin into each knot to position it, following the instructions for fringe with a woven top *(page 56, Box D, Steps 17 and 18)*. Leave the second half of the cluster at the right of the section unknotted; you will knot it into the beginning of the next section.

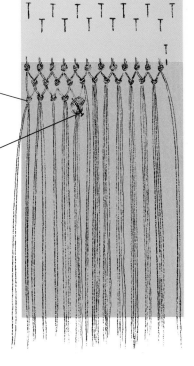

18. To create the third row of knots, start by tying the leftmost set of strands with the adjacent set about 1 inch below the garment edge.

19. Continue across the row, knotting adjacent sets of strands and inserting a pin into each knot to position it evenly with the knot tied in the preceding step.

20. Repeat Steps 16-19 to complete the desired number of rows of knots.

21. To fringe each additional section of the garment edge, first unpin the garment from the working surface and repin it, centering the new section on the working surface.

22. Repeat Steps 5-20, making the knots from left to right and picking up unworked strands of fringing material from the preceding section as you go.

23. At the right end of the garment edge, tie the rightmost cluster to the adjacent set of strands even with the knots in the third, fifth, and successive odd-numbered rows.

24. To finish the fringe, trim the ends evenly to the desired length with scissors.

PASSEMENTERIE WITH ONE BRAID

A PREPARING THE GARMENT PATTERN

1. Make a duplicate of the section of the garment pattern you want to trim by inserting dressmaker's carbon, carbon side down, between the pattern and heavy brown paper. If the garment pattern piece is to be laid out and cut on the fold of the fabric, make a mirror-image duplicate pattern (Appendix) and tape it to the pattern piece before copying the section onto the brown paper.

2. Using a tracing wheel, trace all pattern markings onto the brown paper. Remove the carbon pattern piece.

B MAKING THE PASSEMENTERIE PATTERN

3. With a pencil, draw the interlocking loops for the desired passementerie on the brown paper, adapting the design to the garment outline. If the passementerie will be used on adjacent garment sections to form one continuous design, make sure that the drawn pattern touches the seam line between the sections.

4. When you are satisfied with the design and its placement, draw in a second line, close to the first, to indicate the width of the tubular braid you plan to use.

5. Draw over the pencil lines with a dark indelible nonsmudging pen. Then erase the pencil lines.

6. Cut out the design area, leaving about a 1-inch margin around its perimeter.

7. To determine how much braid you need, lay a string along the lines of the design. Cut off the string needed to cover the design and measure it.

C PREPARING THE TUBULAR BRAID

8. Thread a Size 7 darning needle with a single strand of hard, cotton glacé thread the same color as the braid and knot the end. Insert the needle into the braid about 1/2 inch from the end and draw the needle through.

9. Whip the braid by tightly wrapping the thread around the braid four or five times.

10. Push the needle through the whipped section and trim off the fuzzy end of the braid close to the whipping.

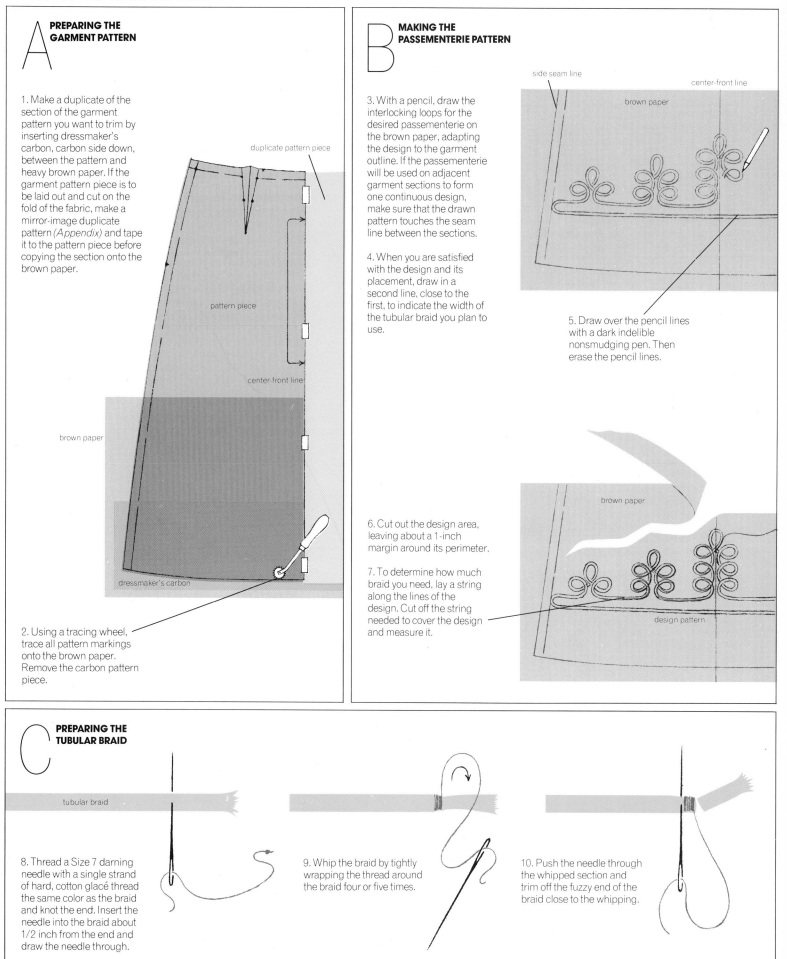

D FORMING THE FIRST LOOP

11. Without cutting the thread, place the whipped end of the braid on one of the loops of the drawn design at the point where two sets of lines intersect.

12. Shape the braid to match the loop with the whipped end on top at the point where the braid crosses. The top surface of the work will be the wrong side of the finished passementerie.

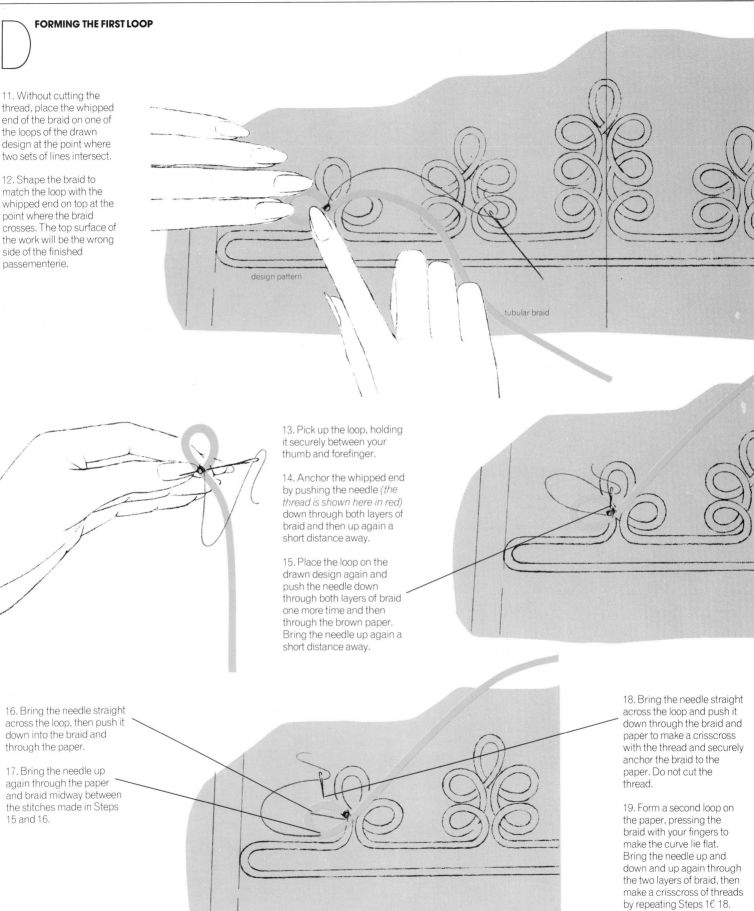

design pattern

tubular braid

13. Pick up the loop, holding it securely between your thumb and forefinger.

14. Anchor the whipped end by pushing the needle *(the thread is shown here in red)* down through both layers of braid and then up again a short distance away.

15. Place the loop on the drawn design again and push the needle down through both layers of braid one more time and then through the brown paper. Bring the needle up again a short distance away.

16. Bring the needle straight across the loop, then push it down into the braid and through the paper.

17. Bring the needle up again through the paper and braid midway between the stitches made in Steps 15 and 16.

18. Bring the needle straight across the loop and push it down through the braid and paper to make a crisscross with the thread and securely anchor the braid to the paper. Do not cut the thread.

19. Form a second loop on the paper, pressing the braid with your fingers to make the curve lie flat. Bring the needle up and down and up again through the two layers of braid, then make a crisscross of threads by repeating Steps 1€ 18.

continued

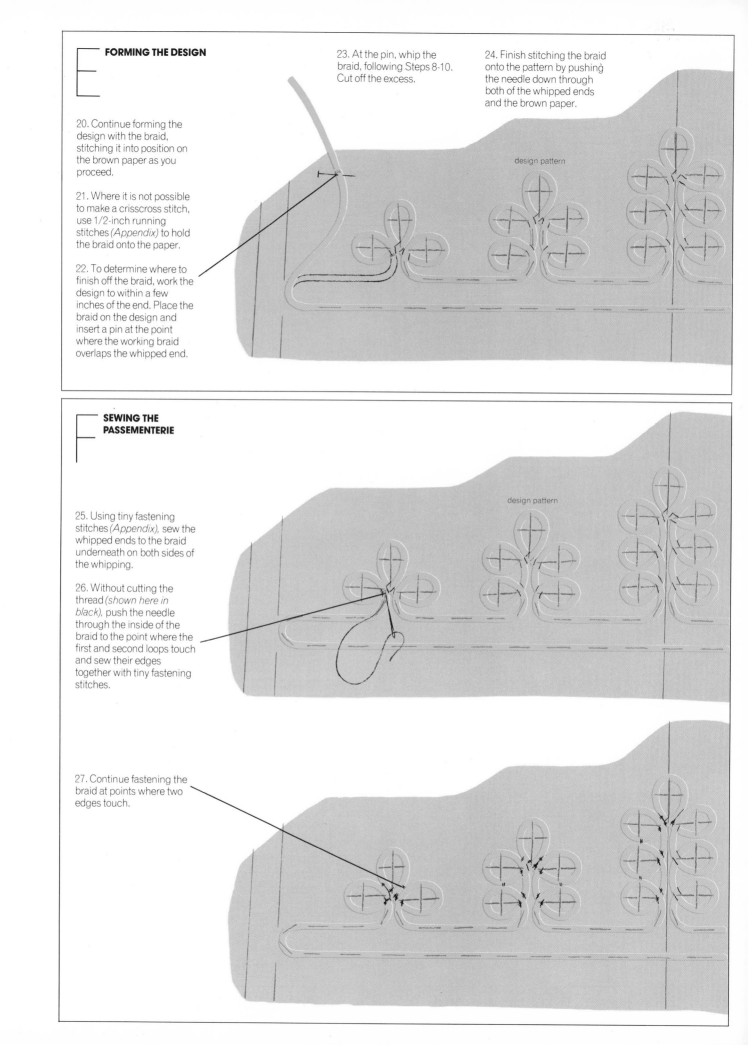

FORMING THE DESIGN

20. Continue forming the design with the braid, stitching it into position on the brown paper as you proceed.

21. Where it is not possible to make a crisscross stitch, use 1/2-inch running stitches *(Appendix)* to hold the braid onto the paper.

22. To determine where to finish off the braid, work the design to within a few inches of the end. Place the braid on the design and insert a pin at the point where the working braid overlaps the whipped end.

23. At the pin, whip the braid, following Steps 8-10. Cut off the excess.

24. Finish stitching the braid onto the pattern by pushing the needle down through both of the whipped ends and the brown paper.

design pattern

SEWING THE PASSEMENTERIE

25. Using tiny fastening stitches *(Appendix),* sew the whipped ends to the braid underneath on both sides of the whipping.

26. Without cutting the thread *(shown here in black),* push the needle through the inside of the braid to the point where the first and second loops touch and sew their edges together with tiny fastening stitches.

design pattern

27. Continue fastening the braid at points where two edges touch.

G ATTACHING THE PASSEMENTERIE TO THE GARMENT

28. Turn over the brown paper and lightly press it with a steam iron.

29. To detach the passementerie from the brown paper, cut the tacking stitches from the underside. The fastening stitches will keep the loops of the design in place.

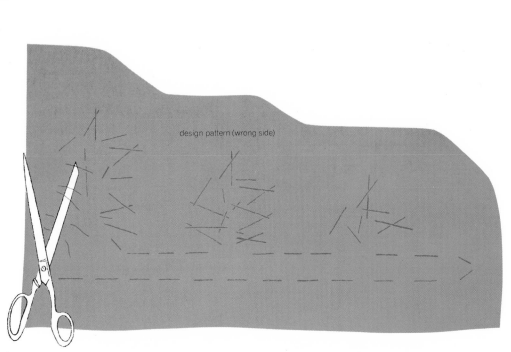

design pattern (wrong side)

30. Arrange the passementerie as desired on the finished garment and use tiny slip stitches (Appendix) to sew the design in place. If the garment calls for a lining, stitch the passementerie in place before adding the lining.

garment

PASSEMENTERIE WITH OVERLAPPING BRAIDS

A ARRANGING THE BRAIDS ON THE DESIGN

1. Make a passementerie pattern by repeating Steps 1-7 for passementerie with one braid (page 60) but work with samples of the two tubular braids you want to use while you plan the design.

2. Attach the braid that you want to have on the top surface of the passementerie first, following the instructions in Steps 8-24.

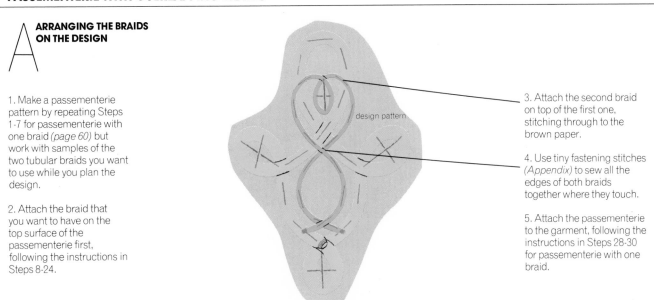

design pattern

3. Attach the second braid on top of the first one, stitching through to the brown paper.

4. Use tiny fastening stitches (Appendix) to sew all the edges of both braids together where they touch.

5. Attach the passementerie to the garment, following the instructions in Steps 28-30 for passementerie with one braid.

3
DASHING ADORNMENTS TO WEAR

Nowadays, in this era of mass-produced clothing, only the woman who buys her clothes from a couturier or who designs her own can be completely sure that she will never meet her fashion double. Yet the essence of style is individuality, and it is still possible to achieve it. The fashionable woman adds decorative accessories—scarves, hats, purses and belts—to mark her costume with her own personality.

ACCESSORIES WITH A PERSONAL AIR

In the projects that follow, two classic vests are embellished, one with a fringe of leather strips, in American Indian style, the other with curlicues of passementerie braid as splendid as a turn-of-the-century bandmaster's uniform. Operating on the principle that if one scarf is decorative, several are more so, four scarves in related patterns are combined into a fluttering cover-up top that could be the main accessory for any number of basic skirts or dresses.

Perhaps the most elegant of all accessories is a beaded bag like the one on page 76, its shimmering bisecting curves and ovals sewed by a method that has not changed for a century. The backing fabric is stretched over a frame; then prestrung beads are held underneath, while a beading hook passes through the fabric from the top, pulling up and securing the thread between each bead.

This technique was developed to cope with the demand for beaded bags in the 19th Century, when fashion magazines decreed that "the lady of fashion should not appear in public without her little beaded purse, her indispensable reticule." Until that time, beaded bags were mainly woven or knitted with laborious techniques. The new method, which is demonstrated on pages 47-50, became the basis of a flourishing industry, particularly in France, Italy and Belgium.

During World War II, however, most of the women workers put aside their frames to do war-related work. The craft was revived in the late 1940s by an American, Mrs. Hilde Walborg, who decided to use $5,000 (which her husband had given her to buy a mink coat) to travel instead around Europe in search of skilled beadworkers. She not only found the women, but set up workshops, using them to teach beading to a new generation. Within a few years, glass-bead factories in Italy, Czechoslovakia and Austria were reopening to fill her orders, and she was employing thousands of women, many of whom used their mothers' and grandmothers' frames.

The actual work of beading a bag is fairly simple, though speed and dexterity come only with practice. When beading is done by an expert, a small art object seems to take shape as if by magic. The skilled beader who made the bag which is photographed on page 76, Rose Gambino of New York, learned the craft when she was only 14 years old. To establish the basic outline, she first stretches a filmy material—either organdy, net, silk or voile—over the frame, and chalks the outline of a design on the fabric. She then threads the beads on a spool which is attached to the frame.

Holding the threaded beads underneath the fabric, she flicks each bead up to its correct position. At the same time, in a continuous movement almost too fast to see, she inserts the hook through the fabric, catches the thread behind the bead, and with a deft twist of the hand fastens it in a sturdy chain stitch.

The varieties of beads and stitches and their decorative potential not only for bags but all kinds of beaded trim is enormous. Rose Gambino remembers nostalgically the time when elegant women wore suits, gowns and capes covered with intricate beadwork. Such lavish costume decoration is rare today. But the beaded bag lives on, and beaded trim, now generally used with restraint, is gaining renewed popularity —even for such unfancy garments as a leather vest (pages 12-13). The fashionable woman of today, once she has mastered the basically simple techniques, need not lack for ways to make her clothes proclaim her own individuality.

Perky vests to enliven a wardrobe

Cascades of knotted fringe and curlicues of passementerie braid ornament these two vests. Although they are quite different in personality, both are made from the same basic pattern, adapted from a simple dartless cardigan jacket pattern labeled suitable for knits.

The sportive vest on the left is cut from washable chamois, a relatively inexpensive suedelike leather found in craft and leather supply stores. Four or five skins are required for this vest and its fringe, depending on the pattern size. The bolero, trimmed with passementerie, needs no more than a yard of fabric and the same amount of lining material. The design pictured here requires about 3 yards of 3/16-inch braid and 2 yards of 1/4-inch braid.

THE FRINGED CHAMOIS VEST

A PREPARING THE PATTERNS

1. Tape paper under the armhole and shoulder of the jacket front pattern. Then extend the shoulder seam and cutting lines 2 5/8 inches beyond the armhole seam line.

2. Make a mark on the drawn shoulder seam line 2 inches beyond the armhole seam line and another mark on the side seam line 1 1/2 inches below the armhole seam line.

3. Draw a new armhole seam line by making a smooth curve between the shoulder seam-line mark, the armhole pattern notch and the side seam-line mark. Then draw a new cutting line 5/8 inch outside and parallel to the new seam line.

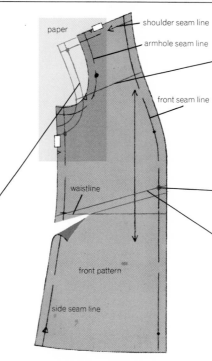

4. Draw a guide line for the upper fringe parallel to the shoulder seam line from the armhole pattern notch to the front edge.

5. To shorten the pattern, first draw a line across the pattern perpendicular to the grain-line arrow from the waistline marking to the front edge.

6. Make a mark on the front seam line 2 inches above the line drawn in Step 5.

7. Draw a new hem seam line by connecting the mark made in Step 6 with the point where the waistline intersects the side seam line. Mark a new cutting line 5/8 inch outside the new seam line.

8. Trim the pattern along the new cutting lines.

9. To make a pattern for the front facing, pin paper under the front edge of the modified front pattern.

10. Using a tracing wheel and carbon paper, trace the front seam line. Trace 2 inches along the shoulder seam and cutting lines and the hem seam line. Remove the pattern.

11. Mark the inner edge of the facing pattern by drawing a line from the shoulder to the hem 2 inches inside and parallel to the front seam line.

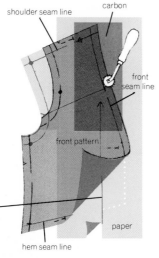

12. Cut out the facing pattern along the markings.

13. To modify the armhole of the back pattern, repeat Steps 1-3.

14. If your pattern has a center-back seam, skip to Step 16. If your pattern has a center-back fold line, tape a strip of paper under the line. Then draw a new center-back cutting line 5/8 inch outside and parallel to the fold line.

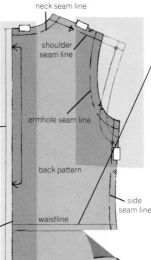

15. Draw a new hem seam line perpendicular to the center-back fold line or the grain-line arrow by extending the waistline marking from the center back to the side edge. Then draw a new cutting line 5/8 inch outside and parallel to the new seam line.

16. Trim the pattern along the new hem, center-back, shoulder and armhole cutting lines.

B CUTTING AND MARKING THE GARMENT SECTIONS

17. Place a chamois skin wrong side down. With the marked sides up, arrange the patterns for the front and front facing lengthwise on the skin, shifting the patterns slightly if necessary to avoid mars. Place both patterns in the same direction, with the top edges closest to the front legs of the skin and the hem edges closest to the hind legs so the nap will run downward on the finished garment. Arrange the back pattern piece on another chamois skin in a similar manner.

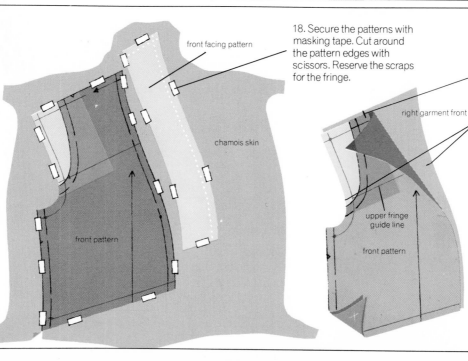

18. Secure the patterns with masking tape. Cut around the pattern edges with scissors. Reserve the scraps for the fringe.

19. Mark the pattern notches along the shoulder and side seams by making 1/4-inch clips into the edges of the front and back patterns and chamois sections.

20. Make a 1/4-inch clip into the front and armhole edges of the chamois at the ends of the upper fringe guide line on the front pattern.

21. Mark the wrong side of each garment section with a chalk X.

22. Remove the pattern pieces; then, using two additional skins, repeat Steps 17-21 to cut the other front, facing and back sections of the garment. In this case, however, place the pattern pieces with the marked sides down.

C PREPARING THE FRONT GARMENT SECTIONS

23. Place one front garment section wrong side up and draw the upper fringe guide line with chalk by connecting the clip mark made in Step 20. Cut a strip of chamois the length of the guide line and 1 inch wide, then place it on the garment front, wrong side down, and center it over the guide line.

24. Trim the strip 3/4 inch inside the armhole and front edges, following the curves of the garment.

25. Apply leather cement to the wrong side of the strip and in 1/2-inch bands on each side of the fringe guide line. Let the cement set; press the strip in place.

26. To make slits for the fringe, first place the garment front wrong side down on a heavy cardboard. Mark the upper fringe guide line on the finished side by repeating Step 23.

27. Position the cutting edges of a multiple 1/8-inch slit cutter on the guide line 1 inch inside the center-front edge. Hold the tool at a right angle to the garment and hammer down on the end until you pierce both the garment and the strip beneath it.

28. Reposition the cutting edges of the tool, inserting the first prong in the last slit punched. Repeat along the guide line, up to about 1 inch from the armhole edge, but make sure to punch an even number of slits.

29. Repeat Steps 23-28 to prepare the other garment front.

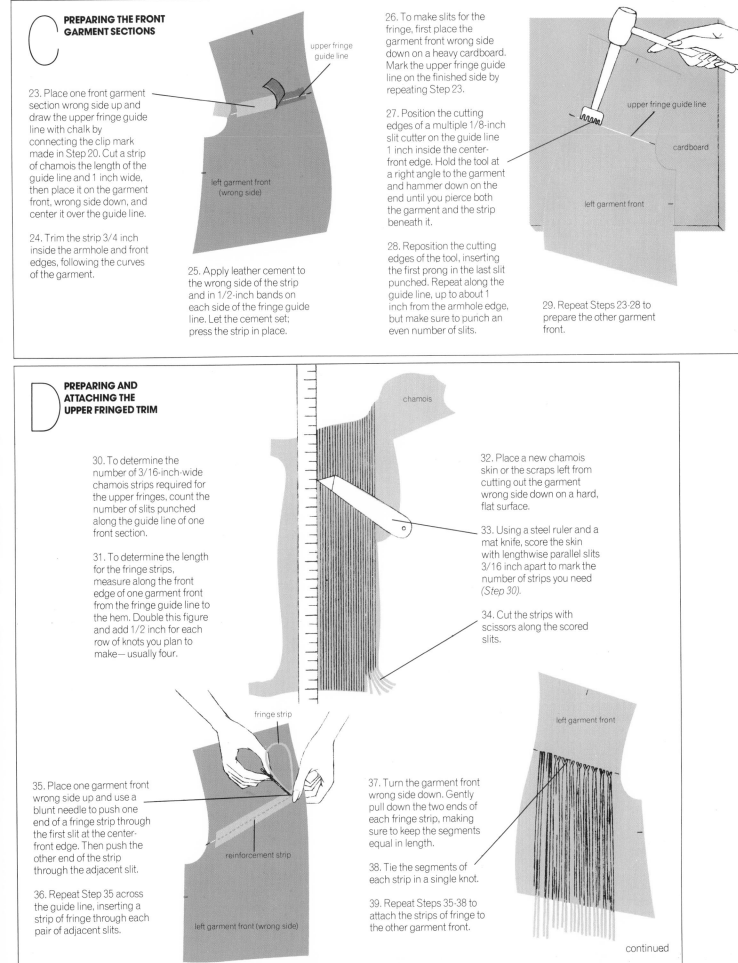

D PREPARING AND ATTACHING THE UPPER FRINGED TRIM

30. To determine the number of 3/16-inch-wide chamois strips required for the upper fringes, count the number of slits punched along the guide line of one front section.

31. To determine the length for the fringe strips, measure along the front edge of one garment front from the fringe guide line to the hem. Double this figure and add 1/2 inch for each row of knots you plan to make—usually four.

32. Place a new chamois skin or the scraps left from cutting out the garment wrong side down on a hard, flat surface.

33. Using a steel ruler and a mat knife, score the skin with lengthwise parallel slits 3/16 inch apart to mark the number of strips you need (Step 30).

34. Cut the strips with scissors along the scored slits.

35. Place one garment front wrong side up and use a blunt needle to push one end of a fringe strip through the first slit at the center-front edge. Then push the other end of the strip through the adjacent slit.

36. Repeat Step 35 across the guide line, inserting a strip of fringe through each pair of adjacent slits.

37. Turn the garment front wrong side down. Gently pull down the two ends of each fringe strip, making sure to keep the segments equal in length.

38. Tie the segments of each strip in a single knot.

39. Repeat Steps 35-38 to attach the strips of fringe to the other garment front.

continued

71

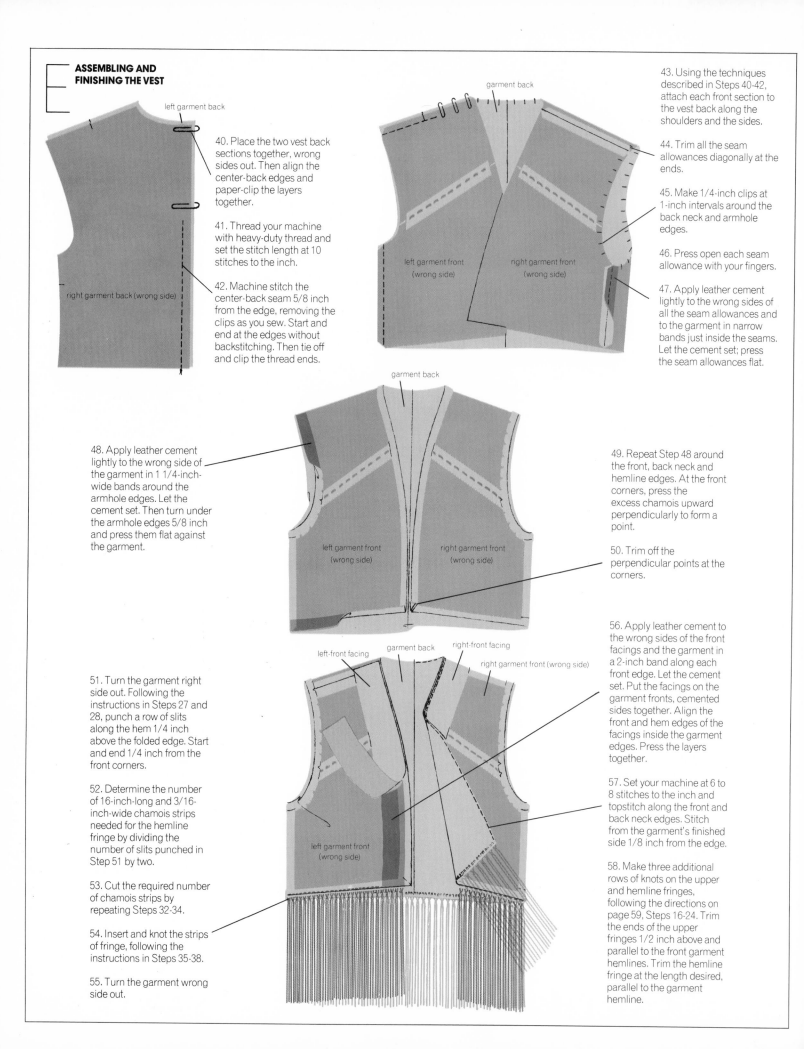

ASSEMBLING AND FINISHING THE VEST

left garment back

right garment back (wrong side)

40. Place the two vest back sections together, wrong sides out. Then align the center-back edges and paper-clip the layers together.

41. Thread your machine with heavy-duty thread and set the stitch length at 10 stitches to the inch.

42. Machine stitch the center-back seam 5/8 inch from the edge, removing the clips as you sew. Start and end at the edges without backstitching. Then tie off and clip the thread ends.

garment back

left garment front (wrong side)

right garment front (wrong side)

43. Using the techniques described in Steps 40-42, attach each front section to the vest back along the shoulders and the sides.

44. Trim all the seam allowances diagonally at the ends.

45. Make 1/4-inch clips at 1-inch intervals around the back neck and armhole edges.

46. Press open each seam allowance with your fingers.

47. Apply leather cement lightly to the wrong sides of all the seam allowances and to the garment in narrow bands just inside the seams. Let the cement set; press the seam allowances flat.

garment back

left garment front (wrong side)

right garment front (wrong side)

48. Apply leather cement lightly to the wrong side of the garment in 1 1/4-inch-wide bands around the armhole edges. Let the cement set. Then turn under the armhole edges 5/8 inch and press them flat against the garment.

49. Repeat Step 48 around the front, back neck and hemline edges. At the front corners, press the excess chamois upward perpendicularly to form a point.

50. Trim off the perpendicular points at the corners.

left-front facing

garment back

right-front facing

right garment front (wrong side)

left garment front (wrong side)

51. Turn the garment right side out. Following the instructions in Steps 27 and 28, punch a row of slits along the hem 1/4 inch above the folded edge. Start and end 1/4 inch from the front corners.

52. Determine the number of 16-inch-long and 3/16-inch-wide chamois strips needed for the hemline fringe by dividing the number of slits punched in Step 51 by two.

53. Cut the required number of chamois strips by repeating Steps 32-34.

54. Insert and knot the strips of fringe, following the instructions in Steps 35-38.

55. Turn the garment wrong side out.

56. Apply leather cement to the wrong sides of the front facings and the garment in a 2-inch band along each front edge. Let the cement set. Put the facings on the garment fronts, cemented sides together. Align the front and hem edges of the facings inside the garment edges. Press the layers together.

57. Set your machine at 6 to 8 stitches to the inch and topstitch along the front and back neck edges. Stitch from the garment's finished side 1/8 inch from the edge.

58. Make three additional rows of knots on the upper and hemline fringes, following the directions on page 59, Steps 16-24. Trim the ends of the upper fringes 1/2 inch above and parallel to the front garment hemlines. Trim the hemline fringe at the length desired, parallel to the garment hemline.

THE BOLERO VEST WITH PASSEMENTERIE TRIM

A MODIFYING THE PATTERN PIECES

1. Mark the shoulder seam of the jacket front pattern 3/4 inch inside the armhole seam line. Make a second mark 1 inch inside and on a level with the pattern dot on the armhole seam line. Then mark the side seam 2 1/2 inches below the armhole seam line.

2. Draw a new armhole seam line by connecting the marks made in Step 1 with a smooth curve.

3. Draw a new hem seam line perpendicular to the grain-line arrow from the waistline marking to the side edge.

4. Make a mark on the new hem seam line 1/2 inch inside the side seam line. Then draw a new side seam line by connecting this mark with the end of the new armhole seam line.

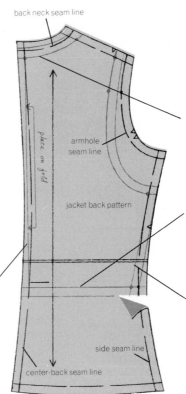

shoulder seam line

armhole seam line

front seam line

jacket front pattern

waistline

side seam line

5. Mark the shoulder seam 3 inches inside the new armhole seam line. Then draw a new front seam line parallel to the printed seam line from this mark to the new hemline.

6. To shape the front corners of the vest, mark the new front seam line and the new hemline 2 inches from the point where the lines intersect. Then connect the marks with a smooth curve.

7. Draw cutting lines 5/8 inch outside and parallel to the new seam lines. Then trim the pattern along the cutting lines.

8. If your jacket back pattern has a center-back fold line, skip to Step 9. If your pattern has a center-back seam, straighten it by drawing a line from the point where the back and neck seams intersect to the waistline marking. Then label the drawn line "place on fold."

back neck seam line

place on fold

armhole seam line

jacket back pattern

side seam line

center-back seam line

9. To modify the armhole, repeat Steps 1 and 2.

10. Mark the shoulder seam line 3 inches inside the new armhole seam line and mark the center-back fold line 1/2 inch below the neck seam line. Then draw a new back neck seam line by connecting the marks with a smooth curve.

11. Measure the length of the side seam line on the front pattern and mark this distance from the armhole on the side seam line of the back pattern. Then draw a new hem seam line perpendicular to the center-back fold line from this mark to the center-back edge.

12. Mark a new side seam line by repeating Step 4.

13. Draw new cutting lines 5/8 inch outside the new neck, armhole side and hem seam lines.

14. Trim the pattern along the cutting lines and the center-back fold line.

B LAYING OUT, CUTTING AND MARKING

15. On a flat surface, arrange string to form three sides of a rectangle representing the fabric you plan to use. Make the width of the rectangle equal to half the width of the fabric and use a yard of string as a first approximation of length.

16. Arrange the back and front patterns inside the string, lining up the center-back fold line of the back pattern along one lengthwise string and keeping the grain-line arrow of the front pattern parallel to the lengthwise strings.

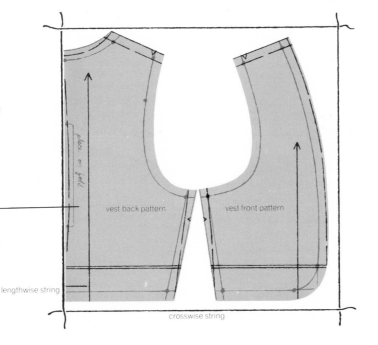

place on fold

vest back pattern

vest front pattern

lengthwise string

crosswise string

17. Close off the open end of the string rectangle near the patterns. Then measure the length of the rectangle to get the amount of fabric you will need for the vest.

18. Straighten the fabric (Appendix), then fold the fabric in half lengthwise, wrong sides out, aligning the selvages. Arrange the patterns on the fabric as in the string layout and cut them out. Transfer the pattern markings, using a tracing wheel and dressmaker's carbon.

19. Repeat Steps 15-18 to prepare the lining for the vest, but mark only the side seams. Then trim 1/8 inch from the hem, center-front, back neck and armhole edges.

continued

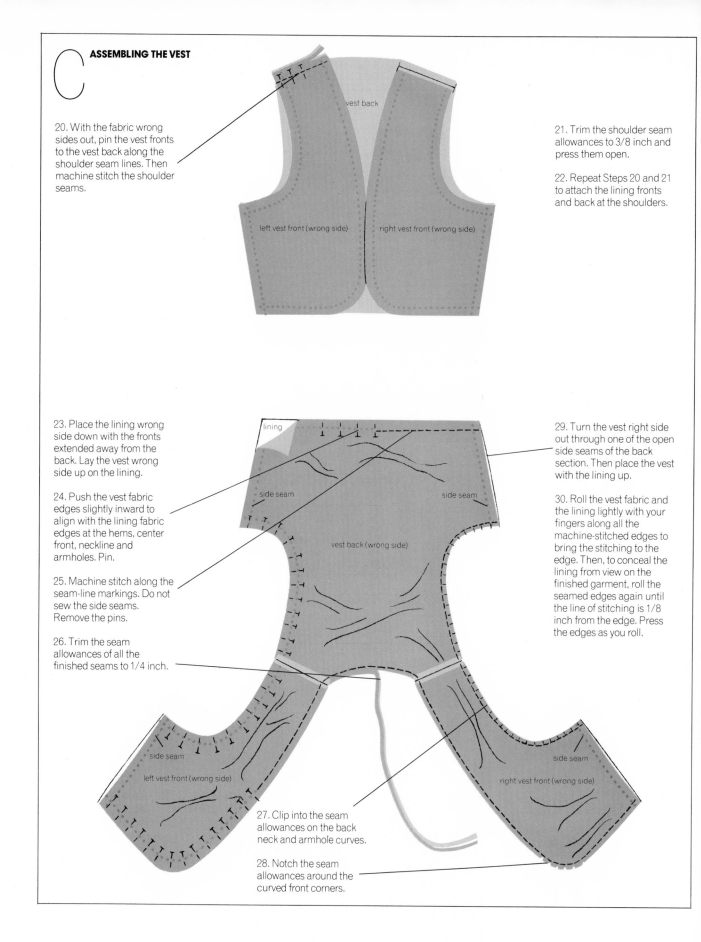

C ASSEMBLING THE VEST

20. With the fabric wrong sides out, pin the vest fronts to the vest back along the shoulder seam lines. Then machine stitch the shoulder seams.

21. Trim the shoulder seam allowances to 3/8 inch and press them open.

22. Repeat Steps 20 and 21 to attach the lining fronts and back at the shoulders.

23. Place the lining wrong side down with the fronts extended away from the back. Lay the vest wrong side up on the lining.

24. Push the vest fabric edges slightly inward to align with the lining fabric edges at the hems, center front, neckline and armholes. Pin.

25. Machine stitch along the seam-line markings. Do not sew the side seams. Remove the pins.

26. Trim the seam allowances of all the finished seams to 1/4 inch.

27. Clip into the seam allowances on the back neck and armhole curves.

28. Notch the seam allowances around the curved front corners.

29. Turn the vest right side out through one of the open side seams of the back section. Then place the vest with the lining up.

30. Roll the vest fabric and the lining lightly with your fingers along all the machine-stitched edges to bring the stitching to the edge. Then, to conceal the lining from view on the finished garment, roll the seamed edges again until the line of stitching is 1/8 inch from the edge. Press the edges as you roll.

Labels in illustration: vest back; left vest front (wrong side); right vest front (wrong side); lining; side seam; vest back (wrong side); side seam

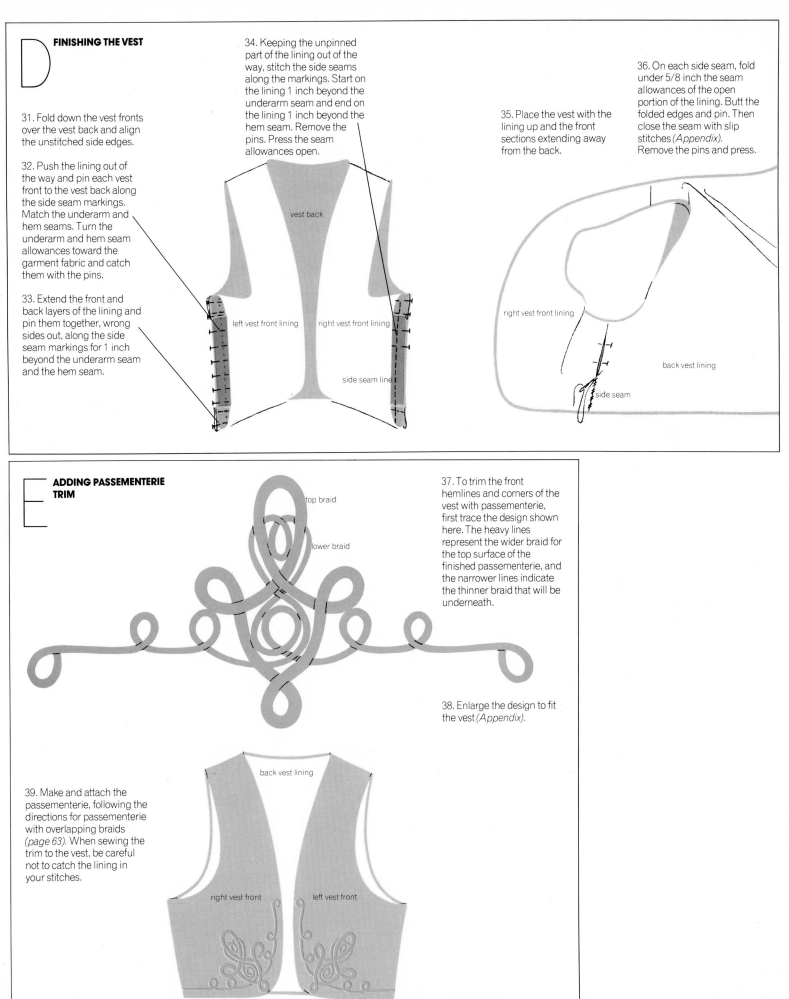

D FINISHING THE VEST

31. Fold down the vest fronts over the vest back and align the unstitched side edges.

32. Push the lining out of the way and pin each vest front to the vest back along the side seam markings. Match the underarm and hem seams. Turn the underarm and hem seam allowances toward the garment fabric and catch them with the pins.

33. Extend the front and back layers of the lining and pin them together, wrong sides out, along the side seam markings for 1 inch beyond the underarm seam and the hem seam.

34. Keeping the unpinned part of the lining out of the way, stitch the side seams along the markings. Start on the lining 1 inch beyond the underarm seam and end on the lining 1 inch beyond the hem seam. Remove the pins. Press the seam allowances open.

vest back

left vest front lining

right vest front lining

side seam line

35. Place the vest with the lining up and the front sections extending away from the back.

36. On each side seam, fold under 5/8 inch the seam allowances of the open portion of the lining. Butt the folded edges and pin. Then close the seam with slip stitches (Appendix). Remove the pins and press.

right vest front lining

back vest lining

side seam

E ADDING PASSEMENTERIE TRIM

top braid

lower braid

37. To trim the front hemlines and corners of the vest with passementerie, first trace the design shown here. The heavy lines represent the wider braid for the top surface of the finished passementerie, and the narrower lines indicate the thinner braid that will be underneath.

38. Enlarge the design to fit the vest (Appendix).

39. Make and attach the passementerie, following the directions for passementerie with overlapping braids (page 63). When sewing the trim to the vest, be careful not to catch the lining in your stitches.

back vest lining

right vest front

left vest front

Iridescent beads for a dazzling bag

As glamorous as the turn-of-the-century painting in the background, this scintillating bead-encrusted bag uses a traditional technique. The beads were attached one by one to a backing of organza with a slim beading hook. But a somewhat simpler variant of this method, using a crochet hook and netting, will produce about the same result; the net should be finer than the beads to prevent their pushing through.

The handbag frame, which must have holes along the inner edge, can be bought at needlework equipment shops or handbag repair shops; it can also be retrieved from an old bag. A 1/4-yard piece of backing fabric is needed, and for the pattern here, about 1/2 kilogram each of prestrung copper cylindrical bugle beads, transparent bugle beads and square-cut steel beads. Beads are usually sold by the kilogram.

A MAKING THE HANDBAG PATTERN

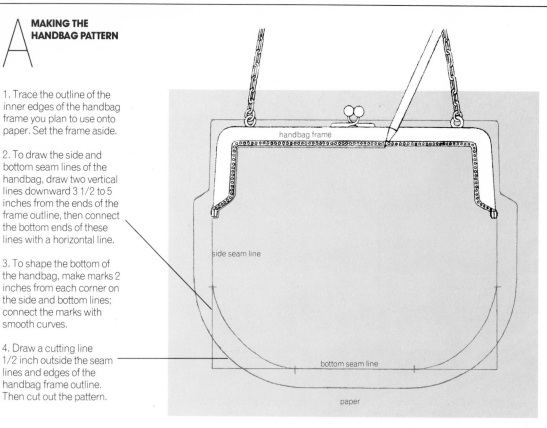

1. Trace the outline of the inner edges of the handbag frame you plan to use onto paper. Set the frame aside.

2. To draw the side and bottom seam lines of the handbag, draw two vertical lines downward 3 1/2 to 5 inches from the ends of the frame outline, then connect the bottom ends of these lines with a horizontal line.

3. To shape the bottom of the handbag, make marks 2 inches from each corner on the side and bottom lines; connect the marks with smooth curves.

4. Draw a cutting line 1/2 inch outside the seam lines and edges of the handbag frame outline. Then cut out the pattern.

5. Use the pattern to cut two pieces of backing fabric for the handbag, following the instructions for beading on a frame *(page 47, Box A)*, but in this case use Steps 1A-5A for both net fabric and opaque fabrics. Set the handbag pattern aside.

handbag frame

side seam line

bottom seam line

paper

B BEADING THE HANDBAG

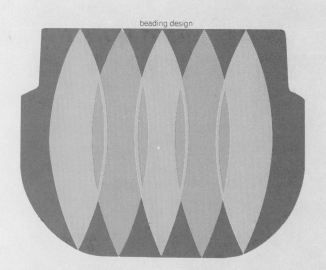

6. Trace the outer edges of the oval motifs and the outline of the bag from the beading design shown here. Enlarge the tracing or reduce it to fit the size of your handbag, following the instructions in the Appendix.

7. Transfer the design to the wrong sides of both pieces of backing fabric, centering the motifs on the fabric. If your fabric is opaque, use dressmaker's carbon and a pencil to transfer the design. If your fabric is net, trace the design—visible through the mesh—with a soft lead pencil.

8. Bead the design, following the instructions for beading on a frame *(pages 47-49)*. Bead the motifs, following the curved contours of the motifs and using steel beads for areas shown in dark gray, copper beads for areas shown in beige and clear beads for areas shown in light gray. After beading the motifs, fill in the background fabric with steel beads.

beading design

paper

C CUTTING THE LINING PIECES

9. Using the handbag pattern *(Step 5)*, make a pattern for the side gussets by first measuring the length of the straight segment of a side seam line from the point where the frame outline ends to the top of the corner curve.

10. Fold a small piece of paper in half and then into quarters.

11. Measure the distance found in Step 9 from the folded corner of the paper along one folded edge; make a mark. Measure half of that distance along the adjoining folded edge; make another mark.

12. Draw a diagonal seam line by connecting the marks made in Step 11.

13. Draw a cutting line 1/2 inch outside and parallel to the seam line. Then cut out and unfold the pattern.

14. Fold 1/4 yard of lining fabric widthwise, wrong sides out. Adjust the folded section so it just holds the handbag and gusset patterns and pin them to the double fabric thickness.

15. Cut the lining pieces; mark seam lines on the fabric's wrong side with dressmaker's carbon and a tracing wheel. Remove the pins; set aside the scraps for the pocket.

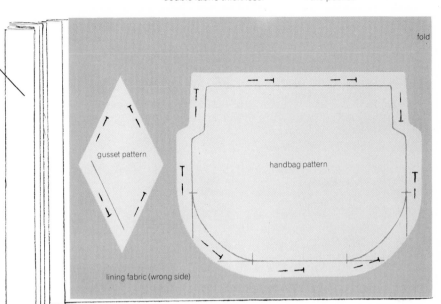

D MAKING THE INNER POCKET

16. Use chalk to draw a 3-by-7-inch rectangle on the wrong side of a scrap of lining fabric.

17. Cut out the pocket.

18. To mark the inner folds of the pocket, draw a line 1 1/4 inches inside and parallel to each end.

19. To mark the outer folds of the pocket, draw a line 1 1/4 inches inside and parallel to each inner line.

20. To hem the top of the pocket, turn the fabric wrong side up and fold the raw edge 1/8 inch along one long side. Press. Fold the edge over another 1/8 inch and press again. Then machine stitch just inside the bottom fold.

21. Fold up the raw edges along the other three sides of the pocket 1/4 inch and press.

22. To make the pleat, first fold the pocket toward the center along one of the inner fold lines and align the fold with the corresponding outer fold line. Press. Then fold the pocket similarly, using the opposite fold lines.

23. To hold the pleats closed, baste across the pocket about 1/2 inch above the unstitched bottom edge.

24. Slip stitch *(Appendix)* the top of the pleat between the inner and outer folds.

25. Place one lining piece wrong side down and center the pocket on top of it, right side up. Pin the pocket in place.

26. Machine stitch 1/8 inch inside the unstitched side and bottom edges of the pocket, backstitching at the beginning and end of the stitching, and pivoting *(Glossary)* at the corners. Remove the pins and bastings.

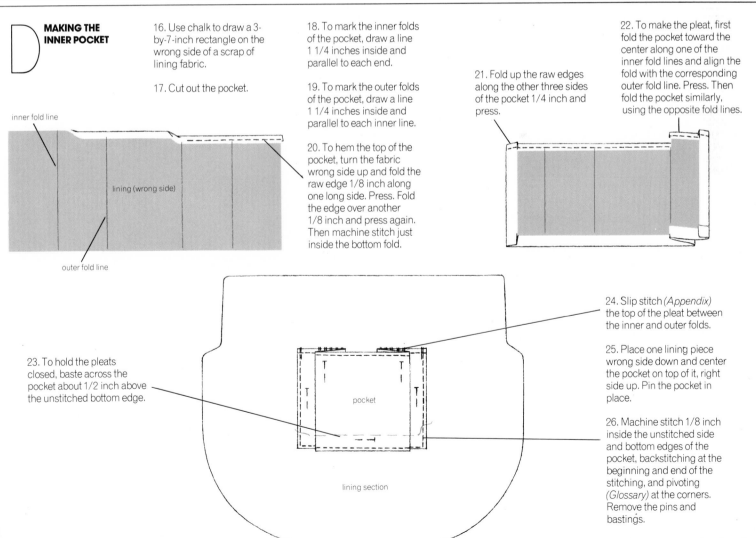

continued

ASSEMBLING THE HANDBAG

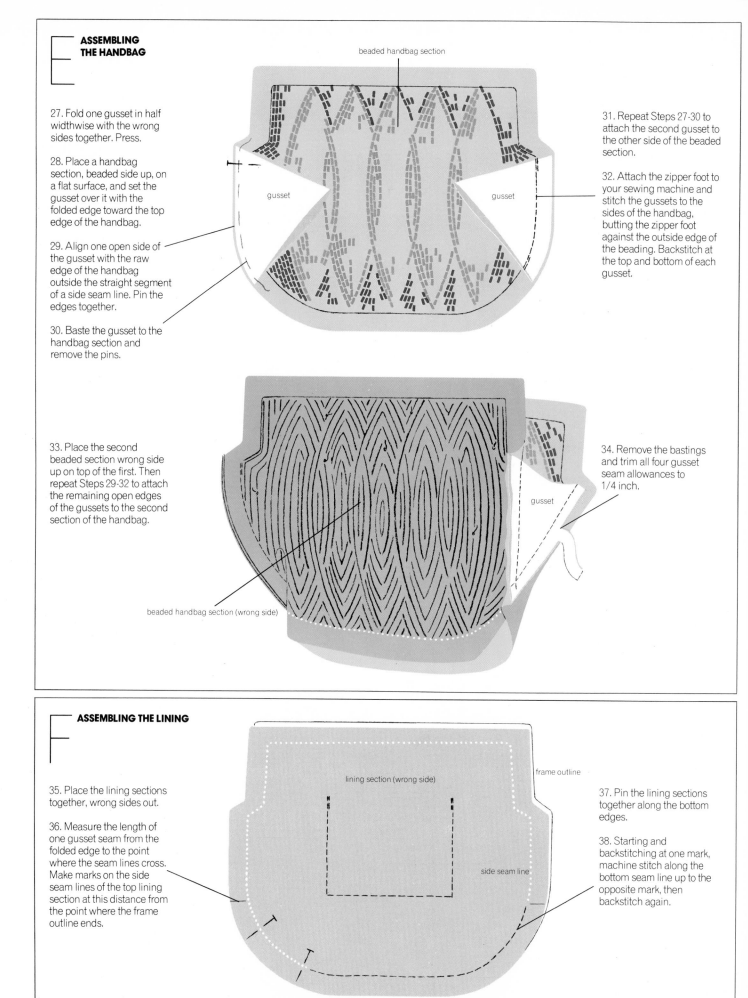

beaded handbag section

gusset

gusset

beaded handbag section (wrong side)

gusset

27. Fold one gusset in half widthwise with the wrong sides together. Press.

28. Place a handbag section, beaded side up, on a flat surface, and set the gusset over it with the folded edge toward the top edge of the handbag.

29. Align one open side of the gusset with the raw edge of the handbag outside the straight segment of a side seam line. Pin the edges together.

30. Baste the gusset to the handbag section and remove the pins.

31. Repeat Steps 27-30 to attach the second gusset to the other side of the beaded section.

32. Attach the zipper foot to your sewing machine and stitch the gussets to the sides of the handbag, butting the zipper foot against the outside edge of the beading. Backstitch at the top and bottom of each gusset.

33. Place the second beaded section wrong side up on top of the first. Then repeat Steps 29-32 to attach the remaining open edges of the gussets to the second section of the handbag.

34. Remove the bastings and trim all four gusset seam allowances to 1/4 inch.

ASSEMBLING THE LINING

lining section (wrong side)

frame outline

side seam line

35. Place the lining sections together, wrong sides out.

36. Measure the length of one gusset seam from the folded edge to the point where the seam lines cross. Make marks on the side seam lines of the top lining section at this distance from the point where the frame outline ends.

37. Pin the lining sections together along the bottom edges.

38. Starting and backstitching at one mark, machine stitch along the bottom seam line up to the opposite mark, then backstitch again.

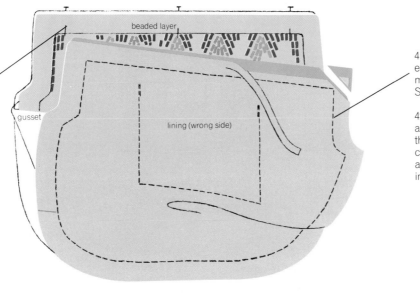

39. Turn the lining and the beaded layer wrong side out.

40. Insert the beaded layer into the lining and align the raw edges. Pin each beaded section to the adjacent lining section along the top edge and down the sides to the gussets.

41. Machine stitch along each pinned edge, using the machine's zipper foot as in Step 32.

42. Trim the lining seam allowances to 1/4 inch at the top of the handbag and clip the corners of the seam allowances up to but not into the stitching.

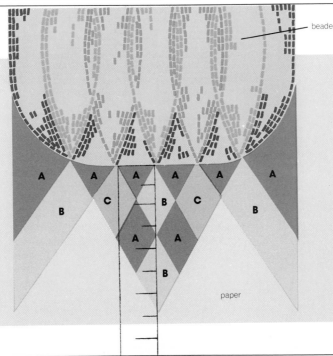

43. Turn the purse lining side out through the opening at the bottom of the beaded layers.

44. Fold under the lining seam allowances at the edges of the gussets, then pin the lining to the gusset so the folded edge just covers the machine stitching.

45. Slip stitch the lining to the gussets on both sides of the purse.

H | **MAKING THE FRINGE DESIGN**

46. Turn the handbag beaded side out, then trace the outline of the bottom edge onto paper.

47. Draw the fringe design as shown onto the paper. The length of the outside lines of the fringe design should be at least as long as the depth of the bag at the center. Make sure the lines on the fringe segments align with the bottom of the motifs in the handbag. Then use a ruler to measure the length required for the center strand of fringe.

48. Mark each section of the design to indicate the colors for the beads. On the design shown here, the dark gray areas indicate steel beads, beige areas copper beads, and light gray areas clear beads.

continued

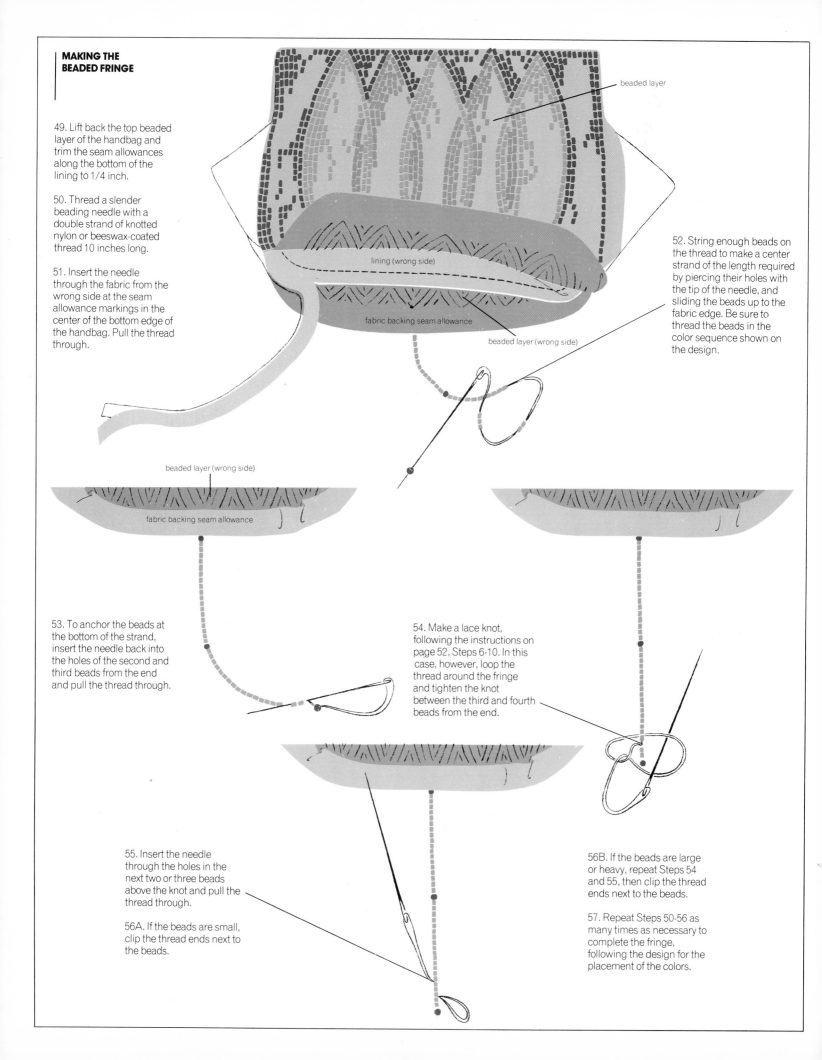

MAKING THE BEADED FRINGE

49. Lift back the top beaded layer of the handbag and trim the seam allowances along the bottom of the lining to 1/4 inch.

50. Thread a slender beading needle with a double strand of knotted nylon or beeswax-coated thread 10 inches long.

51. Insert the needle through the fabric from the wrong side at the seam allowance markings in the center of the bottom edge of the handbag. Pull the thread through.

beaded layer

lining (wrong side)

fabric backing seam allowance

beaded layer (wrong side)

52. String enough beads on the thread to make a center strand of the length required by piercing their holes with the tip of the needle, and sliding the beads up to the fabric edge. Be sure to thread the beads in the color sequence shown on the design.

beaded layer (wrong side)

fabric backing seam allowance

53. To anchor the beads at the bottom of the strand, insert the needle back into the holes of the second and third beads from the end and pull the thread through.

54. Make a lace knot, following the instructions on page 52, Steps 6-10. In this case, however, loop the thread around the fringe and tighten the knot between the third and fourth beads from the end.

55. Insert the needle through the holes in the next two or three beads above the knot and pull the thread through.

56A. If the beads are small, clip the thread ends next to the beads.

56B. If the beads are large or heavy, repeat Steps 54 and 55, then clip the thread ends next to the beads.

57. Repeat Steps 50-56 as many times as necessary to complete the fringe, following the design for the placement of the colors.

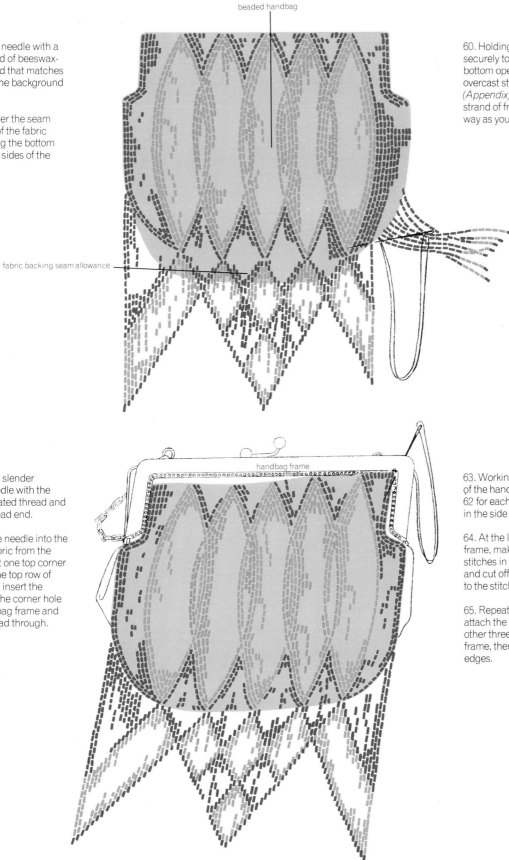

beaded handbag

fabric backing seam allowance

handbag frame

58. Thread a needle with a double strand of beeswax-coated thread that matches the color of the background fabric.

59. Turn under the seam allowances of the fabric backing along the bottom edge of both sides of the handbag.

60. Holding the edges securely together, close the bottom opening with overcast stitches (*Appendix*), flopping each strand of fringe out of the way as you proceed.

61. Thread a slender beading needle with the beeswax-coated thread and knot the thread end.

62. Insert the needle into the handbag fabric from the lining side at one top corner just below the top row of beads. Then insert the needle into the corner hole in the handbag frame and pull the thread through.

63. Working down the side of the handbag, repeat Step 62 for each subsequent hole in the side of the frame.

64. At the lower end of the frame, make 2 tiny fastening stitches in the lining fabric and cut off the thread next to the stitches.

65. Repeat Steps 61-64 to attach the handbag to the other three sides of the frame, then to the top two edges.

An assemblage of scarves

Wrapped and tied snugly around the body, springing into butterfly wing sleeves, this fluttering blouse is made from four scarves in a matter of hours. The sleeves can be one design, the body another, but the two should be related in style and color — small, allover motifs work best; if the scarves have a border, as here, its design becomes an element of the blouse.

The body, front and back, is cut from a pattern for a simple bodice back. All parts use the scarves' finished edges, eliminating the need for hems. If ordinary fabric is substituted for the scarves, cut four 28-inch squares and hem all edges.

SCARF TOP

A CUTTING OUT THE BACK BODICE

1. Eliminate any shoulder or neck darts from the bodice back pattern by folding along the dart lines and pinning the darts closed. Do not close any waist darts.

2. Place one scarf on a flat surface. Fold the wrong sides together; pin along the finished edges.

3. Position the bodice back pattern on the scarf and align the center-back line with the fold. If the center-back line of your pattern is curved, place the high point of the curve on the fold of the scarf. Make sure the grain-line arrow, if there is one on the pattern, is parallel to the fold.

4. To make the scarf top waist length, shift the pattern until the waistline marking at the center back is 1 inch above the bottom edge of the scarf. Pin the pattern to the scarf.

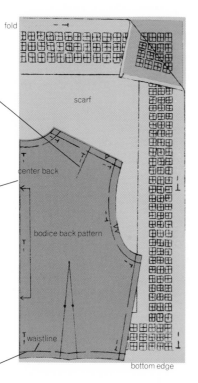

5. To draw a new side cutting line, first measure the pattern at the widest part just below the armhole curve and use dressmaker's chalk to make a mark on the bottom edge of the scarf at this distance from the fold.

6. Make a second mark on the bottom edge 1 inch inside the first one, removing the pins and turning away the bottom side corner of the pattern if necessary.

7. Draw a line to connect the mark made in the preceding step with the widest point of the pattern at the bustline.

8. Cut out the bodice back along only the new side cutting line and the original neck, shoulder and armhole cutting lines of the pattern. Do not cut along the waistline cutting line and do not transfer any pattern markings to the scarf.

9. Remove the pattern and set it aside. Remove the pins around the edges of the scarf.

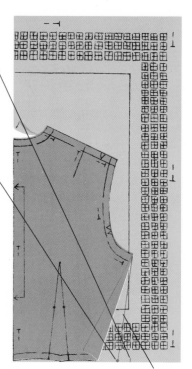

B CUTTING OUT THE FRONT BODICE PIECES

10. Place a second scarf on the flat surface and fold the scarf in half diagonally, wrong sides together. Pin along the finished edges.

11. Measure the side of the bodice back along the cut edge and make a chalk mark on the open side edge of the scarf at this distance from the bottom edge.

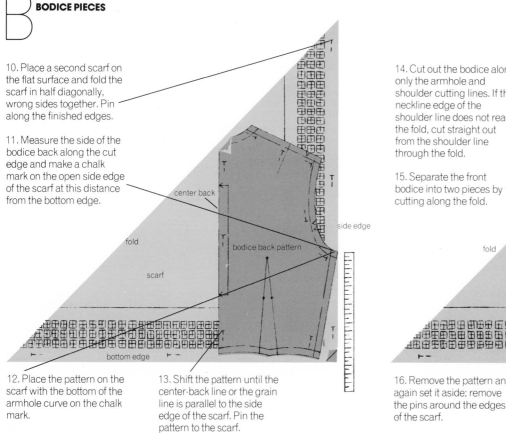

12. Place the pattern on the scarf with the bottom of the armhole curve on the chalk mark.

13. Shift the pattern until the center-back line or the grain line is parallel to the side edge of the scarf. Pin the pattern to the scarf.

14. Cut out the bodice along only the armhole and shoulder cutting lines. If the neckline edge of the shoulder line does not reach the fold, cut straight out from the shoulder line through the fold.

15. Separate the front bodice into two pieces by cutting along the fold.

16. Remove the pattern and again set it aside; remove the pins around the edges of the scarf.

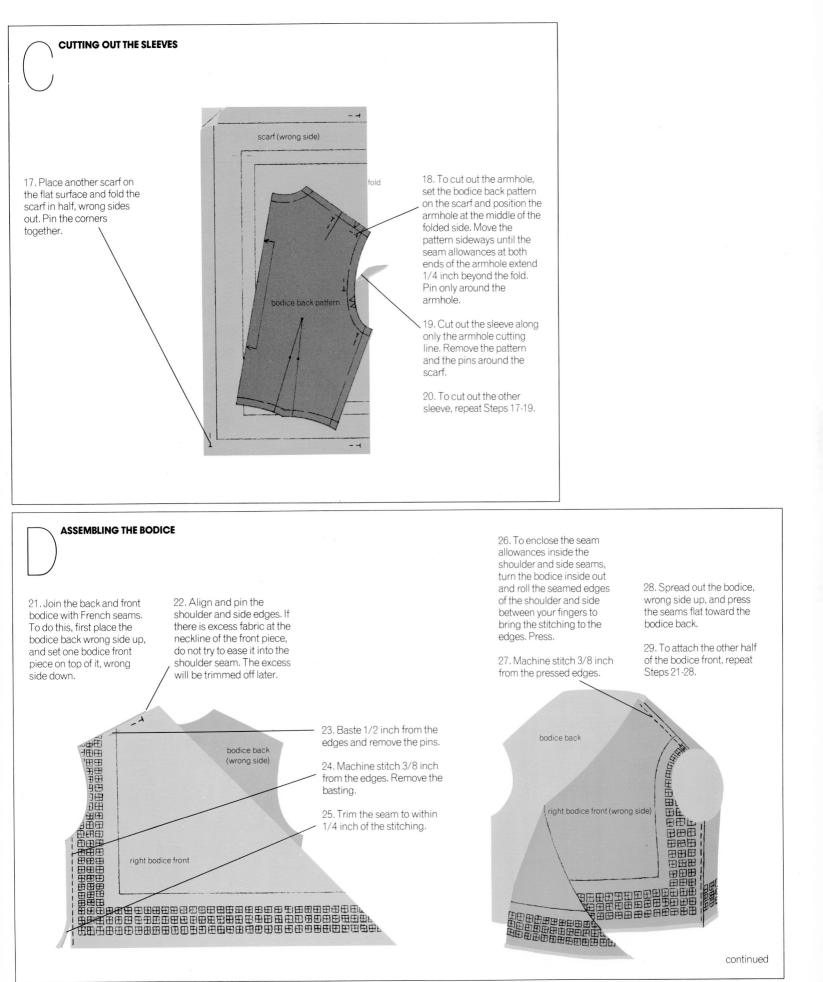

C CUTTING OUT THE SLEEVES

scarf (wrong side)

fold

bodice back pattern

17. Place another scarf on the flat surface and fold the scarf in half, wrong sides out. Pin the corners together.

18. To cut out the armhole, set the bodice back pattern on the scarf and position the armhole at the middle of the folded side. Move the pattern sideways until the seam allowances at both ends of the armhole extend 1/4 inch beyond the fold. Pin only around the armhole.

19. Cut out the sleeve along only the armhole cutting line. Remove the pattern and the pins around the scarf.

20. To cut out the other sleeve, repeat Steps 17-19.

D ASSEMBLING THE BODICE

21. Join the back and front bodice with French seams. To do this, first place the bodice back wrong side up, and set one bodice front piece on top of it, wrong side down.

22. Align and pin the shoulder and side edges. If there is excess fabric at the neckline of the front piece, do not try to ease it into the shoulder seam. The excess will be trimmed off later.

26. To enclose the seam allowances inside the shoulder and side seams, turn the bodice inside out and roll the seamed edges of the shoulder and side between your fingers to bring the stitching to the edges. Press.

27. Machine stitch 3/8 inch from the pressed edges.

28. Spread out the bodice, wrong side up, and press the seams flat toward the bodice back.

29. To attach the other half of the bodice front, repeat Steps 21-28.

bodice back (wrong side)

right bodice front

23. Baste 1/2 inch from the edges and remove the pins.

24. Machine stitch 3/8 inch from the edges. Remove the basting.

25. Trim the seam to within 1/4 inch of the stitching.

bodice back

right bodice front (wrong side)

continued

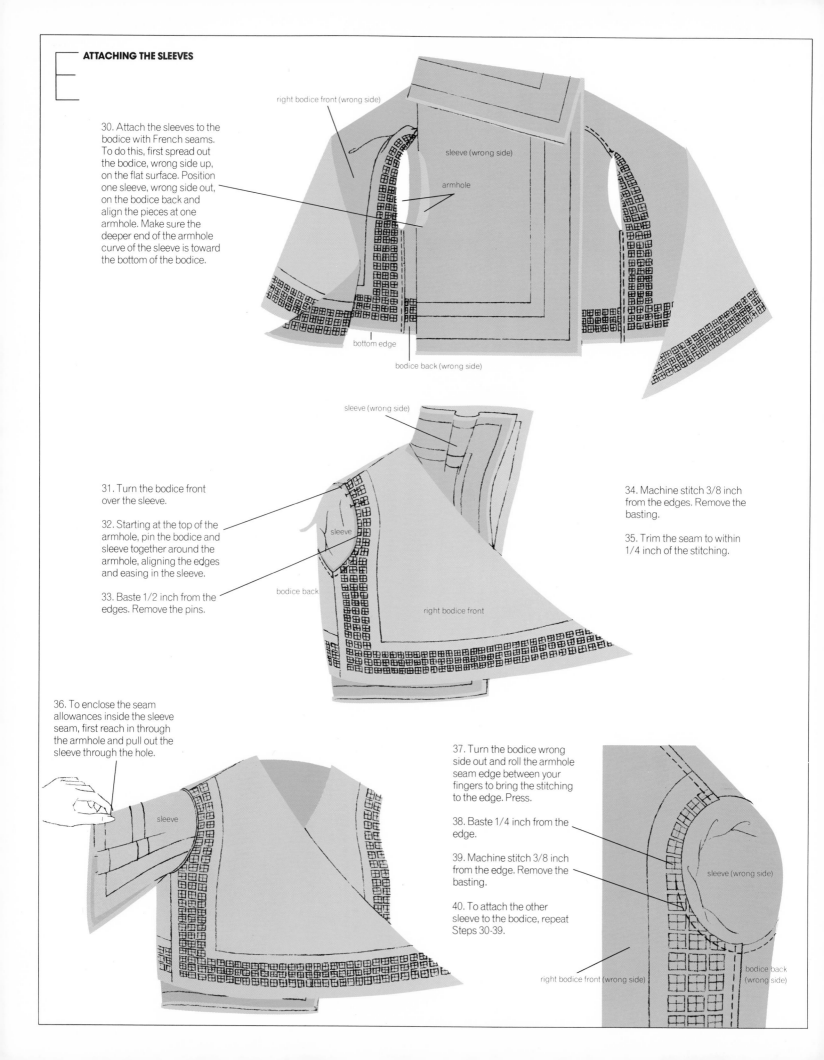

30. Attach the sleeves to the bodice with French seams. To do this, first spread out the bodice, wrong side up, on the flat surface. Position one sleeve, wrong side out, on the bodice back and align the pieces at one armhole. Make sure the deeper end of the armhole curve of the sleeve is toward the bottom of the bodice.

right bodice front (wrong side)

sleeve (wrong side)

armhole

bottom edge

bodice back (wrong side)

sleeve (wrong side)

31. Turn the bodice front over the sleeve.

32. Starting at the top of the armhole, pin the bodice and sleeve together around the armhole, aligning the edges and easing in the sleeve.

33. Baste 1/2 inch from the edges. Remove the pins.

sleeve

bodice back

right bodice front

34. Machine stitch 3/8 inch from the edges. Remove the basting.

35. Trim the seam to within 1/4 inch of the stitching.

36. To enclose the seam allowances inside the sleeve seam, first reach in through the armhole and pull out the sleeve through the hole.

sleeve

37. Turn the bodice wrong side out and roll the armhole seam edge between your fingers to bring the stitching to the edge. Press.

38. Baste 1/4 inch from the edge.

39. Machine stitch 3/8 inch from the edge. Remove the basting.

40. To attach the other sleeve to the bodice, repeat Steps 30-39.

sleeve (wrong side)

right bodice front (wrong side)

bodice back (wrong side)

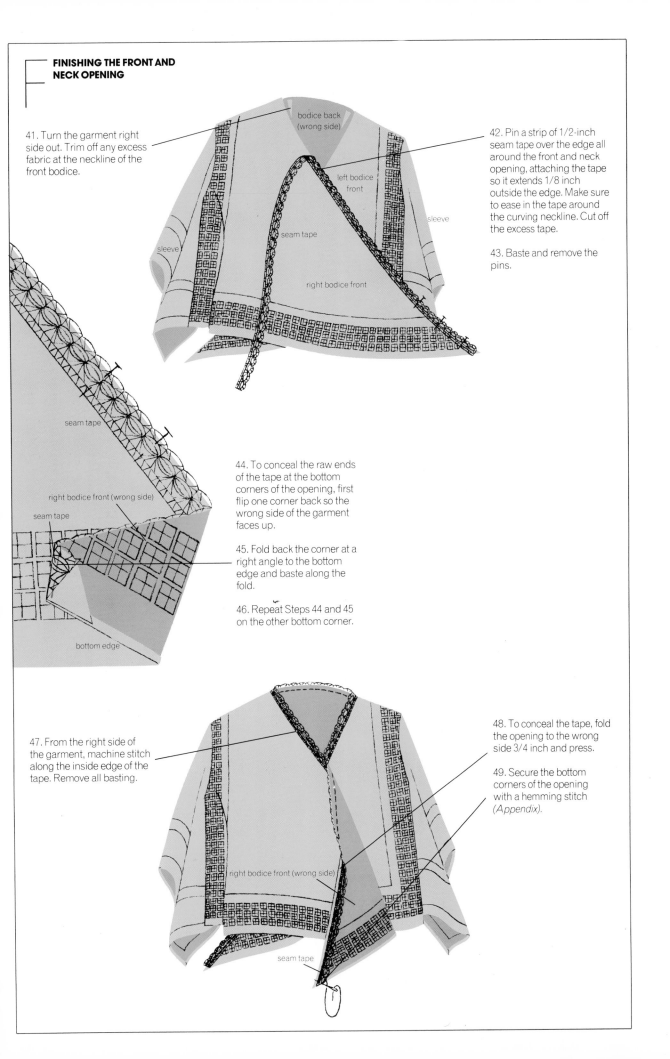

41. Turn the garment right side out. Trim off any excess fabric at the neckline of the front bodice.

42. Pin a strip of 1/2-inch seam tape over the edge all around the front and neck opening, attaching the tape so it extends 1/8 inch outside the edge. Make sure to ease in the tape around the curving neckline. Cut off the excess tape.

43. Baste and remove the pins.

bodice back (wrong side)

left bodice front

seam tape

sleeve

sleeve

right bodice front

seam tape

right bodice front (wrong side)

seam tape

bottom edge

44. To conceal the raw ends of the tape at the bottom corners of the opening, first flip one corner back so the wrong side of the garment faces up.

45. Fold back the corner at a right angle to the bottom edge and baste along the fold.

46. Repeat Steps 44 and 45 on the other bottom corner.

47. From the right side of the garment, machine stitch along the inside edge of the tape. Remove all basting.

48. To conceal the tape, fold the opening to the wrong side 3/4 inch and press.

49. Secure the bottom corners of the opening with a hemming stitch (*Appendix*).

right bodice front (wrong side)

seam tape

4
CRAFTS FOR
DECORATING

Among all the accessories that have decorated human households—rugs, pillows, mats and lamps—none is more venerable than the rug. Rugs date back at least to the Sixth Millennium B.C., when peoples of the Near East wove mats out of rushes. Like other decorative furnishings, rugs filled many practical needs, serving as blankets, saddlebags, tent dividers and canopies. The ancient Greeks covered their

HEIRLOOM CRAFTS TO WARM THE HOME

graves with rugs; Muslims kneel upon them in prayer. But from the very beginning, rugs have been valued equally—or more—for their beauty. The walls of buildings in the Turkish city of Catal Hüyük, 8,000 years old, were painted with designs like those in the rugs called kilim.

Colonial Americans in the cold New England climate had a practical need for rugs and—thriftily using materials at hand—they made a local art form of the hooked rug. It was made by employing a hook to draw loops of fabric (either yarn or strips of cloth) through the interstices of a coarse-woven backing, such as burlap.

Early American women hooked their rugs from outworn clothing scraps, and worked them into patterns drawn onto backings made of used flour and feed sacks. Their designs ran from simple circles, squares and diagonal lines to more elaborate pictures —landscapes, ships, the family cat on the hearth. Like most folk arts, rug hooking was an independent enterprise, carried out with nothing but family ingenuity to guide the artist—until the latter half of the 19th Century. About 1868 an inventive Maine tinker named Edward Sands Frost had a brainstorm that suddenly made rug hooking a good deal simpler.

Frost, who was a peddler of tin and calico, took to sketching patterns of flowers and scrolls on burlap for his wife. Soon he found himself making designs for the neighbors as well, and, as he later wrote, "I began, Yankee-like, to study some way to do them quicker. Then the idea of stenciling presented itself to me." And so, he continued, "I went out to the stable where I had some old iron and some old wash boilers I had bought for their copper bottoms, took the old tin off of them and made my first stencil."

For the job of committing the design sketch to the backing, Frost had reduced 10 hours' worth of labor to two and a half hours; he found he could go into business providing ready-patterned backing, eliminating an entire step in the old rugmaking process. Soon he was peddling printed burlaps all over the region and calling himself "Frost, the rug man." When he retired he left in his workshop some four tons of stencils that today are owned by the Henry Ford Museum in Dearborn, Michigan.

Edward Frost's designs did not alter the basic rug-hooking technique. But modern tools and materials have speeded up the job and added variations to the product. The traditional hook—shaped like a crochet hook—has a wooden handle for easier grasping. The newer latch hook has a metal strip that secures the yarn while the rugmaker works it in and out of the backing.

It is still possible, of course, to make rugs from tattered old clothes just as was done in colonial days, and many women do just that. Overcoats, bathrobes and blankets are ideal for traditional hooking; the wool in them is soft and pliable and it wears well.

By following the same linear pattern but using different fabric and hooks, surprising effects are achieved. "Hooking low"—making loops no higher than 1/8 inch—gives a nubby or grainy look (page 94); this type of rug is made with a traditional hook, and either yarn or cloth strips will do. "Hooking high"—making loops as big as four inches, then splitting them on top—creates a shaggy effect. Latch hooking, using precut yarn, gives a similar result (page 95). Loops made either way can be sheared close for an even, velvety pile. It is even possible to create textured patterns in bas-relief by clipping the loops in different heights. In floor rugs, however, the uneven surface is easy to trip on; reserve this refinement for the ultimate decorative use as a wall hanging.

Two looks with rug hooks

The same design—swirling clouds, borrowed from Chinese painting—floats across two different versions of rug hooking. The bench is covered with a close-looped pile of thin wool strips, pulled with a traditional rug hook through a backing of burlap or monk's cloth. The modern shag rug is made with an easy-to-use contemporary device, a hinged latch hook, with which pre-cut lengths of yarn are knotted onto open-mesh canvas.

Instructions for hooking and latch hooking

Both the traditional hooked bench cover and the latch-hooked rug on pages 94-95 are based on the design in the chart below. While the bench cover is in solid colors as indicated by the letters in the key at right, the rug is hooked with various shades of these colors to produce a mottled effect.

To make a 36-by-17-inch bench cover like the one shown, you will need a 40-by-21-inch closely woven backing—preferably a 13-ounce burlap, which weighs 13 ounces to the 40-inch-wide yard, or a two-by-two monk's cloth, in which two threads act as one in both the warp and weft. In addition, you will need a large wooden hoop or frame (even a picture frame) to stretch the backing, 4 yards of 1 1/2-inch cotton twill rug tape to bind it, and a medium-sized rug hook. The bench cover requires about 2 1/2

yards or 3,700 strips of new or used wool flannel in the amounts given in the key. Each strip should be cut 3/32 inch wide and 12 inches long. Such strips come precut in bunches of 30, but the cloth can be cut with scissors or a special slitting machine available through craft suppliers.

To make the 2-by-4-foot rug shown, you will need a 28-by-52-inch backing of stiff double-mesh (leno weave) rug canvas, a latch hook and a total of 32 three-ounce skeins of 4-ply wool yarn or 27 four-ounce skeins of acrylic rug yarn in the colors listed below. Cut the yarn into strips 1 3/4 to 2 1/2 inches long or use yarn that is precut in the 1 3/4-inch length.

MATERIALS REQUIRED

Color	Bench Cover flannel strips	Rug ounces of yarn
A blue	360	9
B dark green	540	14
C light green	360	12
D brown	420	7
E light brown	390	12
F yellow	300	12
G light yellow	360	6
H yellow-green	360	6
I beige	450	9
J pink	120	6

TRADITIONAL HOOKING

A PREPARING THE BACKING

1. Cut a backing of closely woven burlap or monk's cloth 4 inches longer and wider than the size you want the finished project to be; do not cut off the selvages.

2. Turn under the raw edges of the backing 1/4 inch. Machine stitch 1/8 inch from the folds.

3. Enlarge your design and transfer it to the backing, following the instructions in the Appendix. Use a waterproof marker to indicate the color for each area of the design.

4. Run two rows of straight or zigzag machine stitches 1/8 inch apart about 3/4 inch outside the design area, pivoting (Glossary) at corners.

5. Measure around the outside of the design area and add 1 inch for every 8 inches measured to determine the total length of binding you need. Cut that amount of 1 1/2-inch-wide cotton twill rug tape and preshrink it.

6. Place the binding on the backing, starting inside the center top of the design area and aligning the edge of the tape with the edges of the design.

7. Pin the binding to the backing, mitering corners.

8. Overlap the ends of the binding 1 inch and cut off the excess. Fold under the top end 1/2 inch. Pin.

9. Machine stitch along the binding 1/8 inch from the outside edge, pivoting at corners. Remove the pins. The binding will stand up away from the design area.

B ATTACHING THE BACKING TO THE HOOP OR FRAME

10. Center the backing, design side up, on your hoop or frame.

11. Tighten the thumbscrew if you are using a hoop. Attach the backing securely with thumbtacks if you are using a frame. As you hook, restretch and secure the backing whenever it begins to sag.

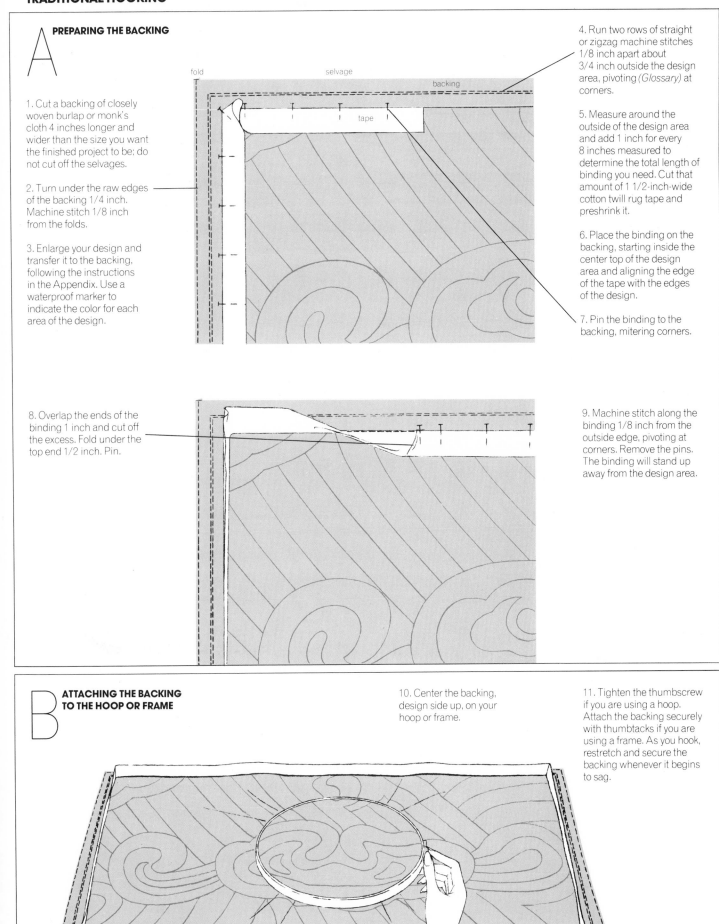

continued

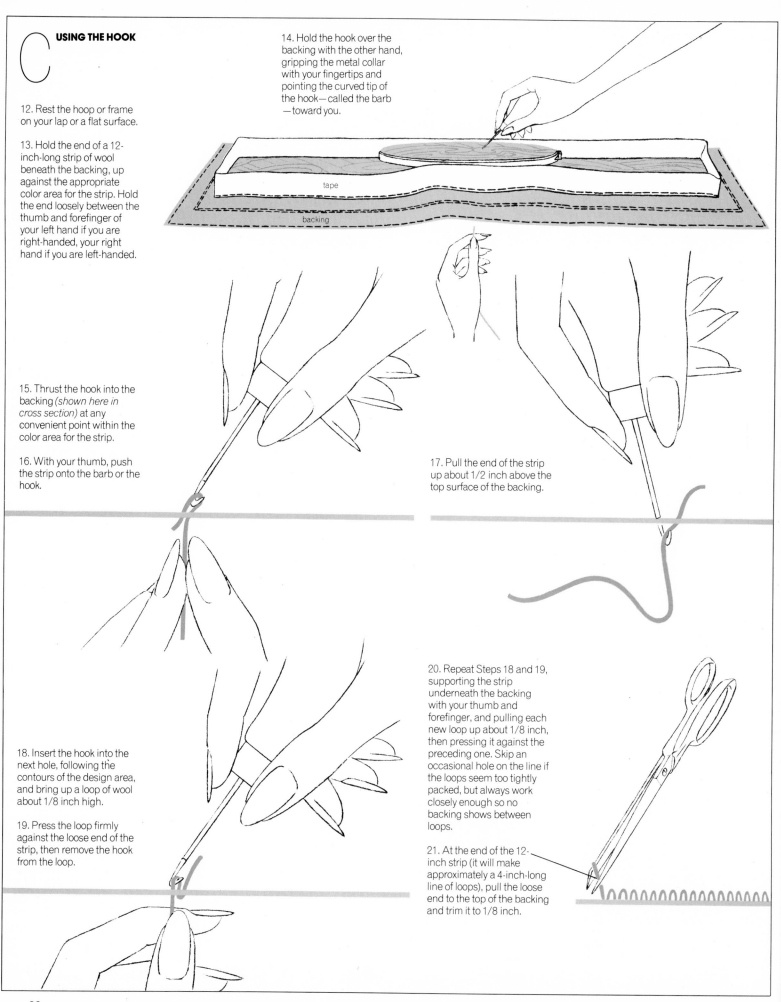

C USING THE HOOK

12. Rest the hoop or frame on your lap or a flat surface.

13. Hold the end of a 12-inch-long strip of wool beneath the backing, up against the appropriate color area for the strip. Hold the end loosely between the thumb and forefinger of your left hand if you are right-handed, your right hand if you are left-handed.

14. Hold the hook over the backing with the other hand, gripping the metal collar with your fingertips and pointing the curved tip of the hook—called the barb —toward you.

tape

backing

15. Thrust the hook into the backing (shown here in cross section) at any convenient point within the color area for the strip.

16. With your thumb, push the strip onto the barb or the hook.

17. Pull the end of the strip up about 1/2 inch above the top surface of the backing.

18. Insert the hook into the next hole, following the contours of the design area, and bring up a loop of wool about 1/8 inch high.

19. Press the loop firmly against the loose end of the strip, then remove the hook from the loop.

20. Repeat Steps 18 and 19, supporting the strip underneath the backing with your thumb and forefinger, and pulling each new loop up about 1/8 inch, then pressing it against the preceding one. Skip an occasional hole on the line if the loops seem too tightly packed, but always work closely enough so no backing shows between loops.

21. At the end of the 12-inch strip (it will make approximately a 4-inch-long line of loops), pull the loose end to the top of the backing and trim it to 1/8 inch.

98

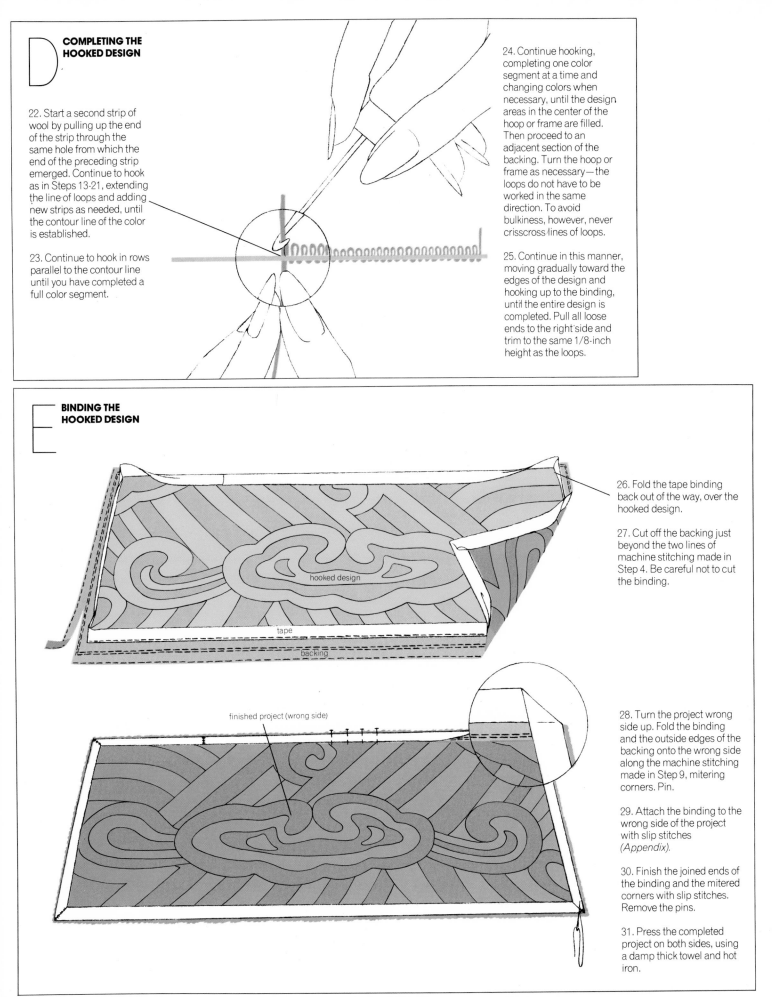

D COMPLETING THE HOOKED DESIGN

22. Start a second strip of wool by pulling up the end of the strip through the same hole from which the end of the preceding strip emerged. Continue to hook as in Steps 13-21, extending the line of loops and adding new strips as needed, until the contour line of the color is established.

23. Continue to hook in rows parallel to the contour line until you have completed a full color segment.

24. Continue hooking, completing one color segment at a time and changing colors when necessary, until the design areas in the center of the hoop or frame are filled. Then proceed to an adjacent section of the backing. Turn the hoop or frame as necessary—the loops do not have to be worked in the same direction. To avoid bulkiness, however, never crisscross lines of loops.

25. Continue in this manner, moving gradually toward the edges of the design and hooking up to the binding, until the entire design is completed. Pull all loose ends to the right side and trim to the same 1/8-inch height as the loops.

E BINDING THE HOOKED DESIGN

hooked design

tape

backing

26. Fold the tape binding back out of the way, over the hooked design.

27. Cut off the backing just beyond the two lines of machine stitching made in Step 4. Be careful not to cut the binding.

finished project (wrong side)

28. Turn the project wrong side up. Fold the binding and the outside edges of the backing onto the wrong side along the machine stitching made in Step 9, mitering corners. Pin.

29. Attach the binding to the wrong side of the project with slip stitches (Appendix).

30. Finish the joined ends of the binding and the mitered corners with slip stitches. Remove the pins.

31. Press the completed project on both sides, using a damp thick towel and hot iron.

LATCH HOOKING

A PREPARING THE BACKING

1. Cut a backing of double-mesh rug canvas 4 inches longer and wider than the size you want the finished project to be; it is not necessary to cut off the selvages.

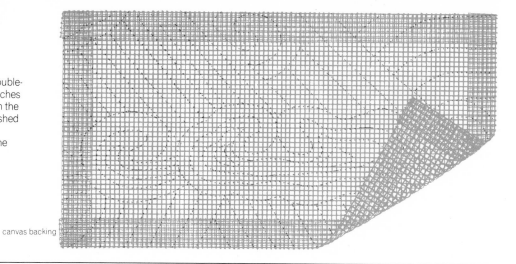

canvas backing

2. Enlarge your design and transfer it to the canvas (*Appendix*). Use a waterproof marker to indicate the color for each area of the design.

3. Fold a 2-inch hem all around the canvas, turning up the short end while turning down the long sides. Be sure to align the mesh holes of all layers in the folded areas.

B USING THE LATCH HOOK

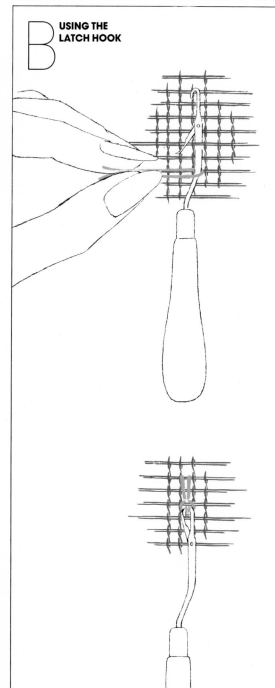

4. Place the canvas on a flat surface. Fold a 1 3/4- to 2 1/2-inch length of yarn around the shank of the latch hook and hold the yarn horizontally, at right angles to the hook.

5. Start near the center of the design. With the hinged latch open and the curved tip of the hook pointed toward the ends of the yarn, insert the tip of the hook in a hole.

6. Push the hook forward and then up through the next hole directly above, until the latch is all the way through both holes and the tip lies flat on the surface of the canvas.

7. Pull the hook toward you — as you do this, the latch will begin to close. When it is about halfway closed, cross the ends of the yarn over the latch and under the curved tip of the hook.

8. Continue to pull the hook toward you until the ends of the yarn slip out of your fingers and begin to slide under the double strand of canvas between the 2 holes.

9. Keeping your wrist low, yank the hook hard and flick the tip upward. The ends of the yarn will emerge from the first hole through the loop of the yarn, forming a knot.

10. Tug the ends of the yarn to tighten the knot.

11. Make a second knot alongside the first knot. Then continue latch hooking horizontally, working to the left and right of the preceding knots, until you have completed a line of knots within a color segment.

canvas backing

12. Continue to make horizontal lines upward, one above the other, until you have completed a full color segment. As you work upward on the canvas, pull the completed part of the design toward you and roll it under on your lap. Change colors as necessary to complete the top part of the canvas. When you reach the hems, insert the hook and yarn through both of their two layers.

13. When the entire top of the design is completed, unroll the bottom part and complete that area, starting at the bottom hem edge and working up.

14. Check the wrong side; if any parts of the canvas have been missed, fill them in. It is not necessary to bind or finish the hems of the backing, because the hooking of the knots provides its own finish.

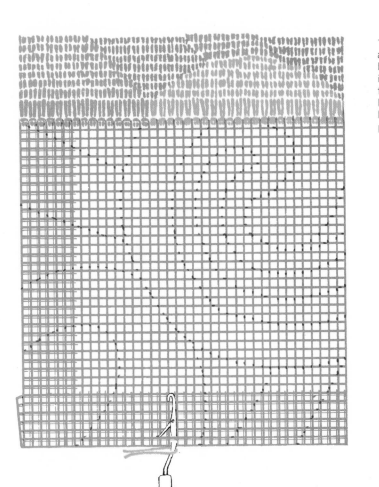

An old-world design in cross-stitch

Long popular as a trimming for household linens and peasant costumes—and once used on the traditional samplers that taught young girls both the alphabet and the needle arts—counted-thread embroidery radiates the cheerful charm of another age. But counted-thread embroidery can also be as crisply modern as the Scandinavian design that decorates the lid of this contemporary sewing box. The work is done simply by counting off threads on any even-weave fabric, usually cotton or linen, following a grid-marked paper pattern; the cross-stitch is most often employed.

Instructions for counted-thread embroidery

In counted-thread embroidery, fabric threads are the working grid for the design; each stitch is made over a square formed by vertical and horizontal threads. Therefore, this technique calls for fabric woven with the same number of vertical and horizontal threads per inch.

Two types of linen or cotton fabrics are suitable. One, called even weave, is a plain woven fabric with a smooth surface; it may be as fine as 40 threads per inch or as coarse as 10 per inch. The other fabric is a square weave *(right)* in which clusters of threads form small textured squares—of from 6 to 14 per inch —separated at the corners by holes. Counting thread is simpler with square-weave fabric—each stitch is worked over one of the squares formed by the weave.

Though many stitches are used in counted-thread embroidery, the cross-stitch is among the most popular. Because it is simple to do and works up quickly, cross-stitch is often used to fill in the entire design area. For adding details such as fine lines, the Holbein stitch, a form of double running stitch, is ideal.

1. Using a soft pencil, draw a rectangle onto the right side of the embroidery fabric with sides at least 2 inches larger than the design area. Draw each line along a row of the holes formed by the weave of the fabric.

2. Trim the fabric along the drawn lines.

3. To avoid fraying, run a line of machine zigzag stitching along the edges of the fabric, or hand stitch the edges with overcast stitches *(Appendix)*.

4. To make guide lines indicating the center of the fabric, use a ruler and pencil to mark the hole in the weave that is closest to the center point of two adjacent sides.

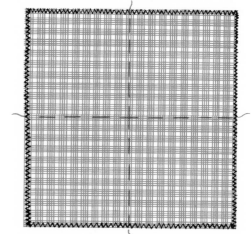

5. Starting from each marked central hole, run basting stitches lengthwise and widthwise across the rectangle along a row of holes. Take long stitches on the visible side of the fabric so the guide lines will be easy to follow; be sure the two lines cross on the visible side at the center of the fabric.

THE COUNTED-THREAD CROSS-STITCH

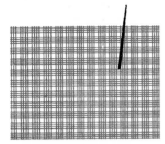

1. Whether you are right-handed or left-handed, start the first row at the right edge of the design area. Using knotted thread, bring the needle up from the wrong side of the fabric through the second hole from the top of the area. Pull the thread through.

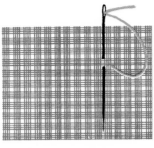

2. To make the first half cross-stitch, insert the needle into the fabric 1 hole above and 1 hole to the left of the hole from which the thread last emerged. Turn the needle downward and bring it out 1 hole to the left of the hole from which the thread last emerged. Pull the thread through.

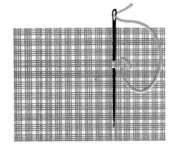

3. Working to the left, repeat Step 2 as many times as necessary to make the remaining half cross-stitches in the row.

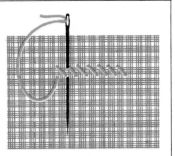

4. At the left-hand end of the row, complete the first cross-stitch by reversing the direction and inserting the needle into the fabric 1 hole above and 1 hole to the right of the hole from which the thread last emerged. Turn the needle downward and bring it out 1 hole to the right of the hole from which the thread last emerged. Pull the thread through.

5. Repeat Step 4 across the row to complete the remaining cross-stitches. On the last stitch, insert the needle into the fabric 1 hole above and 1 hole to the right of the hole from which the thread last emerged and pull the thread through to the wrong side of the fabric.

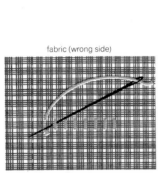

6. To start each subsequent row, bring the needle up from the wrong side of the fabric 2 holes below the hole into which the thread last entered and pull the thread through. Then repeat Steps 2-5.

fabric (wrong side)

7. To end off, turn the fabric wrong side up. Insert the needle under the embroidery threads forming the last stitch, but not into the fabric. Then pull the thread partially through, leaving a small loop.

fabric (wrong side)

8. Insert the needle through the loop made in Step 7 and over the thread. Draw the thread through and pull it tight to close the loop. Clip off the excess thread.

THE COUNTED-THREAD HOLBEIN STITCH

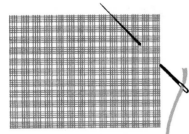

1. Start the line of stitches at the right of the design area. If the line is vertical or diagonal, turn the fabric and the instruction chart so that you can work horizontally. Using knotted thread, bring the needle up from the wrong side of the fabric through the hole in which you wish to begin. Pull the thread through.

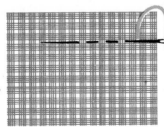

2. Insert the needle into the fabric 1 hole to the left, then bring it up in the next hole and weave it in and out of the fabric several times through succeeding holes. Pull the thread through. Repeat until you fill in the line.

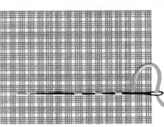

3. Turn the fabric 180° so the bottom edge is on top and the thread emerges at the right end of the line again. Repeat Step 2 to fill in the empty spaces between stitches and complete the line. Secure the last stitch on the wrong side of the fabric as shown for the cross-stitch, Steps 7 and 8.

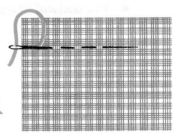

IF YOU ARE LEFT-HANDED...
Follow Steps 1-3 but begin at the left edge of the design area and work to the right as shown.

Quickly done cross-stitches on an even weave

The counted-thread embroidery design pictured on pages 102-103 and detailed in the chart at right measures 12 1/2 inches square—13 1/2 inches when edged with a half-inch-wide plain border. The design requires 1/2 yard of white or cream-colored square-weave fabric, sometimes known as Aida cloth, with a count of 14 squares to the linear inch; alternatively, use even-weave cotton or linen with a thread count of 28 threads to the inch. You will also need several Size 6 or 7 embroidery needles and 10 skeins of six-strand cotton embroidery thread. To match the colors shown in the chart, use five skeins of dark blue thread, two of medium pink, and one each of light blue, medium blue, light gray and dark red.

An embroidery hoop is not essential—the fabric will not pull out of shape—but it helps hold the work comfortably. A magnifying lens especially mounted for use in needlework makes it easier to count the fabric squares or threads.

Preparing the fabric: Cut the fabric at least 2 inches wider on each side than the desired finished size of your project. Follow the instructions on page 104 to cut out the fabric, secure the edges and baste guide lines for the divisions between the four quarters.

Using the design chart: The design is divided into quarters and is completed, from the center outward, one quarter at a time. The chart opposite shows the upper-right quarter. After you have worked this first quarter of the design, rotate the chart to complete each one of the remaining three quarters successively. The center vertical and horizontal rows are marked with arrows and correspond to the guide lines basted on the fabric. Work these marked center rows only once, in the quarter of the design in which they first appear. After you have completed the upper-right quarter, finish the remaining quarters in whichever order you prefer. For the upper-left quarter, simply rotate the chart 90° to the left of its original position; for the lower-right quarter, 90° to the right; and for the lower-left quarter, 180°.

Stitches in counted-thread embroidery are placed differently from those in most embroidery, in which the design is transferred to the fabric. For this type, the placement of stitches is determined by counting off squares or threads on the design chart, then counting off a like number of squares or threads on the fabric and working the stitches over them. Each square of the grid represents a square formed by the intersecting threads of the fabric. On square-weave Aida cloth, the holes in the weave through which you will insert the needle will correspond to the points where the design grid lines intersect; on even-weave fabrics, you will need groups of two or more intersecting threads to form a square of equivalent size. The squares marked by an X on the chart represent cross-stitches; those marked by a straight line represent Holbein stitches. Each stitch is indicated in the color of thread to be used.

Stitching the design: Thread the needle with two strands of the six-strand embroidery thread. If possible, use a different needle for each thread color, to minimize rethreading. When working with any given color, you can carry the thread to an adjacent area of the same color if it is no more than 1/4 inch away; otherwise, end off the thread and begin the adjacent area anew.

Working outward from the center, make the first stitch at the basted center point of the fabric and work the stylized cross in pink, light blue, dark red and dark blue.

Then, proceeding toward the outer edges of the project, complete the double lines in dark blue that form the inner border. Next, work the six lines in medium blue, dark red, pink, light blue and dark blue that form the middle border with the gap-toothed edge.

Continue with the single line of light blue stitches at the outer border; then work the dark blue Greek key design around the outer edge.

Now working back toward the center of the piece, fill in the remaining design areas as follows: Embroider the gray X's on both sides of the light blue outer border line; the pink, dark blue and gray diamonds between the outer and middle border lines; the pink, gray and dark blue pattern of crosses between the middle and inner borders; and the ornamental tracery in pink, light blue and dark blue adjacent to the inner border. Next embroider the flowers in light blue, pink and gray. Do the dark blue flower stems last, working them in a combination of cross-stitch and Holbein stitch as marked on the chart.

Pressing the embroidery: Place the finished embroidery wrong side up on several layers of soft dry toweling. Then press with a dry iron and a wet cloth.

Pillows to put on show

Radiating glamor and luxurious softness, these eight plump pillows are
made with careful attention to detail.
Each cover is stretched over a larger
inner pillow for extra fullness, and
square styles are imperceptibly contoured for truly square corners.

Clockwise, beginning below, are
pillows with shirred Turkish corners, round shirring, pleated Turkish
corners, double flange edges, box
edges, mitered pattern and (center)
knife edges and bolster shape.

THE KNIFE-EDGED PILLOW

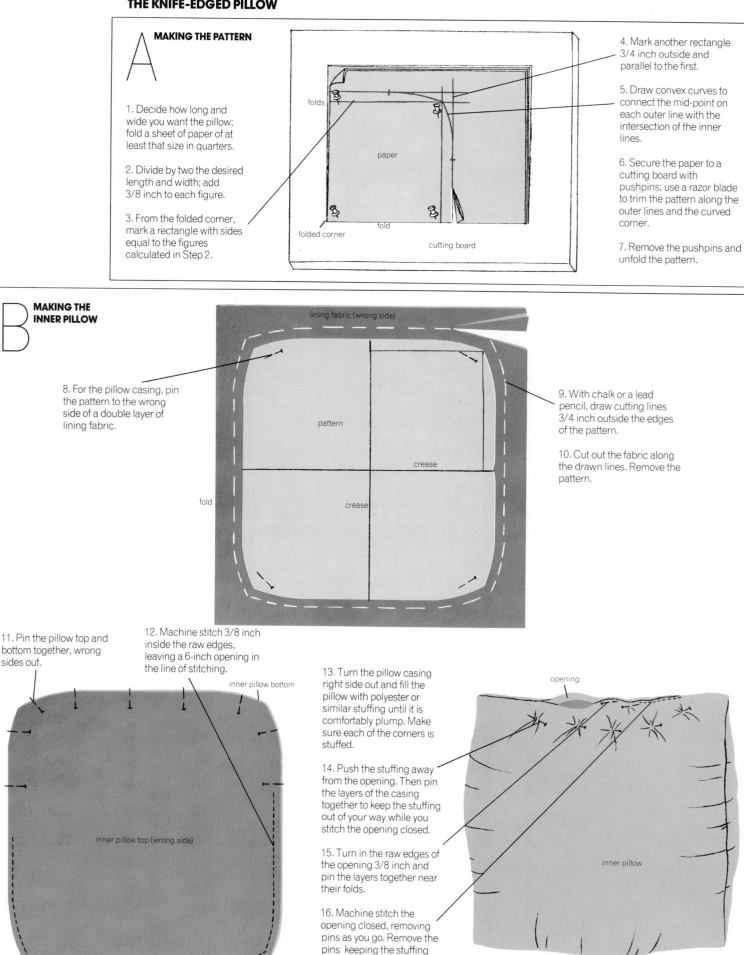

A MAKING THE PATTERN

1. Decide how long and wide you want the pillow; fold a sheet of paper of at least that size in quarters.

2. Divide by two the desired length and width; add 3/8 inch to each figure.

3. From the folded corner, mark a rectangle with sides equal to the figures calculated in Step 2.

folds

paper

folded corner

fold

cutting board

4. Mark another rectangle 3/4 inch outside and parallel to the first.

5. Draw convex curves to connect the mid-point on each outer line with the intersection of the inner lines.

6. Secure the paper to a cutting board with pushpins; use a razor blade to trim the pattern along the outer lines and the curved corner.

7. Remove the pushpins and unfold the pattern.

B MAKING THE INNER PILLOW

lining fabric (wrong side)

pattern

crease

crease

fold

8. For the pillow casing, pin the pattern to the wrong side of a double layer of lining fabric.

9. With chalk or a lead pencil, draw cutting lines 3/4 inch outside the edges of the pattern.

10. Cut out the fabric along the drawn lines. Remove the pattern.

11. Pin the pillow top and bottom together, wrong sides out.

12. Machine stitch 3/8 inch inside the raw edges, leaving a 6-inch opening in the line of stitching.

inner pillow bottom

inner pillow top (wrong side)

13. Turn the pillow casing right side out and fill the pillow with polyester or similar stuffing until it is comfortably plump. Make sure each of the corners is stuffed.

14. Push the stuffing away from the opening. Then pin the layers of the casing together to keep the stuffing out of your way while you stitch the opening closed.

15. Turn in the raw edges of the opening 3/8 inch and pin the layers together near their folds.

16. Machine stitch the opening closed, removing pins as you go. Remove the pins keeping the stuffing compressed, and evenly distribute the stuffing.

opening

inner pillow

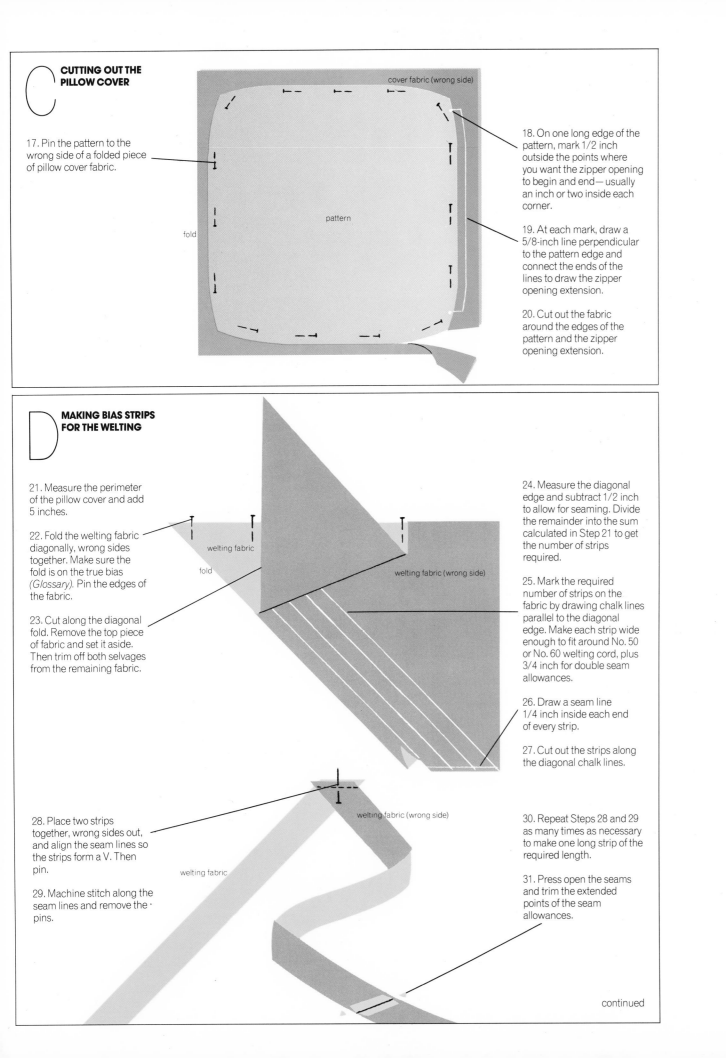

C CUTTING OUT THE PILLOW COVER

17. Pin the pattern to the wrong side of a folded piece of pillow cover fabric.

cover fabric (wrong side)

pattern

fold

18. On one long edge of the pattern, mark 1/2 inch outside the points where you want the zipper opening to begin and end—usually an inch or two inside each corner.

19. At each mark, draw a 5/8-inch line perpendicular to the pattern edge and connect the ends of the lines to draw the zipper opening extension.

20. Cut out the fabric around the edges of the pattern and the zipper opening extension.

D MAKING BIAS STRIPS FOR THE WELTING

21. Measure the perimeter of the pillow cover and add 5 inches.

22. Fold the welting fabric diagonally, wrong sides together. Make sure the fold is on the true bias (Glossary). Pin the edges of the fabric.

23. Cut along the diagonal fold. Remove the top piece of fabric and set it aside. Then trim off both selvages from the remaining fabric.

welting fabric

fold

welting fabric (wrong side)

24. Measure the diagonal edge and subtract 1/2 inch to allow for seaming. Divide the remainder into the sum calculated in Step 21 to get the number of strips required.

25. Mark the required number of strips on the fabric by drawing chalk lines parallel to the diagonal edge. Make each strip wide enough to fit around No. 50 or No. 60 welting cord, plus 3/4 inch for double seam allowances.

26. Draw a seam line 1/4 inch inside each end of every strip.

27. Cut out the strips along the diagonal chalk lines.

welting fabric (wrong side)

28. Place two strips together, wrong sides out, and align the seam lines so the strips form a V. Then pin.

29. Machine stitch along the seam lines and remove the pins.

welting fabric

30. Repeat Steps 28 and 29 as many times as necessary to make one long strip of the required length.

31. Press open the seams and trim the extended points of the seam allowances.

continued

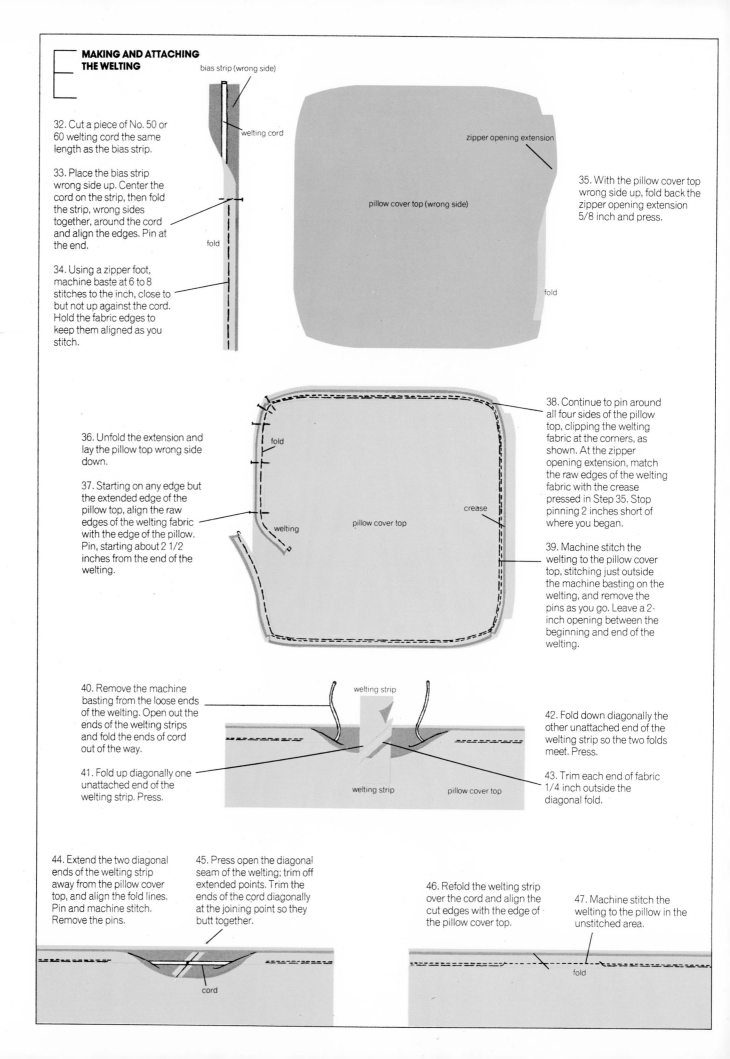

MAKING AND ATTACHING THE WELTING

bias strip (wrong side)

welting cord

32. Cut a piece of No. 50 or 60 welting cord the same length as the bias strip.

33. Place the bias strip wrong side up. Center the cord on the strip, then fold the strip, wrong sides together, around the cord and align the edges. Pin at the end.

fold

34. Using a zipper foot, machine baste at 6 to 8 stitches to the inch, close to but not up against the cord. Hold the fabric edges to keep them aligned as you stitch.

zipper opening extension

pillow cover top (wrong side)

35. With the pillow cover top wrong side up, fold back the zipper opening extension 5/8 inch and press.

fold

36. Unfold the extension and lay the pillow top wrong side down.

37. Starting on any edge but the extended edge of the pillow top, align the raw edges of the welting fabric with the edge of the pillow. Pin, starting about 2 1/2 inches from the end of the welting.

fold

welting

pillow cover top

crease

38. Continue to pin around all four sides of the pillow top, clipping the welting fabric at the corners, as shown. At the zipper opening extension, match the raw edges of the welting fabric with the crease pressed in Step 35. Stop pinning 2 inches short of where you began.

39. Machine stitch the welting to the pillow cover top, stitching just outside the machine basting on the welting, and remove the pins as you go. Leave a 2-inch opening between the beginning and end of the welting.

40. Remove the machine basting from the loose ends of the welting. Open out the ends of the welting strips and fold the ends of cord out of the way.

41. Fold up diagonally one unattached end of the welting strip. Press.

welting strip

welting strip

pillow cover top

42. Fold down diagonally the other unattached end of the welting strip so the two folds meet. Press.

43. Trim each end of fabric 1/4 inch outside the diagonal fold.

44. Extend the two diagonal ends of the welting strip away from the pillow cover top, and align the fold lines. Pin and machine stitch. Remove the pins.

45. Press open the diagonal seam of the welting; trim off extended points. Trim the ends of the cord diagonally at the joining point so they butt together.

cord

46. Refold the welting strip over the cord and align the cut edges with the edge of the pillow cover top.

47. Machine stitch the welting to the pillow in the unstitched area.

fold

48. Place the pillow cover top and bottom together, wrong sides out. With the top section facing up, pin along the edges of the zipper opening extension.

49. Machine stitch inside the welting stitches from each corner to 1/2 inch inside each end of the extension.

50. Flop the pillow cover so the unwelted bottom section is facing up. Push the fabric out of the way along the zipper opening.

51. Open the zipper and place one side of it face down on the welted zipper extension with the outer edge of the zipper tape toward the fabric edge.

52. Place the top stop of the zipper just below the stitched portion of the seam and midway on the corded part of the welting. Insert a pin at the top end of the tape.

53. Using a zipper foot, stitch 1/4 inch from the zipper teeth. Stitch from the top zipper stop to the bottom stop. Hold the zipper in place with your hand to keep the teeth lined up along the middle of the corded part of the welting. Remove the pin.

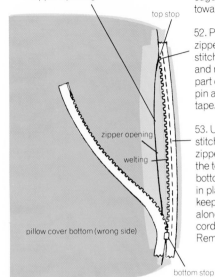

pillow cover bottom

pillow cover top (wrong side)

zipper opening extension

top stop

zipper opening

welting

pillow cover bottom (wrong side)

bottom stop

54. Open out the fabric so both the top and bottom sections are wrong side down.

55. Close the zipper and fold under the seam allowance of the top section to turn the zipper face up.

56. Lap the unattached folded edge of the bottom section of the pillow over the zipper teeth, covering them completely. Pin, making sure to catch the zipper tape underneath.

57. Using a zipper foot, machine stitch the zipper to the pillow bottom. Sew from the finished side starting at the welting just below the bottom zipper stop. Stitch to 1/2 inch outside the welt. Pivot (Glossary) and stitch parallel to the welt, stopping just above the top zipper stop. Pivot again and stitch to the welting. Remove the pins. Press.

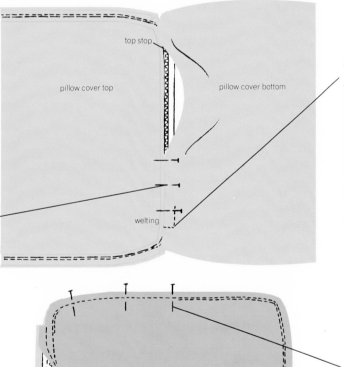

top stop

pillow cover top

pillow cover bottom

welting

58. Open the zipper and fold the pillow cover along the zipper so the wrong sides are facing out.

59. Align the remaining unstitched edges of the pillow. Pin with the pillow top facing up.

60. Using a zipper foot machine, stitch the pillow together, stitching against the welting cord inside the row of stitches holding the welting in place.

pillow cover top (wrong side)

THE MITERED-PATTERN KNIFE-EDGED PILLOW

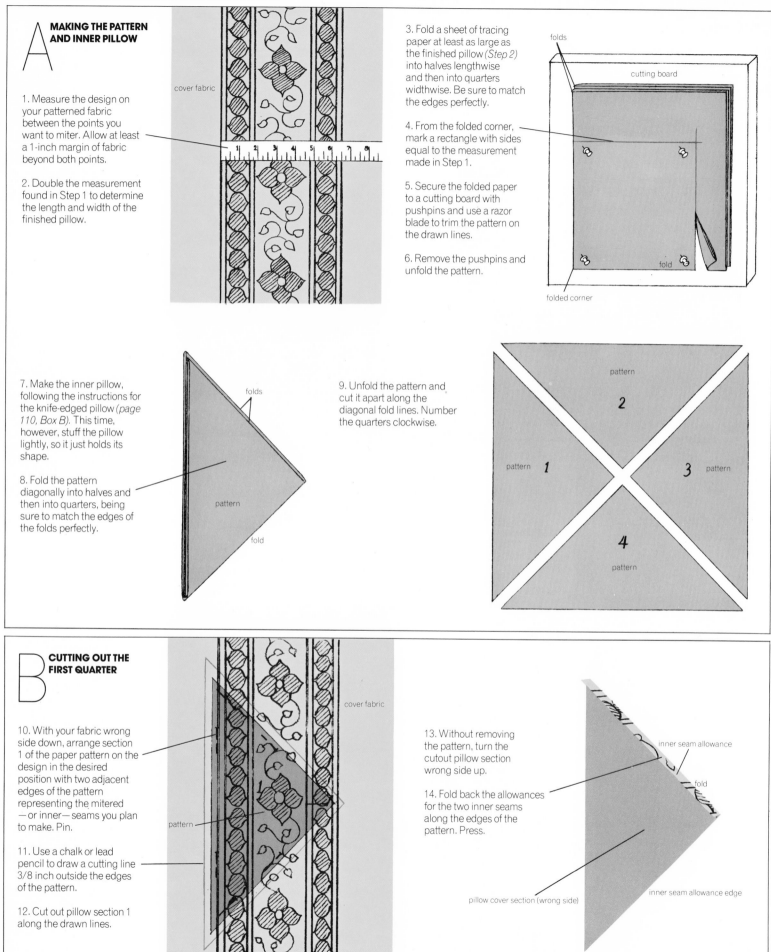

A MAKING THE PATTERN AND INNER PILLOW

1. Measure the design on your patterned fabric between the points you want to miter. Allow at least a 1-inch margin of fabric beyond both points.

2. Double the measurement found in Step 1 to determine the length and width of the finished pillow.

cover fabric

3. Fold a sheet of tracing paper at least as large as the finished pillow (Step 2) into halves lengthwise and then into quarters widthwise. Be sure to match the edges perfectly.

4. From the folded corner, mark a rectangle with sides equal to the measurement made in Step 1.

5. Secure the folded paper to a cutting board with pushpins and use a razor blade to trim the pattern on the drawn lines.

6. Remove the pushpins and unfold the pattern.

folds

cutting board

fold

folded corner

7. Make the inner pillow, following the instructions for the knife-edged pillow (page 110, Box B). This time, however, stuff the pillow lightly, so it just holds its shape.

8. Fold the pattern diagonally into halves and then into quarters, being sure to match the edges of the folds perfectly.

folds

pattern

fold

9. Unfold the pattern and cut it apart along the diagonal fold lines. Number the quarters clockwise.

pattern

2

pattern 1   3 pattern

4

pattern

B CUTTING OUT THE FIRST QUARTER

cover fabric

10. With your fabric wrong side down, arrange section 1 of the paper pattern on the design in the desired position with two adjacent edges of the pattern representing the mitered — or inner — seams you plan to make. Pin.

11. Use a chalk or lead pencil to draw a cutting line 3/8 inch outside the edges of the pattern.

12. Cut out pillow section 1 along the drawn lines.

pattern

13. Without removing the pattern, turn the cutout pillow section wrong side up.

14. Fold back the allowances for the two inner seams along the edges of the pattern. Press.

inner seam allowance

fold

pillow cover section (wrong side)

inner seam allowance edge

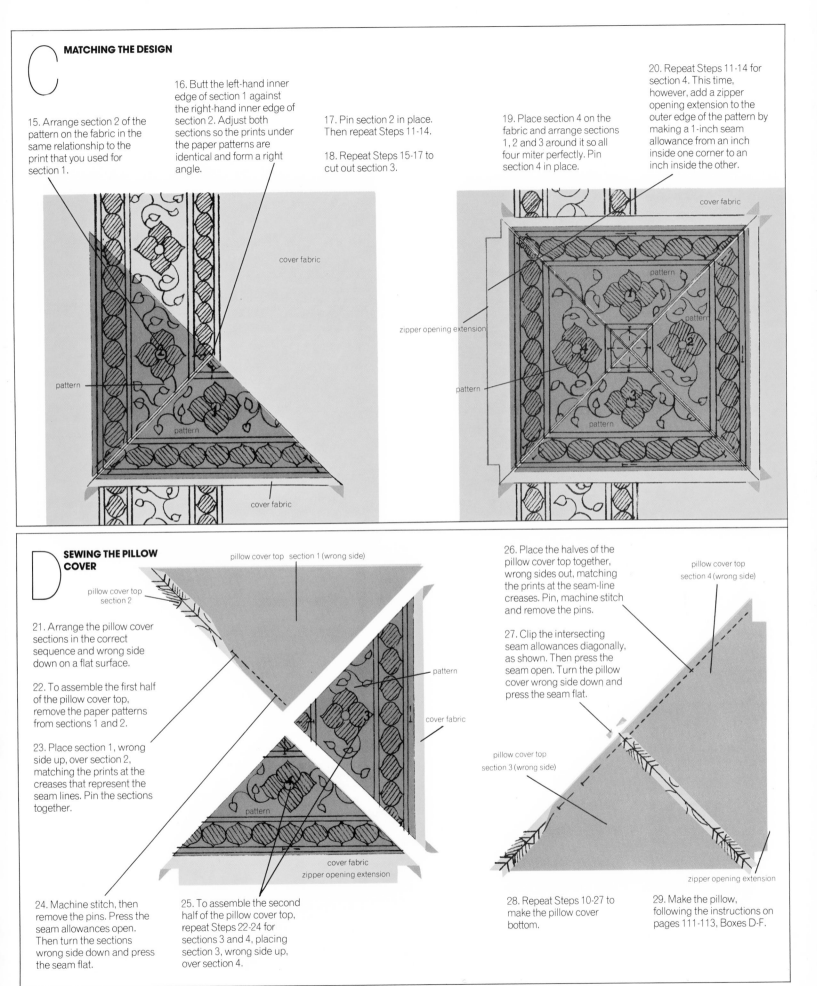

C MATCHING THE DESIGN

15. Arrange section 2 of the pattern on the fabric in the same relationship to the print that you used for section 1.

16. Butt the left-hand inner edge of section 1 against the right-hand inner edge of section 2. Adjust both sections so the prints under the paper patterns are identical and form a right angle.

17. Pin section 2 in place. Then repeat Steps 11-14.

18. Repeat Steps 15-17 to cut out section 3.

19. Place section 4 on the fabric and arrange sections 1, 2 and 3 around it so all four miter perfectly. Pin section 4 in place.

20. Repeat Steps 11-14 for section 4. This time, however, add a zipper opening extension to the outer edge of the pattern by making a 1-inch seam allowance from an inch inside one corner to an inch inside the other.

cover fabric

pattern

pattern

cover fabric

cover fabric

zipper opening extension

pattern

pattern

D SEWING THE PILLOW COVER

pillow cover top section 1 (wrong side)

pillow cover top section 2

21. Arrange the pillow cover sections in the correct sequence and wrong side down on a flat surface.

22. To assemble the first half of the pillow cover top, remove the paper patterns from sections 1 and 2.

23. Place section 1, wrong side up, over section 2, matching the prints at the creases that represent the seam lines. Pin the sections together.

pattern

cover fabric

pattern

cover fabric
zipper opening extension

24. Machine stitch, then remove the pins. Press the seam allowances open. Then turn the sections wrong side down and press the seam flat.

25. To assemble the second half of the pillow cover top, repeat Steps 22-24 for sections 3 and 4, placing section 3, wrong side up, over section 4.

26. Place the halves of the pillow cover top together, wrong sides out, matching the prints at the seam-line creases. Pin, machine stitch and remove the pins.

27. Clip the intersecting seam allowances diagonally, as shown. Then press the seam open. Turn the pillow cover wrong side down and press the seam flat.

pillow cover top section 4 (wrong side)

pillow cover top section 3 (wrong side)

zipper opening extension

28. Repeat Steps 10-27 to make the pillow cover bottom.

29. Make the pillow, following the instructions on pages 111-113, Boxes D-F.

THE BOX PILLOW

A MAKING THE PATTERN

1. Draw the desired shape of the pillow on paper, following the instructions for the knife-edged pillow *(page 110, Box A, Steps 1-3).*

2. To ensure that the corners of the finished pillow will look square, contour the corners of the pattern by first making a mark 1/8 inch inside the corner of the drawn lines of the rectangle.

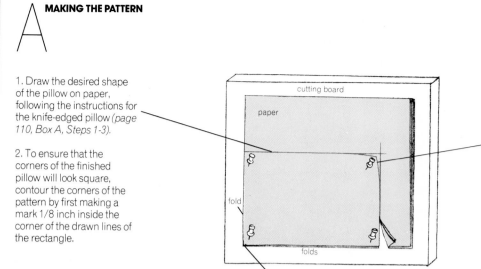

cutting board

paper

fold

folds

folded corner

3. Make a mark on each line 3 inches from the corner.

4. Finally, draw slightly convex curves to connect each of the marks made in Step 3 with the mark made in Step 2.

5. Secure the folded pattern to a cutting board with pushpins and use a razor blade to trim the pattern along the drawn lines and contoured corner. Remove the pushpins and unfold the pattern.

B ATTACHING THE BOXING STRIP

6. Cut out the top and bottom of the inner pillow, following the instructions for the knife-edged pillow *(page 110, Box B, Steps 8-10).*

7. Cut a boxing strip for the inner pillow 1 1/4 inches wider than the desired finished width and 4 inches longer than the perimeter of the pillow sections.

8. With the wrong sides facing out, place one end of the boxing strip along one side of the inner pillow top so it overlaps the first corner of the pillow top. Align the side edges.

short end

first corner

inner pillow top

boxing strip (wrong side)

9. Machine stitch 3/8 inch in from the side edges, starting inside the short end of the boxing strip at a distance equal to the width of the strip. End the line of stitches 3/8 inch from the opposite corner of the pillow top.

10. Clip 1/4 inch into the seam allowance of the boxing strip next to the last stitch made in Step 9.

11. Turn the long end of the boxing strip at a right angle on the clip mark so the outer edge of the strip aligns with the adjacent side of the pillow top.

12. Pivot *(Glossary),* then machine stitch 3/8 inch in from the side edges from the last stitch made in Step 9 to within 3/8 inch of the opposite corner. Clip the seam allowance next to the last stitch in this line.

13. Repeat Steps 11 and 12 to attach the boxing strip to the third and fourth sides of the pillow top. On the fourth side, however, stop stitching short of the first corner at a distance equal to the width of the boxing strip.

14. Smooth the ends of the boxing strip flat, and trim them off even with the sides of the pillow top.

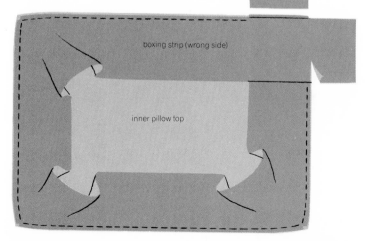

boxing strip (wrong side)

inner pillow top

15. Extend the ends of the strip away from the pillow top. Match the ends, wrong sides out, and pin.

16. Machine stitch the ends 3/8 inch inside the raw edges. Press the seam allowance open. Then finish machine stitching the strip to the pillow top.

C FINISHING THE INNER PILLOW

17. Clip open 1/4 inch at the unattached end of the boxing strip seam.

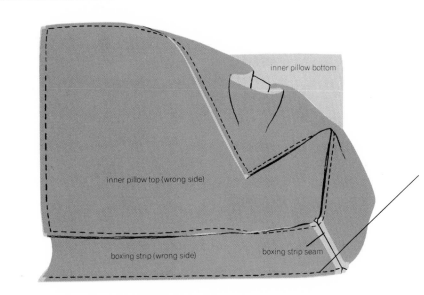

inner pillow bottom

inner pillow top (wrong side)

boxing strip (wrong side)

boxing strip seam

18. Place one corner of the inner pillow bottom against the boxing strip seam, wrong sides out.

19. Starting at the seam, machine stitch the pillow bottom to the boxing strip 3/8 inch inside their matching raw edges, clipping the boxing at the corners. Leave a 6-inch opening in the line of stitching so the pillow can be stuffed.

20. Complete the inner pillow by following the instructions for the knife-edged pillow *(page 110, Box B, Steps 13-16).*

D MAKING THE PILLOW COVER

21. Cut out the pillow cover top and bottom, following the instructions for the knife-edged pillow *(page 111, Box C, Steps 17-20).* Then cut out a pillow cover boxing of the desired finished width plus 3/4 inch and of the length determined in Step 7.

22. Trim the 5/8-inch zipper extension from the pillow cover top.

23. Repeat Steps 8-16 to stitch the boxing to the pillow cover top.

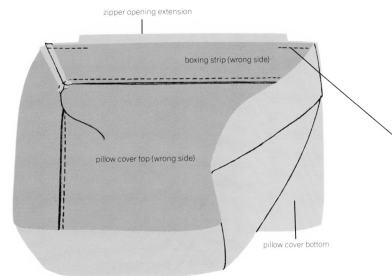

zipper opening extension

boxing strip (wrong side)

pillow cover top (wrong side)

pillow cover bottom

24. Align the zipper opening side of the pillow cover bottom with the long side of the boxing.

25. Stitch the ends of the zipper opening edge, following the instructions for the knife-edged pillow *(page 113, Box F, Step 49).*

26. Press open the seam allowances and press back the zipper opening allowance on the boxing and the 1-inch allowance on the pillow cover bottom.

27. Open out the pillow cover so both the top and bottom sections are wrong side down.

28. Open the zipper and place one side of it face up under the folded zipper opening edge of the boxing.

29. Align the top stop of the zipper just below the stitched portion of the seam. The folded edge should be close to the zipper teeth. Pin.

30. Using a zipper foot, machine stitch from the top zipper stop to the bottom stop as close to the fold as possible, removing the pins as you go.

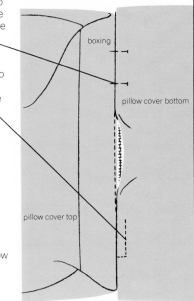

pillow cover top

boxing

pillow cover bottom

top stop

opening edge

fold

bottom stop

boxing

pillow cover bottom

pillow cover top

31. Close the zipper and lap the unattached folded edge of the pillow bottom over the edge of the boxing. Pin.

32. Using a zipper foot, machine stitch the zipper to the pillow bottom in the manner described on page 113, Box F, Step 57.

33. Open the zipper, and fold the pillow cover sections, wrong sides out.

34. Align the edges of the pillow bottom and boxing. Pin, clipping the boxing at the corners.

35. Machine stitch the pillow bottom to the boxing; start and stop at the ends of the zipper opening edge.

THE TURKISH CORNER PILLOW

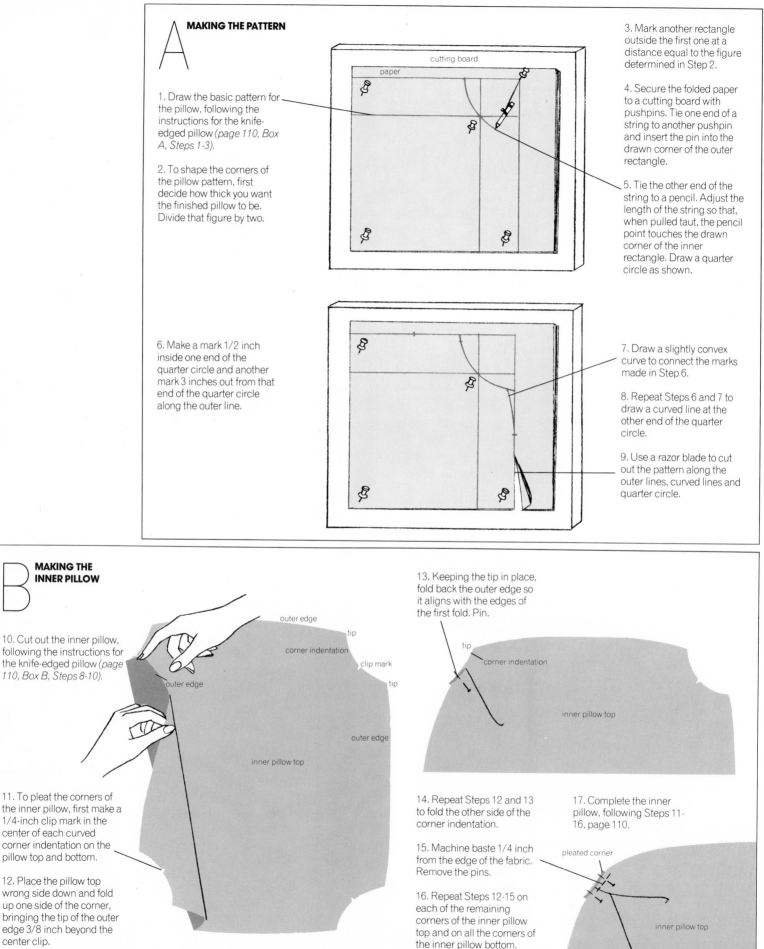

A MAKING THE PATTERN

1. Draw the basic pattern for the pillow, following the instructions for the knife-edged pillow (page 110, Box A, Steps 1-3).

2. To shape the corners of the pillow pattern, first decide how thick you want the finished pillow to be. Divide that figure by two.

cutting board

paper

3. Mark another rectangle outside the first one at a distance equal to the figure determined in Step 2.

4. Secure the folded paper to a cutting board with pushpins. Tie one end of a string to another pushpin and insert the pin into the drawn corner of the outer rectangle.

5. Tie the other end of the string to a pencil. Adjust the length of the string so that, when pulled taut, the pencil point touches the drawn corner of the inner rectangle. Draw a quarter circle as shown.

6. Make a mark 1/2 inch inside one end of the quarter circle and another mark 3 inches out from that end of the quarter circle along the outer line.

7. Draw a slightly convex curve to connect the marks made in Step 6.

8. Repeat Steps 6 and 7 to draw a curved line at the other end of the quarter circle.

9. Use a razor blade to cut out the pattern along the outer lines, curved lines and quarter circle.

B MAKING THE INNER PILLOW

10. Cut out the inner pillow, following the instructions for the knife-edged pillow (page 110, Box B, Steps 8-10).

outer edge

tip

corner indentation

clip mark

outer edge

tip

outer edge

inner pillow top

13. Keeping the tip in place, fold back the outer edge so it aligns with the edges of the first fold. Pin.

tip

corner indentation

inner pillow top

11. To pleat the corners of the inner pillow, first make a 1/4-inch clip mark in the center of each curved corner indentation on the pillow top and bottom.

12. Place the pillow top wrong side down and fold up one side of the corner, bringing the tip of the outer edge 3/8 inch beyond the center clip.

14. Repeat Steps 12 and 13 to fold the other side of the corner indentation.

15. Machine baste 1/4 inch from the edge of the fabric. Remove the pins.

16. Repeat Steps 12-15 on each of the remaining corners of the inner pillow top and on all the corners of the inner pillow bottom.

17. Complete the inner pillow, following Steps 11-16, page 110.

pleated corner

inner pillow top

C MAKING THE PILLOW COVER

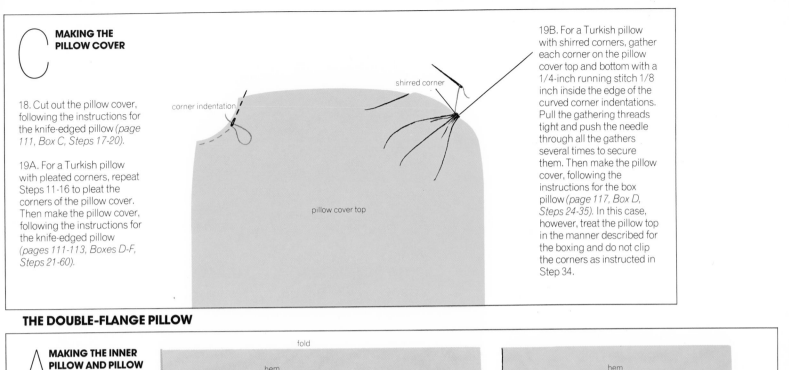

18. Cut out the pillow cover, following the instructions for the knife-edged pillow (*page 111, Box C, Steps 17-20*).

19A. For a Turkish pillow with pleated corners, repeat Steps 11-16 to pleat the corners of the pillow cover. Then make the pillow cover, following the instructions for the knife-edged pillow (*pages 111-113, Boxes D-F, Steps 21-60*).

19B. For a Turkish pillow with shirred corners, gather each corner on the pillow cover top and bottom with a 1/4-inch running stitch 1/8 inch inside the edge of the curved corner indentations. Pull the gathering threads tight and push the needle through all the gathers several times to secure them. Then make the pillow cover, following the instructions for the box pillow (*page 117, Box D, Steps 24-35*). In this case, however, treat the pillow top in the manner described for the boxing and do not clip the corners as instructed in Step 34.

THE DOUBLE-FLANGE PILLOW

A MAKING THE INNER PILLOW AND PILLOW COVER

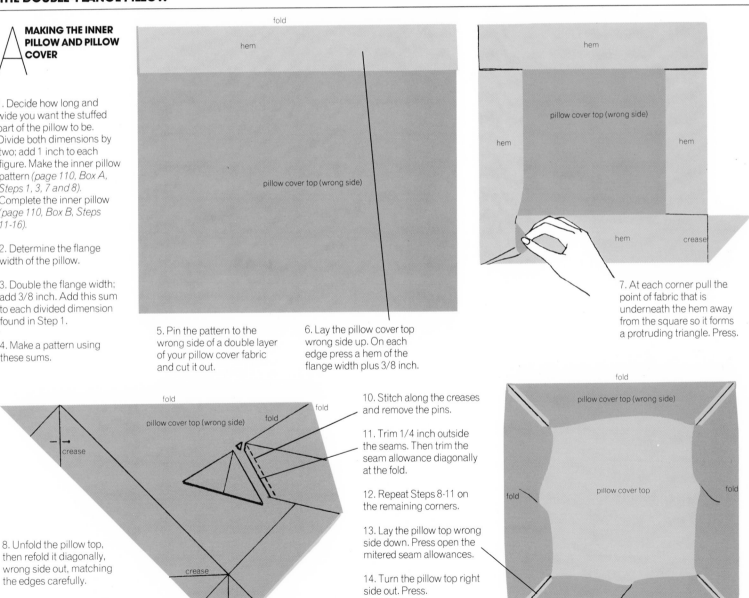

1. Decide how long and wide you want the stuffed part of the pillow to be. Divide both dimensions by two; add 1 inch to each figure. Make the inner pillow pattern (*page 110, Box A, Steps 1, 3, 7 and 8*). Complete the inner pillow (*page 110, Box B, Steps 11-16*).

2. Determine the flange width of the pillow.

3. Double the flange width; add 3/8 inch. Add this sum to each divided dimension found in Step 1.

4. Make a pattern using these sums.

5. Pin the pattern to the wrong side of a double layer of your pillow cover fabric and cut it out.

6. Lay the pillow cover top wrong side up. On each edge press a hem of the flange width plus 3/8 inch.

7. At each corner pull the point of fabric that is underneath the hem away from the square so it forms a protruding triangle. Press.

8. Unfold the pillow top, then refold it diagonally, wrong side out, matching the edges carefully.

9. Pin the corners near the fold at the creases that form a right angle to the fold.

10. Stitch along the creases and remove the pins.

11. Trim 1/4 inch outside the seams. Then trim the seam allowance diagonally at the fold.

12. Repeat Steps 8-11 on the remaining corners.

13. Lay the pillow top wrong side down. Press open the mitered seam allowances.

14. Turn the pillow top right side out. Press.

15. Repeat Steps 6-14 on the pillow cover bottom.

continued

B FINISHING THE PILLOW

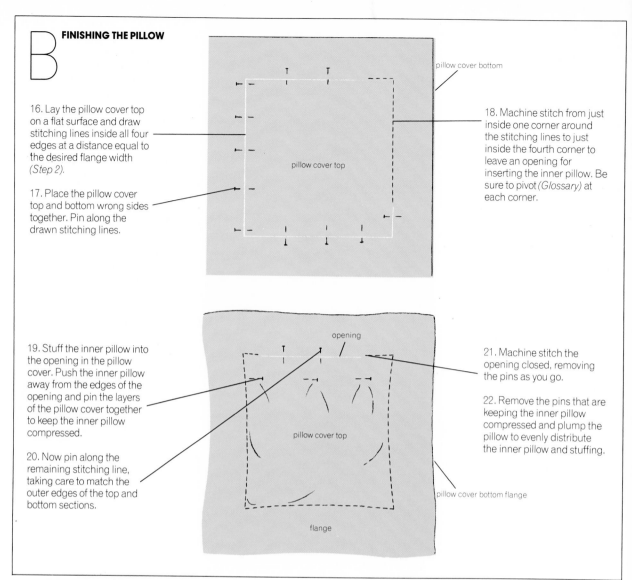

16. Lay the pillow cover top on a flat surface and draw stitching lines inside all four edges at a distance equal to the desired flange width (Step 2).

17. Place the pillow cover top and bottom wrong sides together. Pin along the drawn stitching lines.

18. Machine stitch from just inside one corner around the stitching lines to just inside the fourth corner to leave an opening for inserting the inner pillow. Be sure to pivot (Glossary) at each corner.

19. Stuff the inner pillow into the opening in the pillow cover. Push the inner pillow away from the edges of the opening and pin the layers of the pillow cover together to keep the inner pillow compressed.

20. Now pin along the remaining stitching line, taking care to match the outer edges of the top and bottom sections.

21. Machine stitch the opening closed, removing the pins as you go.

22. Remove the pins that are keeping the inner pillow compressed and plump the pillow to evenly distribute the inner pillow and stuffing.

THE ROUND SHIRRED PILLOW

A MAKING THE PATTERN

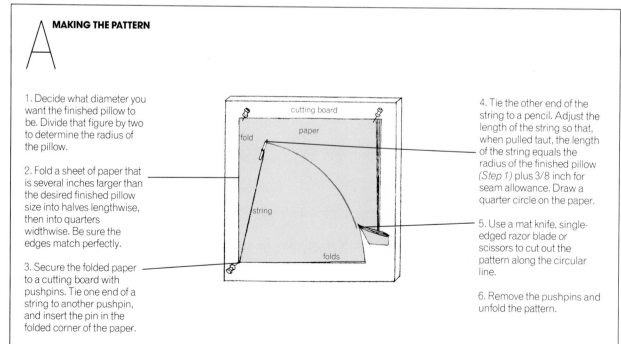

1. Decide what diameter you want the finished pillow to be. Divide that figure by two to determine the radius of the pillow.

2. Fold a sheet of paper that is several inches larger than the desired finished pillow size into halves lengthwise, then into quarters widthwise. Be sure the edges match perfectly.

3. Secure the folded paper to a cutting board with pushpins. Tie one end of a string to another pushpin, and insert the pin in the folded corner of the paper.

4. Tie the other end of the string to a pencil. Adjust the length of the string so that, when pulled taut, the length of the string equals the radius of the finished pillow (Step 1) plus 3/8 inch for seam allowance. Draw a quarter circle on the paper.

5. Use a mat knife, single-edged razor blade or scissors to cut out the pattern along the circular line.

6. Remove the pushpins and unfold the pattern.

MAKING THE INNER PILLOW

7. Cut out the top and bottom sections of the inner pillow, following the instructions for the knife-edged pillow (*page 110, Box B, Steps 8-10*).

8. Turn a pillow section wrong side down and place the pattern over it. Mark the center of the section by piercing the centerfold of the pattern with the point of a pencil. Repeat on the other section.

9. Decide how thick you want the finished pillow to be.

10. Cut a strip of inner pillow boxing 3/4 inch wider than the width determined in Step 9 and 4 inches longer than the circumference of the inner pillow sections.

11. Place one end of the boxing strip inside the inner pillow top with the wrong sides facing out. Align the outside edges and pin the strip and pillow top together, starting about 2 inches from the end of the strip and stopping about 4 inches short of the first pin.

12. Machine stitch 3/8 inch inside the raw outer edge of the boxing strip, removing the pins as you go.

13. Smooth the outer edge of one end of the strip around the edge of the inner pillow top. Pin 2 inches from the end of the stitching.

14. Fold back the strip at the pin, aligning the unstitched inner edges. Press in the fold.

boxing strip (wrong side)

inner pillow top

boxing strip outer edge

boxing strip inner edges

15. Smooth the remaining loose end of the strip toward the folded end and mark the meeting point with a pin.

boxing strip (wrong side)

16. Remove the pin from the folded strip and extend the ends of both strips away from the inner pillow top. Match the crease with the pin inserted in Step 15.

17. Pin the ends together, then machine stitch along the crease. Remove the pins.

18. Trim the seam allowance to 3/8 inch and press it open. Then finish stitching the outer edge of the boxing to the inner pillow top.

crease

boxing strip (wrong side)

19. Pin, then stitch the inner pillow bottom to the other edge of the strip. Leave a 6-inch opening in the line of stitching so the pillow can be stuffed.

20. Complete the inner pillow, following the instructions for the knife-edged pillow (*page 110, Box B, Steps 13-16*).

21. Thread a long needle with a double strand of heavy nylon thread. Tie the ends into a loop.

22. Push the needle through the pillow at the center marks made in Step 8.

23. Cut off the needle and tie the thread ends into a loop.

inner pillow bottom (wrong side)

boxing strip (wrong side)

needle

inner pillow

loop

continued

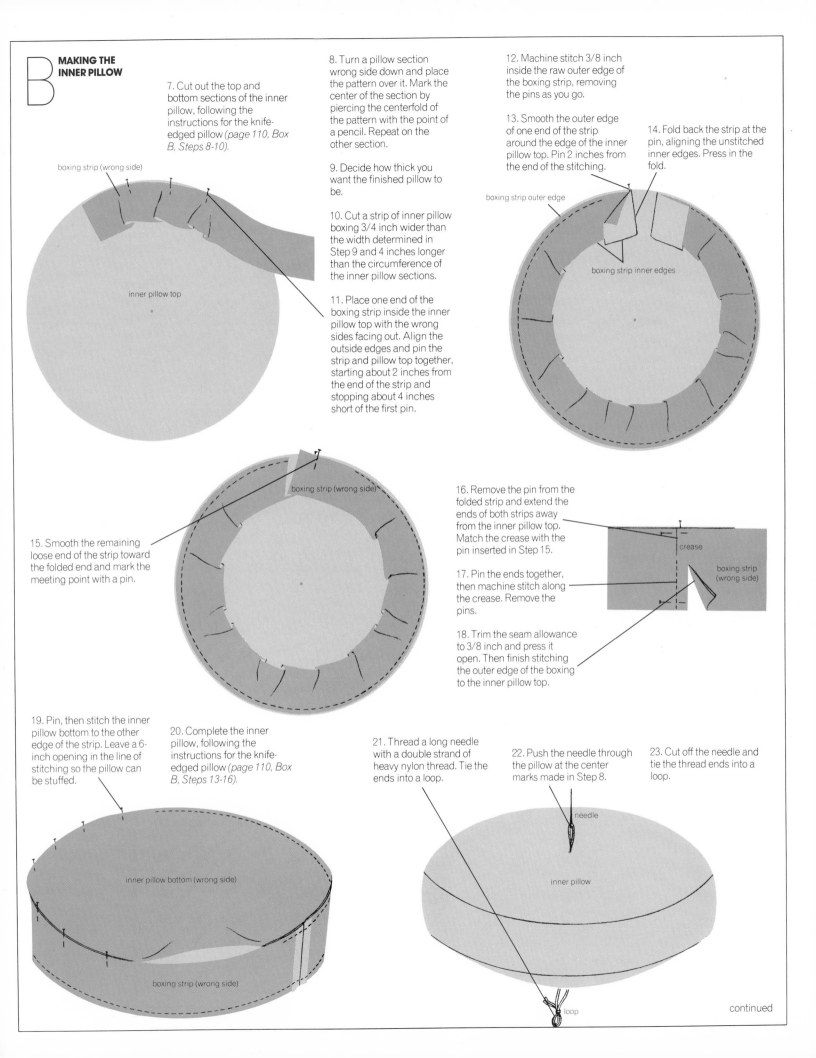

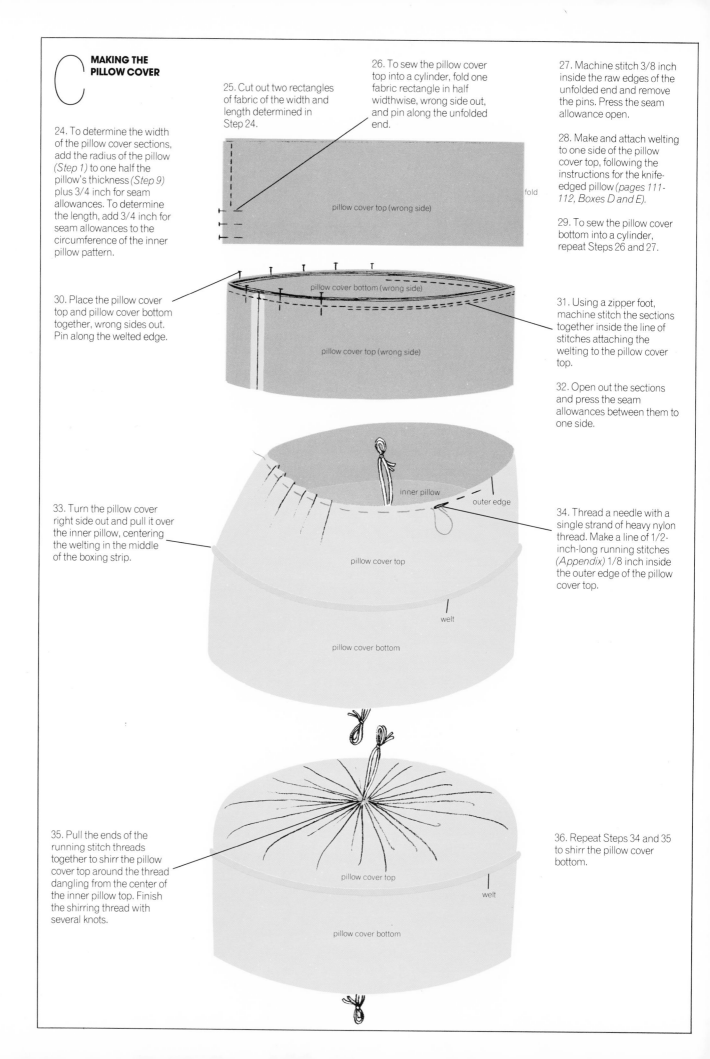

C MAKING THE PILLOW COVER

24. To determine the width of the pillow cover sections, add the radius of the pillow *(Step 1)* to one half the pillow's thickness *(Step 9)* plus 3/4 inch for seam allowances. To determine the length, add 3/4 inch for seam allowances to the circumference of the inner pillow pattern.

25. Cut out two rectangles of fabric of the width and length determined in Step 24.

26. To sew the pillow cover top into a cylinder, fold one fabric rectangle in half widthwise, wrong side out, and pin along the unfolded end.

27. Machine stitch 3/8 inch inside the raw edges of the unfolded end and remove the pins. Press the seam allowance open.

28. Make and attach welting to one side of the pillow cover top, following the instructions for the knife-edged pillow *(pages 111-112, Boxes D and E)*.

29. To sew the pillow cover bottom into a cylinder, repeat Steps 26 and 27.

30. Place the pillow cover top and pillow cover bottom together, wrong sides out. Pin along the welted edge.

31. Using a zipper foot, machine stitch the sections together inside the line of stitches attaching the welting to the pillow cover top.

32. Open out the sections and press the seam allowances between them to one side.

33. Turn the pillow cover right side out and pull it over the inner pillow, centering the welting in the middle of the boxing strip.

34. Thread a needle with a single strand of heavy nylon thread. Make a line of 1/2-inch-long running stitches *(Appendix)* 1/8 inch inside the outer edge of the pillow cover top.

35. Pull the ends of the running stitch threads together to shirr the pillow cover top around the thread dangling from the center of the inner pillow top. Finish the shirring thread with several knots.

36. Repeat Steps 34 and 35 to shirr the pillow cover bottom.

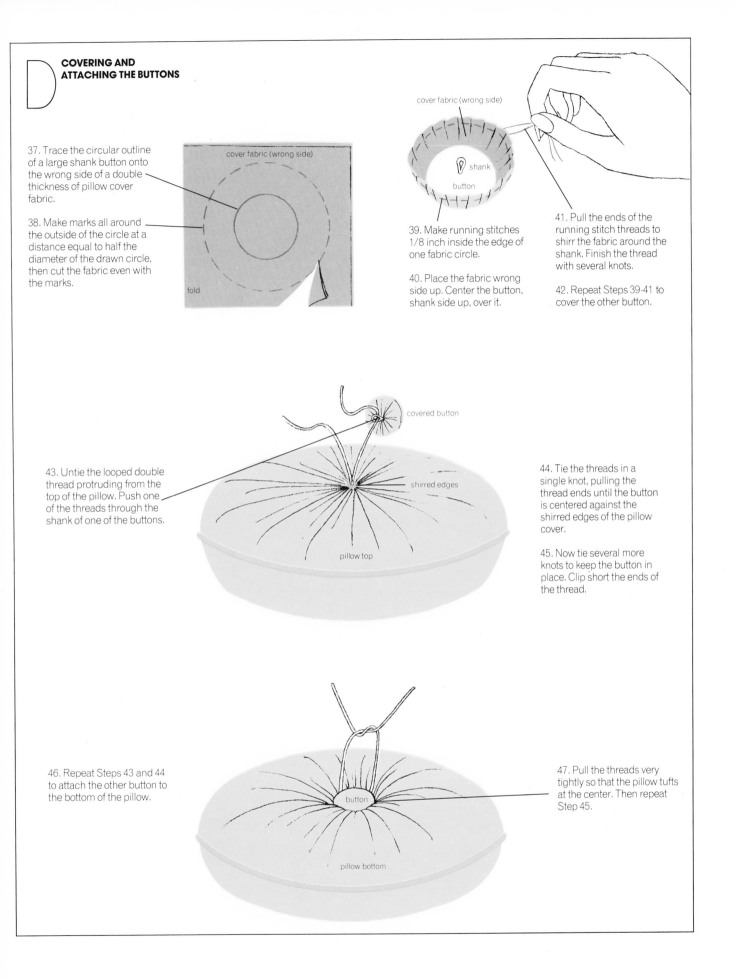

COVERING AND ATTACHING THE BUTTONS

37. Trace the circular outline of a large shank button onto the wrong side of a double thickness of pillow cover fabric.

38. Make marks all around the outside of the circle at a distance equal to half the diameter of the drawn circle, then cut the fabric even with the marks.

cover fabric (wrong side)

fold

cover fabric (wrong side)

shank

button

39. Make running stitches 1/8 inch inside the edge of one fabric circle.

40. Place the fabric wrong side up. Center the button, shank side up, over it.

41. Pull the ends of the running stitch threads to shirr the fabric around the shank. Finish the thread with several knots.

42. Repeat Steps 39-41 to cover the other button.

covered button

shirred edges

pillow top

43. Untie the looped double thread protruding from the top of the pillow. Push one of the threads through the shank of one of the buttons.

44. Tie the threads in a single knot, pulling the thread ends until the button is centered against the shirred edges of the pillow cover.

45. Now tie several more knots to keep the button in place. Clip short the ends of the thread.

button

pillow bottom

46. Repeat Steps 43 and 44 to attach the other button to the bottom of the pillow.

47. Pull the threads very tightly so that the pillow tufts at the center. Then repeat Step 45.

A MAKING THE INNER PILLOW

1. Measure the length, circumference and radius of your urethane foam bolster form.

2. Cut a length of heavy nylon thread about three times as long as the bolster form. Thread it through the eye of a small heavy object such as the fishing weight shown here, or tie it to one end of an untwisted coat hanger.

bolster form

loop

3. Pull the ends of the thread even and insert them through the hole in a spool of thread. Loop the ends together to prevent them from pulling through the spool hole.

4. Drop the weighted end of the thread through the hole in the bolster form, then cut off the weight and attach the thread ends to another spool of thread.

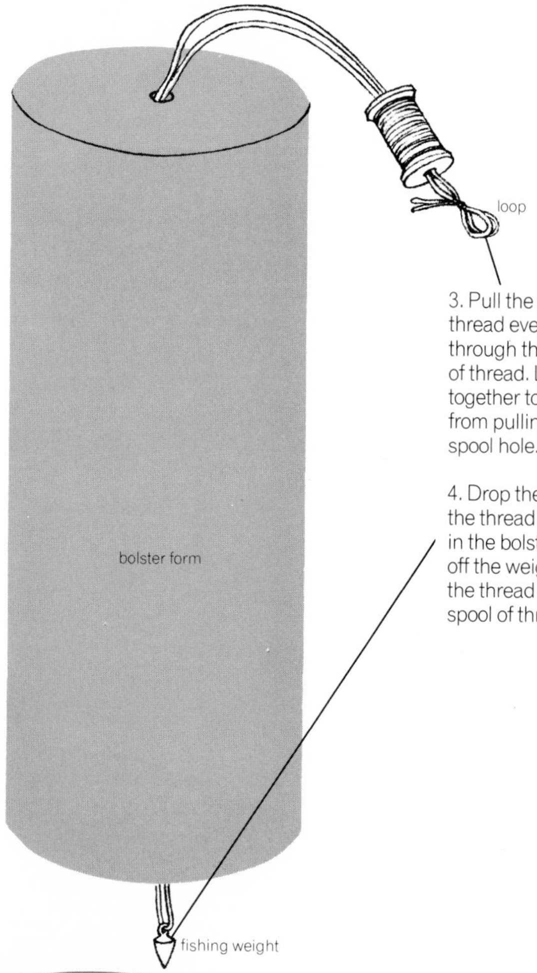

fishing weight

bolster form

batting

5. Cut out a layer of cotton or polyester batting that is as long as the length plus the diameter of the bolster form by twice the circumference of the form.

6. Center the bolster form lengthwise on the batting, then wrap the batting around the form.

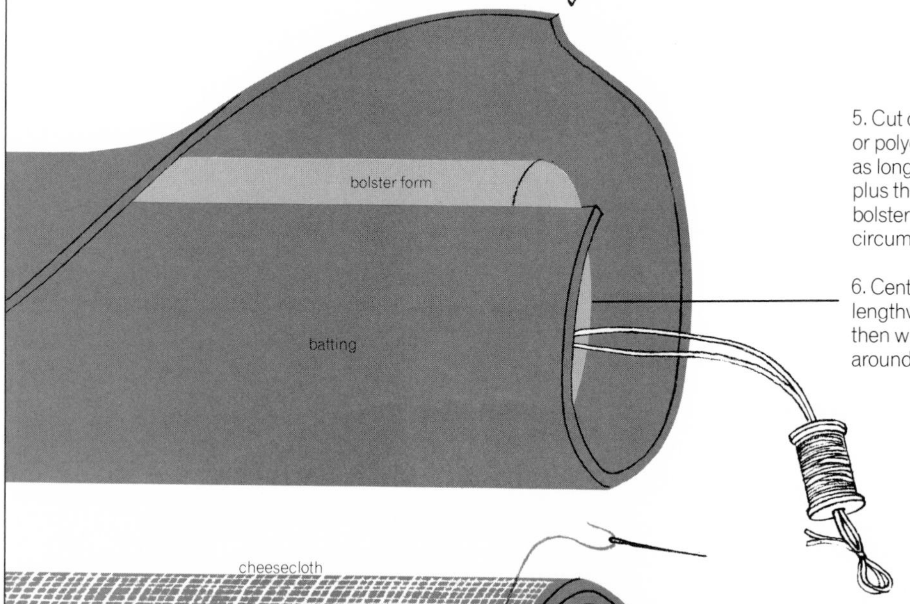

cheesecloth

batting

bolster form

7. Cut a layer of cheesecloth the same size as the batting and wrap it around the batting, securing the long edge with a row of large diagonal basting stitches (Appendix).

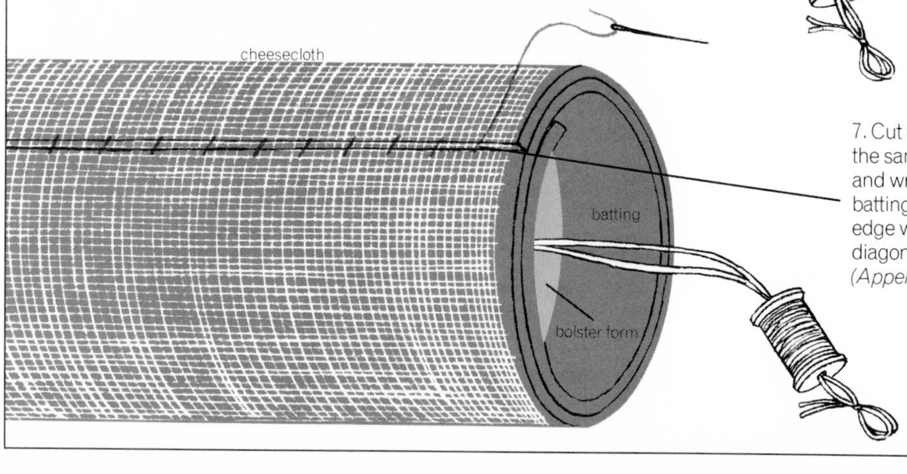

B MAKING THE BOLSTER COVER

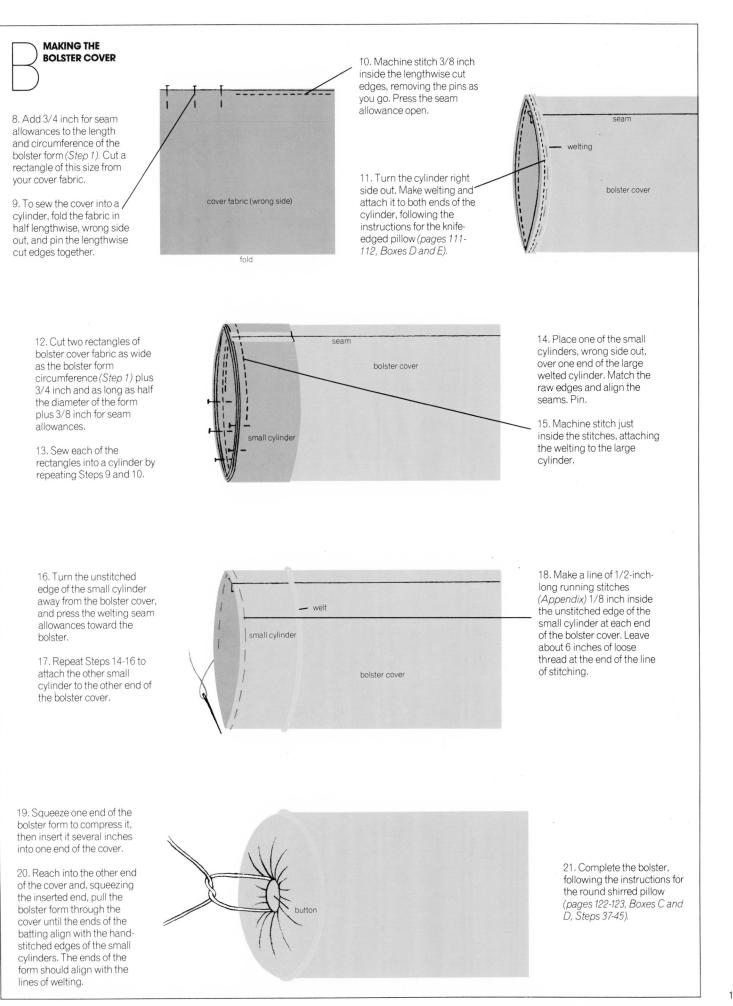

10. Machine stitch 3/8 inch inside the lengthwise cut edges, removing the pins as you go. Press the seam allowance open.

8. Add 3/4 inch for seam allowances to the length and circumference of the bolster form *(Step 1)*. Cut a rectangle of this size from your cover fabric.

9. To sew the cover into a cylinder, fold the fabric in half lengthwise, wrong side out, and pin the lengthwise cut edges together.

11. Turn the cylinder right side out. Make welting and attach it to both ends of the cylinder, following the instructions for the knife-edged pillow *(pages 111-112, Boxes D and E)*.

cover fabric (wrong side)

fold

seam

welting

bolster cover

12. Cut two rectangles of bolster cover fabric as wide as the bolster form circumference *(Step 1)* plus 3/4 inch and as long as half the diameter of the form plus 3/8 inch for seam allowances.

13. Sew each of the rectangles into a cylinder by repeating Steps 9 and 10.

14. Place one of the small cylinders, wrong side out, over one end of the large welted cylinder. Match the raw edges and align the seams. Pin.

15. Machine stitch just inside the stitches, attaching the welting to the large cylinder.

seam

bolster cover

small cylinder

16. Turn the unstitched edge of the small cylinder away from the bolster cover, and press the welting seam allowances toward the bolster.

17. Repeat Steps 14-16 to attach the other small cylinder to the other end of the bolster cover.

18. Make a line of 1/2-inch-long running stitches *(Appendix)* 1/8 inch inside the unstitched edge of the small cylinder at each end of the bolster cover. Leave about 6 inches of loose thread at the end of the line of stitching.

welt

small cylinder

bolster cover

19. Squeeze one end of the bolster form to compress it, then insert it several inches into one end of the cover.

20. Reach into the other end of the cover and, squeezing the inserted end, pull the bolster form through the cover until the ends of the batting align with the hand-stitched edges of the small cylinders. The ends of the form should align with the lines of welting.

21. Complete the bolster, following the instructions for the round shirred pillow *(pages 122-123, Boxes C and D, Steps 37-45)*.

button

Crisp pleats, soft gathers for shades

Accordion pleating and smocking, two classic ways of adding interesting fullness to cloth, here lend their respective crispness and softness to two fabric lampshades. The pleated shade is made of medium-weight fabric lined with iron-on interfacing; a coating of clear acrylic plastic stiffens the pleats.

The smocked shade slips over a standard paper shade, and it can be removed easily for laundering. A lightweight checked fabric is recommended, the 1/8-inch or 1/4-inch checks serving as guide lines for the smocking.

THE PLEATED LAMPSHADE

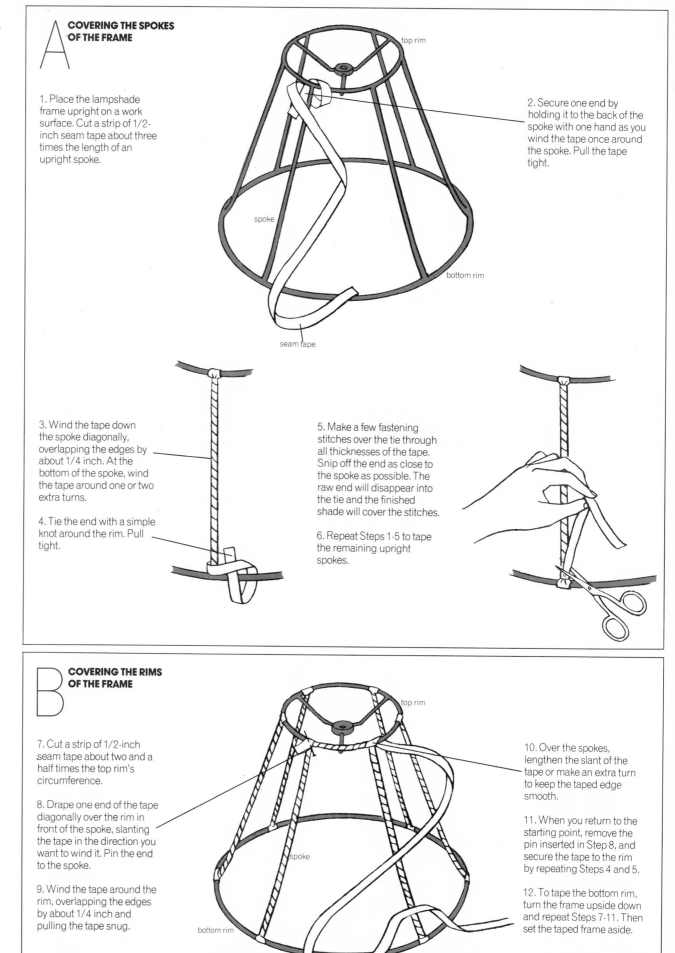

A COVERING THE SPOKES OF THE FRAME

1. Place the lampshade frame upright on a work surface. Cut a strip of 1/2-inch seam tape about three times the length of an upright spoke.

2. Secure one end by holding it to the back of the spoke with one hand as you wind the tape once around the spoke. Pull the tape tight.

3. Wind the tape down the spoke diagonally, overlapping the edges by about 1/4 inch. At the bottom of the spoke, wind the tape around one or two extra turns.

4. Tie the end with a simple knot around the rim. Pull tight.

5. Make a few fastening stitches over the tie through all thicknesses of the tape. Snip off the end as close to the spoke as possible. The raw end will disappear into the tie and the finished shade will cover the stitches.

6. Repeat Steps 1-5 to tape the remaining upright spokes.

B COVERING THE RIMS OF THE FRAME

7. Cut a strip of 1/2-inch seam tape about two and a half times the top rim's circumference.

8. Drape one end of the tape diagonally over the rim in front of the spoke, slanting the tape in the direction you want to wind it. Pin the end to the spoke.

9. Wind the tape around the rim, overlapping the edges by about 1/4 inch and pulling the tape snug.

10. Over the spokes, lengthen the slant of the tape or make an extra turn to keep the taped edge smooth.

11. When you return to the starting point, remove the pin inserted in Step 8, and secure the tape to the rim by repeating Steps 4 and 5.

12. To tape the bottom rim, turn the frame upside down and repeat Steps 7-11. Then set the taped frame aside.

13. With shade fabric wrong side up, use a dressmaker's pencil to draw a rectangle lengthwise along one selvage. Make the length of the rectangle equal to two and a half times the circumference of the bottom rim of the frame, and make the width equal to the height of the frame plus 2 1/4 inches.

14. Cut out the shade fabric along the drawn lines.

15. To line the shade, cut from iron-on interfacing material a rectangle 1 1/4 inches narrower than the one made in Step 13.

fabric (wrong side)

selvage

16. Place the shade fabric wrong side up and center the lining, fusing side down, on top of it, leaving 5/8-inch hem allowances above and below the lining. Fuse the pieces with a medium-hot iron, following the manufacturer's instructions on the fusible lining.

17. Fold in the fabric hem allowances along the edges of the lining and iron.

shade fabric (wrong side)

hem allowance

fusing side

lining

fusing web

hem allowance

18. Cut two strips of 1/2-inch-wide fusing web the length of the shade fabric (*Step 13*).

19. To hem the shade, insert a strip of web under one hem and fuse the pieces together with a medium-hot iron, following the web manufacturer's instructions. Repeat on the opposite hem.

20. To stiffen the shade, first place it fabric side up on brown paper or several sheets of newspaper in a well-ventilated room.

21. Use a paintbrush to brush clear acrylic plastic coating onto the fabric. Let the shade dry completely.

22. Place the shade, lining side up, on a flat surface.

23. Using a yardstick, measure in from one side of the shade a distance equal to the desired pleat depth — usually 1/2, 3/4 or 1 inch. Make a pencil mark just inside one hem at this point.

24. To mark the outer fold lines for the pleats, double the desired pleat depth and make marks at this interval all along the hem.

25. Repeat Steps 22-24 along the opposite hem, beginning from the same end of the shade.

paper

acrylic plastic coating

shade fabric

continued

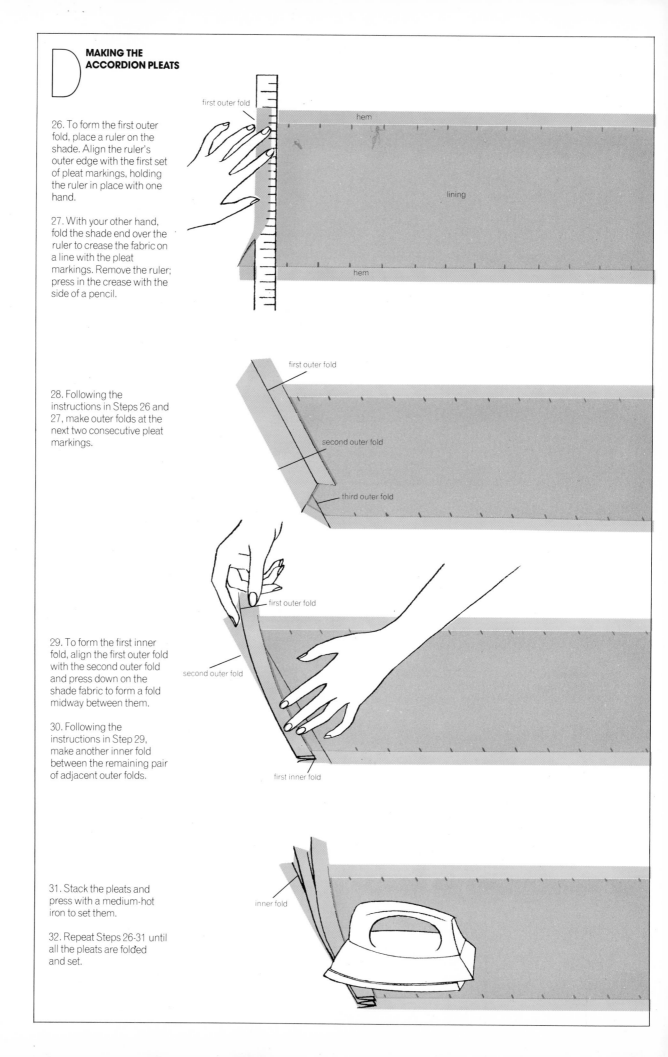

D MAKING THE ACCORDION PLEATS

26. To form the first outer fold, place a ruler on the shade. Align the ruler's outer edge with the first set of pleat markings, holding the ruler in place with one hand.

27. With your other hand, fold the shade end over the ruler to crease the fabric on a line with the pleat markings. Remove the ruler; press in the crease with the side of a pencil.

28. Following the instructions in Steps 26 and 27, make outer folds at the next two consecutive pleat markings.

29. To form the first inner fold, align the first outer fold with the second outer fold and press down on the shade fabric to form a fold midway between them.

30. Following the instructions in Step 29, make another inner fold between the remaining pair of adjacent outer folds.

31. Stack the pleats and press with a medium-hot iron to set them.

32. Repeat Steps 26-31 until all the pleats are folded and set.

33. Form the shade into a cylinder by lapping the first outer fold over the last outer fold. Then trim the excess shade length from the bottom layer.

34. Paper-clip the overlapped folds together.

35. Thread a heavy-duty needle with a double strand of beeswax-coated thread at least 10 inches longer than the circumference of the frame. Knot the thread end.

36. Insert the needle from the fabric side 3/4 inch below the outer edge of the shade bottom and 1/8 inch inside the raw edge of the overlapped folds.

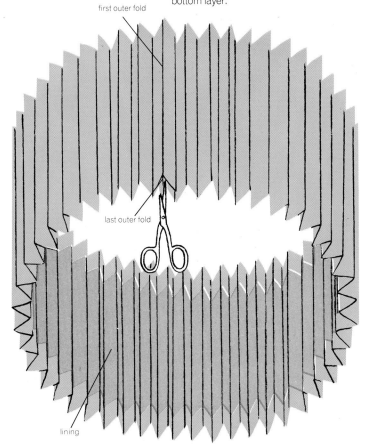

first outer fold

last outer fold

lining

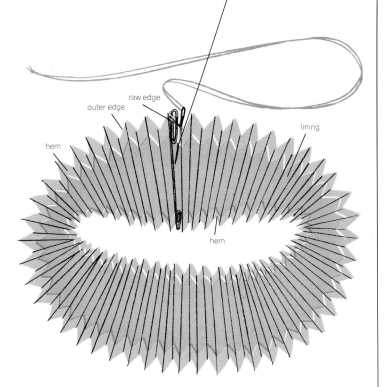

outer edge

raw edge

hem

lining

hem

37. Working from the lining side, pinch together the adjacent pleat and insert the needle through the double thickness of the inner fold of the pleat 1/8 inch from the crease and just below the hem.

38. Repeat Step 37 to thread the pleats all around.

39. To end the threading, insert the needle from the lining side 1/8 inch from the last inner fold, going through only a single thickness of the pleat.

40. Pull the thread out to the fabric side and knot the end.

41. Repeat Steps 35-40 to thread around the pleats along the shade bottom.

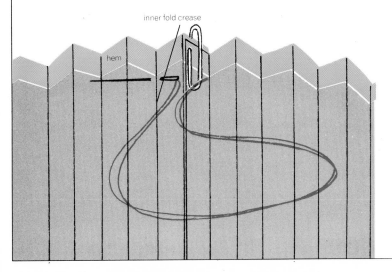

inner fold crease

hem

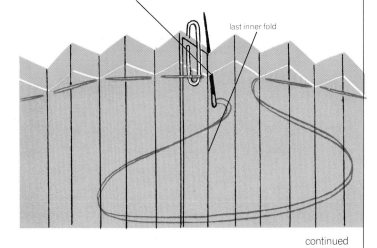

last inner fold

continued

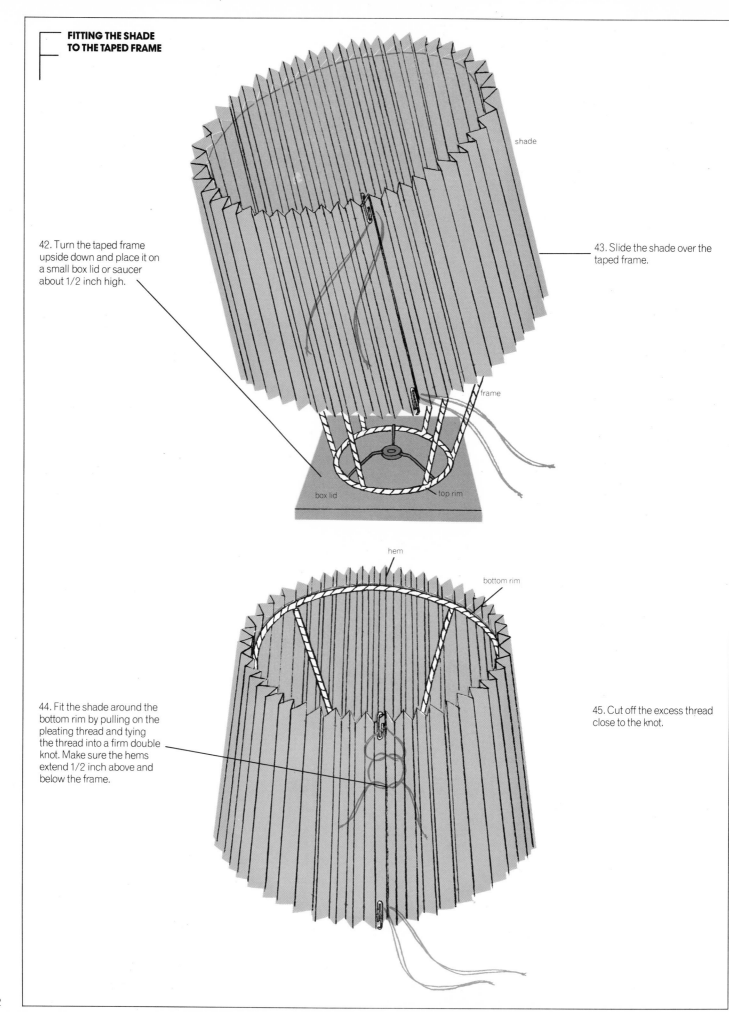

42. Turn the taped frame upside down and place it on a small box lid or saucer about 1/2 inch high.

43. Slide the shade over the taped frame.

shade

frame

box lid

top rim

hem

bottom rim

44. Fit the shade around the bottom rim by pulling on the pleating thread and tying the thread into a firm double knot. Make sure the hems extend 1/2 inch above and below the frame.

45. Cut off the excess thread close to the knot.

TACKING THE SHADE TO THE FRAME

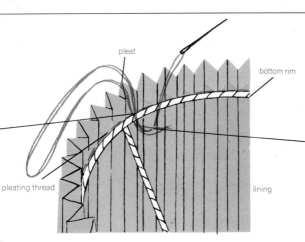

46. Thread a needle with a double strand of beeswax-coated thread about six times the diameter of the rim in length. Knot the thread end, then lower the knot into the space between a pleat and the pleating thread around the bottom rim. Let the knot hang loosely about 2 inches below the rim.

47. Insert the needle from inside the rim between the double strand near the knot and pull up the needle to anchor the thread around the rim.

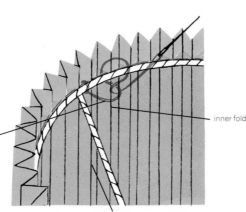

48. To attach the shade to the bottom rim, make tacking stitches by first inserting the needle from under the rim into the space between the adjacent pair of inner folds and the pleating thread to form a loop around the rim.

49. Insert the needle through the loop, and pull the needle horizontally away from the rim to finish the stitch.

50. Tighten the thread, thus pulling up the pleating thread to the bottom rim.

51. Repeat Steps 48-50 all around the bottom rim at regular intervals, spacing the stitches so they fall midway between the inner folds of the pleats.

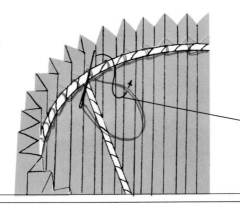

52. When you reach the anchoring stitch made in Step 47, make a tacking stitch over it.

53. Fasten off the thread by first inserting the needle through the last tacking stitch and making a loop. Then insert the needle through the loop and pull it horizontally away from the rim. Cut off the thread.

H FINISHING THE SHADE

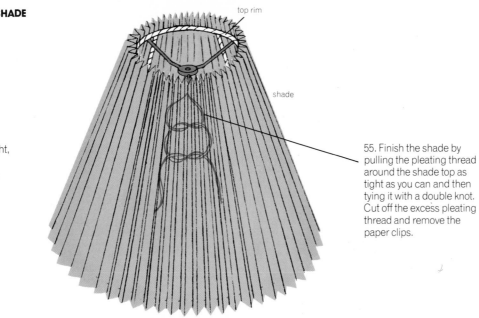

54. Turn the shade upright, removing the box top or saucer from underneath.

55. Finish the shade by pulling the pleating thread around the shade top as tight as you can and then tying it with a double knot. Cut off the excess pleating thread and remove the paper clips.

THE SMOCKED LAMPSHADE

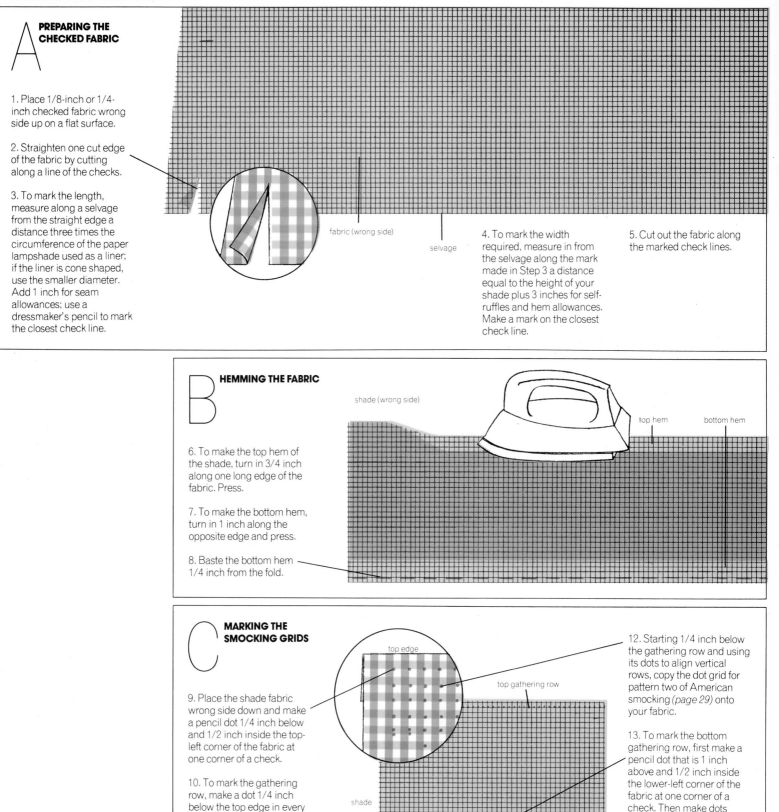

A PREPARING THE CHECKED FABRIC

1. Place 1/8-inch or 1/4-inch checked fabric wrong side up on a flat surface.

2. Straighten one cut edge of the fabric by cutting along a line of the checks.

3. To mark the length, measure along a selvage from the straight edge a distance three times the circumference of the paper lampshade used as a liner; if the liner is cone shaped, use the smaller diameter. Add 1 inch for seam allowances; use a dressmaker's pencil to mark the closest check line.

fabric (wrong side)

selvage

4. To mark the width required, measure in from the selvage along the mark made in Step 3 a distance equal to the height of your shade plus 3 inches for self-ruffles and hem allowances. Make a mark on the closest check line.

5. Cut out the fabric along the marked check lines.

B HEMMING THE FABRIC

shade (wrong side)

top hem

bottom hem

6. To make the top hem of the shade, turn in 3/4 inch along one long edge of the fabric. Press.

7. To make the bottom hem, turn in 1 inch along the opposite edge and press.

8. Baste the bottom hem 1/4 inch from the fold.

C MARKING THE SMOCKING GRIDS

top edge

top gathering row

shade

bottom gathering row

bottom edge

9. Place the shade fabric wrong side down and make a pencil dot 1/4 inch below and 1/2 inch inside the top-left corner of the fabric at one corner of a check.

10. To mark the gathering row, make a dot 1/4 inch below the top edge in every check across the fabric if the design is 1/4 inch wide, in every other check if it is 1/8 inch wide. Be sure to put each dot in the same corner used for the first check in Step 9.

11. End the row with an even-numbered dot 1/2 inch inside the fabric's right-hand edge. Trim it to exactly 1/2 inch.

12. Starting 1/4 inch below the gathering row and using its dots to align vertical rows, copy the dot grid for pattern two of American smocking (page 29) onto your fabric.

13. To mark the bottom gathering row, first make a pencil dot that is 1 inch above and 1/2 inch inside the lower-left corner of the fabric at one corner of a check. Then make dots across the fabric at the same 1/4- or 1/8-inch intervals you used for the top grid.

14. Using pattern two of American smocking as a guide, copy the dots for two cable rows onto the fabric. Start the first row 1/4 inch below the bottom gathering row, the second row 1/8 inch below the first one.

D SMOCKING THE FABRIC SHADE

15. Prepare the top gathering row and vertical bastings, following the instructions on page 26, Box B, Steps 10-17.

16. Make a paper smocking guide, using the circumference of the paper lampshade liner plus 1 inch as the width measurement and the height of the shade plus 1 inch as the length measurement. Then pin the fabric to the paper, following the instructions for pattern one of American smocking, Box B, Steps 18-25.

17. Smock the top of the shade with contrasting or matching embroidery or cotton pearl thread, following the instructions for pattern two of American smocking *(pages 29-31)*, and stitching through the top hem on the first row.

18. Make the bottom gathering row as you did the top one, then smock the two cable rows—stitching through the bottom hem.

19. Remove the basting and gathering rows and steam-press the smocking.

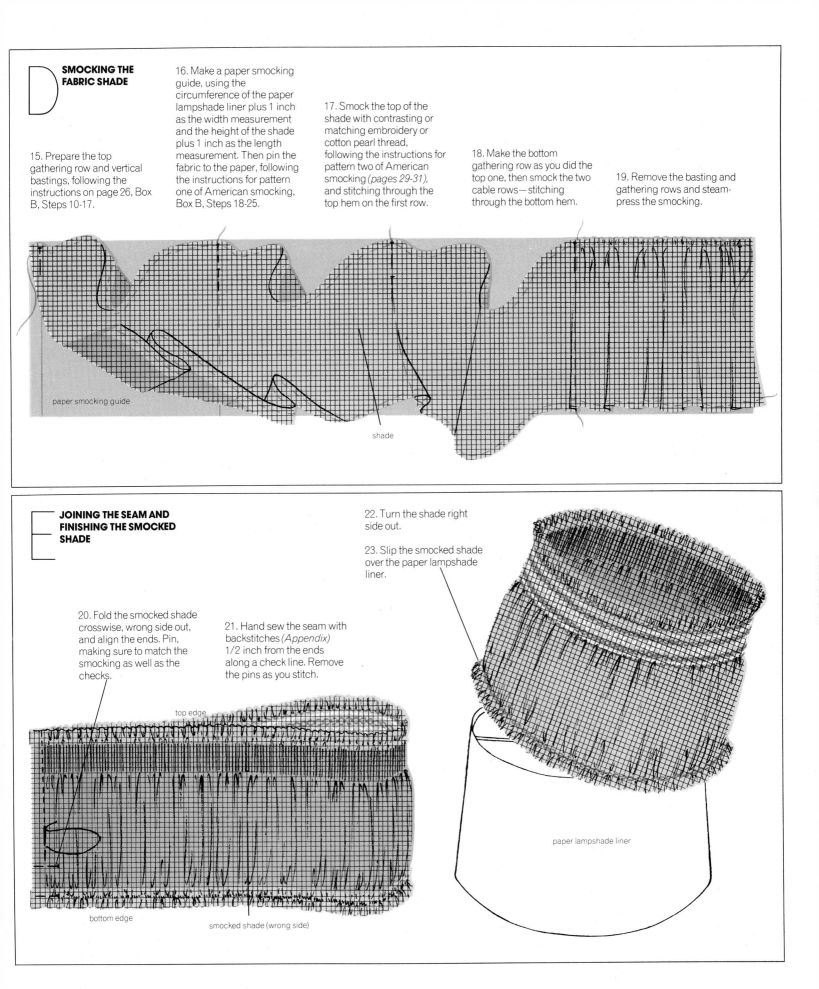

paper smocking guide

shade

E JOINING THE SEAM AND FINISHING THE SMOCKED SHADE

20. Fold the smocked shade crosswise, wrong side out, and align the ends. Pin, making sure to match the smocking as well as the checks.

21. Hand sew the seam with backstitches *(Appendix)* 1/2 inch from the ends along a check line. Remove the pins as you stitch.

22. Turn the shade right side out.

23. Slip the smocked shade over the paper lampshade liner.

top edge

bottom edge

smocked shade (wrong side)

paper lampshade liner

135

5
NOVEL WAYS
TO KNIT
AND CROCHET

With yarn and twine are, top to bottom, an adjustable loom for hairpin lace, a jumbo knitting
needle for broomstick lace, a set of four double-point knitting needles and a crochet hook.

During the craft boom of the 1960s, an array of needlecraft tools and materials appeared on the market —jumbo knitting needles and crochet hooks of lightweight plastic and aluminum, meant for work with thick-textured yarns—designed to make knitting and crocheting fast and easy. Though the craze for jiffy knits and crochets subsided, the intriguing new materials and equipment remained, and so did the delight many

MODERN ACCENTS FROM YARN AND TWINE

found in the rhythmic patterns of handwork.

This delight in needlecraft was indicated by increased interest in such complex knitting as socks fashioned on four needles. And it inspired the adaptation of modern tools and materials to specialized decorative techniques, some of which had languished for half a century or more, so that the old painstaking needlecrafts could be revived without the drudgery they once entailed.

One half-forgotten technique was the

making of hairpin lace, a kind of crocheting originally done—as the name implies—on a hairpin. In times past, the product was a strip of delicate lace that trimmed the edges of everything from pillowcases to pantaloons. Today hairpin lace has graduated in size and bloomed in decorative potential.

A special hairpin lace loom *(page 137)* —a small rectangular frame with two movable posts—can be adjusted to make lace from 1/2 to 4 inches wide. Using the big yarns called quick-point or jiffy knit, or materials like wrapping twine or jute, hairpin lacemaking has been reborn as a technique for making place mats and even small rugs. Strips that emerge from the loom are pliant enough to be shaped into rectangles, triangles, circles and semicircles.

Another old technique given a new lease on life is broomstick lacemaking. It is also a variant of crocheting, once done on a broomstick but now on the big knitting needle created for jiffy knits.

Probably developed by pioneer farm women, in days when free hours were as scarce as they are now, broomstick lace produces a strip of shell-like openwork circles in much less time than the more traditional time-consuming methods of lacemaking. Once it was used to make doilies and antimacassars, but in its modern reincarnation, using contemporary yarns and color combinations, it has become popular as a quick way to make lacy vests and stoles and decorative accessories like the saucy hat and matching bag on pages 156-157.

Unlike broomstick and hairpin lace, old crafts revived, the technique of four-needle knitting has never gone into eclipse. It is the classic way to finish off a crew-neck sweater and one of the standard ways to knit stockings and socks.

Four-needle knitting goes back at least to the 14th Century. An obscure North German altar painting of that date shows the Virgin Mary knitting a tubular gown for the infant Jesus on four wooden knitting needles (according to legend, the gown was supposed to have grown with its wearer). But the technique really came into prominence in the 16th Century, when knitted hose began to replace sewn woven hose all over Europe. Royalty naturally were the first wearers of knitted stockings. Henry VIII is said to have owned six pairs of black silk knitted hose, and Queen Elizabeth I was so delighted with her first pair of knitted silk stockings that she thereafter declined to wear any other kind.

This new fashion in leg coverings was knitted sometimes on four needles, sometimes on two, but the former method—then as now—had one distinct advantage. Stockings knitted on four needles have no seams, and thus are both sleekly contoured and supremely comfortable. This seamless construction is ideal for completing the toe section of socks that have foot and leg sections done on two needles. Such boldly patterned socks as the supersize Argyles and the barber-pole stripes *(pages 140-141),* for instance—designs that must be done on two needles—can be transferred to four needles for the shaping of the toe. Thus, the knitter, by adding a new technique to her repertoire, enlarges the range of decorative possibilities in her craft.

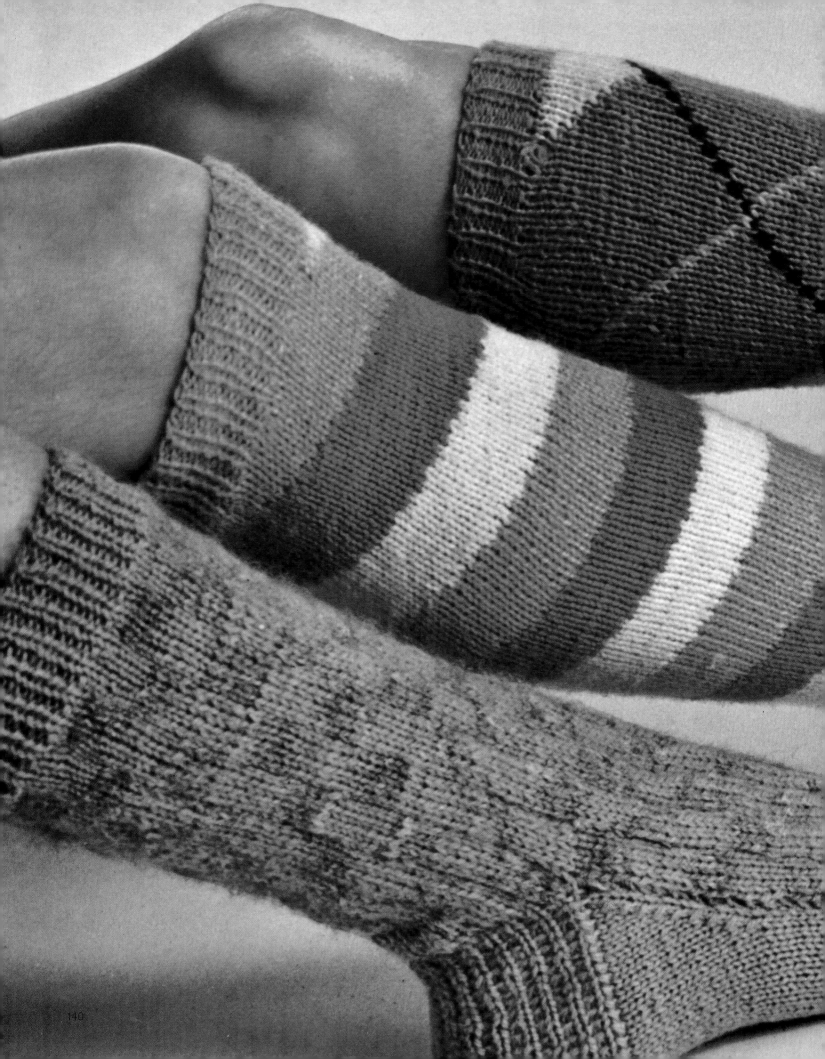

A trio of sporty socks

A four-needle knitting technique helps produce these eye-catching socks. It is used for the leg section of the checkerboard socks, which is knitted in the round to form a continuous tube, thus eliminating the seam at the back. The pattern areas of the barber-pole-stripe and Argyle socks are knitted on two conventional needles and then they are transferred to four double-pointed needles in order to make a toe that is comfortably seamless.

Instructions for knitting the patterned socks

The checkerboard, barber-pole and Argyle socks shown on pages 140-141 are planned to be made to fit the size of the wearer's foot. Measure from the back of the heel to the tip of the longest toe, and knit the instep and sole piece 2 inches shorter than this measurement. The toe sections, regardless of foot size, are all made 2 inches long.

For making the socks you will need a set of four double-pointed Size 3 knitting needles, a tapestry needle and a stitch holder or large safety pin. For the barber-pole and Argyle socks you will also need a pair of Size 3 straight needles, and—for the Argyles—10 yarn bobbins.

Except for 1 1/2 inches of knit-one, purl-one ribbing stitches at the top of each sock, all the work is done in the stockinette stitch. If you are using two needles, you will make the stockinette in the conventional way by alternating knit and purl rows. If you are using four needles, however, you will knit every row. Directions for using four needles precede the instructions for the checkerboard socks. The basic knitting stitches and elementary techniques involved are explained in the Appendix.

For all the patterned socks, the gauge is 7 stitches and 9 rows to the inch. In order to test the gauge, use Size 3 knitting needles and knit a swatch that measures at least 4 inches square. Count the number of stitches and rows to the inch with a ruler; do not use a tape measure.

WORKING WITH FOUR NEEDLES

In four-needle knitting you use three needles, arranged in a triangle, to hold the stitches *(drawing 1)* and a fourth—or spare—needle to work new stitches. Each needle alternates its function, and is referred to in the instructions by the function it is performing—for example, whichever needle is serving as the spare is called the spare needle. Each of the other needles is identified by the group of stitches it holds. The needle holding the first group of cast-on stitches is called the first needle; similarly, the needle that at any time holds the second cast-on group is called the second needle, and the needle holding the third cast-on group is called the third needle. As you knit a row, or a "round," that goes clockwise around the triangle of holding needles, the needles play musical chairs: each needle serves in turn as spare, first group holder, spare, second group holder, spare, third group holder and spare again.

THE SHORT CHECKERBOARD SOCKS

You will need six ounces of sport-weight yarn—four ounces of the main color (light brown in the photograph on pages 140-141) and two ounces of the contrasting color (gray in the photograph).

THE TOP OF THE SOCK

Starting at the top of the sock and using one of the double-pointed needles and the main color yarn, loosely cast on 60 stitches. Be sure that you cast on loosely, or the edge of the cuff will be too tight. Divide the 60 stitches evenly among three double-pointed needles so that you have 20 stitches on each needle. Arrange the three needles in a triangle and make certain that no stitches are twisted on the needles or between them.

Working the ribbing: Position the triangle so that the side closest to you is formed by the needle holding the first group of cast-on stitches. Insert the spare needle into the first cast-on stitch and knit it, pulling the yarn firmly so there will not be a hole in the work between the needles. Position the two needles you are working with—the spare needle and a holding needle—on top of the other two holding needles *(drawing 2)*. Purl 1 stitch, then continue to knit 1 stitch and purl 1 stitch across the first group of cast-on stitches. At this stage, the spare will have taken the place of the first-group holder, which now will serve as the spare or working needle. Insert it into the first stitch of the second group of cast-on stitches and knit, again pulling the yarn firmly. Purl 1 stitch, knit 1 stitch and purl 1 stitch across the row. When this row is completed, another change of needles will have been accomplished; the needle that had held the second group of stitches will now be freed to serve as the new spare needle. Insert it into the first stitch of the third group and knit it, pulling the yarn firmly. Purl 1 stitch, knit 1 stitch and purl 1 stitch across this row to complete the first round. Once again needles switch, the one that had held the third group becoming available to start working an additional row on the first group as another round begins. Repeat the round, alternating needles, until the ribbing measures 1 1/2 inches. Then, still using the main color, knit one round, increasing 4 stitches at evenly spaced intervals so

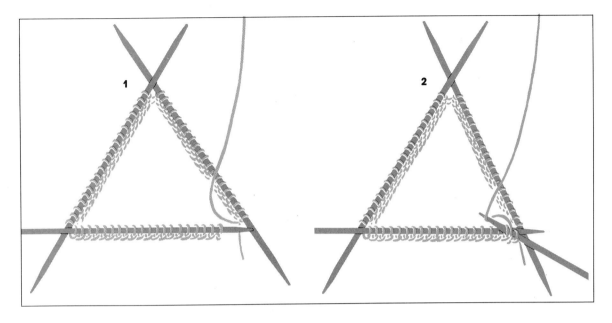

that you have 64 stitches in all. Now shift the stitches among the holding needles, placing 20 stitches on the needle holding the first group, 24 stitches on the needle holding the second group and 20 on the one holding the third. **Making the first pattern sequence:** Make each check in the pattern 4 stitches wide and 6 rows deep *(as shown in the chart below)* in the following manner: without cutting off the main color yarn, attach the contrasting color yarn and knit 4 stitches on the first group. Draw the main color yarn loosely across the back of the contrasting color stitches so

the design does not pucker, and knit 4 stitches in the main color. When changing from one color to another, always bring up the color to be used next from underneath the one previously used. Draw the contrasting color yarn loosely across the back of the main color stitches and knit 4 stitches in the contrasting color. Continue across the first, second and third groups to complete the initial round of the pattern. Repeat this round five more times to finish the first row of checks.

Completing the top of the sock: Now knit 4 stitches of the

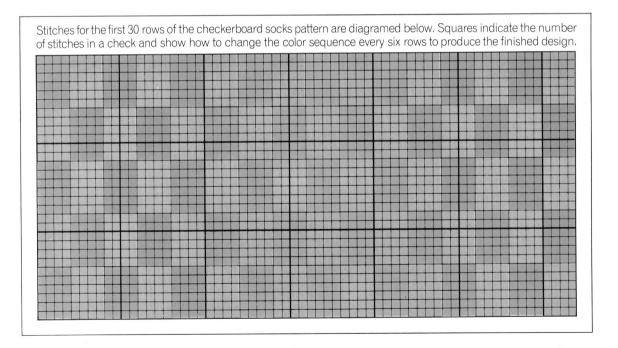

Stitches for the first 30 rows of the checkerboard socks pattern are diagramed below. Squares indicate the number of stitches in a check and show how to change the color sequence every six rows to produce the finished design.

seventh round with the main color yarn, then 4 stitches with the contrasting color yarn. Repeat the color sequence across the round, then repeat this round five more times to finish the second row of checks. Knit alternating checks of main color and contrasting color every six rounds until you have completed 9 rows of checks, or 54 rounds of the pattern.

THE FOOT OF THE SOCK

Establishing the instep: Working with the spare needle and using the main color yarn, knit across 16 stitches of group one. Transfer the remaining 4 stitches in this group onto the needle holding group two. Knit across group two in the checkerboard pattern. Then transfer the first 4 stitches of group three onto the needle holding group two, and work them in the checkerboard pattern. Group two will now have 32 stitches in it; groups one and three, 16 stitches each. Transfer the stitches in group two onto a stitch holder or a large safety pin; eventually they will become the instep. The remainder of the instep, the heel and the sole are not made with four needles but with two or three.

Preparing to make the back of the heel: The back of the heel is made with two double-pointed needles. Dropping the contrasting color yarn, and working with the main color yarn alone, knit across group three as follows: knit 7 stitches, knit 2 stitches together, knit the remaining 7 stitches. Now knit 7 stitches of group one onto this same needle, knit 2 stitches together, then knit the remaining 7 stitches. Groups one and two will now be combined on a single needle holding 30 stitches. These stitches make up the back of the heel, which is knitted on two needles alone.

Fashioning the back of the heel: With the wrong side of the heel facing you, slip 1 stitch as if to purl, and purl across the row. Turn the heel section to the right side, slip the first stitch as if to purl, then knit 1 stitch; repeat this sequence across the row, ending with a knit stitch. Repeat these 2 rows until you have worked 32 rows, ending with the second row of the sequence.

Turning the heel: Two needles are used to turn the heel. With the wrong side of the heel facing you, slip 1 stitch as if to purl, purl the next 16 stitches, then purl 2 stitches together and purl 1 stitch. Now turn the work 180° and begin to work the short rows that will gradually enlarge the center section of the heel without enlarging the edges, thus creating a cup shape for the bottom of the heel.

Row 1: With the right side of the work facing you, slip 1 stitch as if to knit, knit the next 5 stitches, slip 1 stitch as if to knit, knit 1 stitch and pass the slipped stitch over the knit stitch, knit 1 stitch and turn.

Row 2: Slip 1 stitch as if to purl, purl the next 6 stitches, purl 2 stitches together across the hole that has resulted from turning the work, purl 1 stitch and turn.

Row 3: Slip 1 stitch as if to knit, knit the next 7 stitches, slip 1 stitch as if to knit, knit 1 stitch, pass the slipped stitch across the hole made by turning the work and over the knit stitch, knit 1 stitch and turn.

Rows 4-11: Continue in short rows, working 1 more stitch between the decreases on each row, until you reach the outer edges of the heel section and all the stitches on the

back of the heel have been incorporated into what is now the bottom of the heel. End on a knit row; 18 stitches will remain on the needle.

Shaping the gusset: The gusset requires three double-pointed needles. With the right side of the heel facing you, using the main color yarn, pick up with a free needle 16 stitches along the finished left edge of the heel. Purl back across those 16 stitches. Then purl across the 18 stitches on the needle that has been holding the turned heel. Then with another free needle, pick up 16 more stitches along the other finished edge of the heel for a total of 50 stitches on three needles. Divide these 50 stitches onto the two needles that picked up stitches along the finished edges, putting 25 stitches on each. To form the little triangular gussets on each side of the heel, with the wrong side of the heel facing you, work as follows: Knit 1 stitch, slip 1 stitch as if to knit, knit 1 stitch. Pass the slipped stitch over the knit stitch and knit to the end of the needle. Carry the yarn to the other holding needle and knit to within 3 stitches of the end of that needle; knit 2 stitches together, knit 1 stitch. Purl across the next row on both needles. Repeat these two rows, decreasing at the beginning and end of each knit row until you have a total of 28 stitches remaining—14 on each needle.

Knitting the sole: Slip all 28 stitches onto a single needle and work in the stockinette stitch by knitting a row, purling a row until the sole measures 2 inches shorter than the desired foot length; end with a purl row.

Working the instep: Slip the 32 instep stitches from their holder back onto a needle, and, following the pattern, work in the stockinette stitch by knitting a row, purling a row until the instep is the same length as the sole, ending with a purl row. It is not necessary to complete an entire pattern sequence at the end of the instep.

THE TOE OF THE SOCK

The toe, like the leg section of the checkerboard socks, is knitted in the round on four needles. To set up the toe section, divide the 28 sole stitches between two double-pointed needles. The 32 instep stitches, carried as group two through the body of the sock, continues as section two of the toe. The needle preceding this section, now holding 14 stitches from the sole, is designated section one of the toe; the needle holding the other 14 stitches from the sole is designated section three. Slip 1 stitch from each end of section two and place them on sections one and three respectively, so that the distribution of stitches on the three holding needles is as follows: 15 stitches on sections one and three; 30 stitches on section two. Pick up the main color yarn from the point where you left it, at the end of the sole, and knit across section three.

Shaping the toe: Round 1: Knit to within 3 stitches of the end of section one, knit 2 stitches together, knit 1 stitch. On section two, knit 1 stitch, slip 1 stitch as if to knit, knit 1 stitch and pass the slipped stitch over the knit stitch. Knit to within 3 stitches of the end of section two, knit 2 stitches together, knit 1. On section three, knit 1 stitch, slip 1 stitch as if to knit, knit 1 stitch and pass the slipped stitch over the knit stitch. Knit to the end of the section. Round 2: Knit every stitch.

Repeat these two rounds, decreasing as above until you have 16 stitches—4 stitches on the first and third sections, 8 stitches on the second. Knit across 4 stitches on the first section, and slip these stitches onto the needle holding the third section. You will now have 16 stitches on two needles, 8 stitches on each. Break off the yarn, leaving a 20-inch length for weaving.

Weaving the toe: Thread the end of the weaving yarn into a tapestry needle. Place together the two needles, holding the knitting so that they are even and parallel, with the yarn end coming from the back needle; the yarn end should be at your right as you begin to work.

Step 1: Insert the tapestry needle in the first stitch of the front needle as if to purl *(drawing 3)*; draw the yarn through the stitch, leaving the stitch on the knitting needle.

Step 2: Insert the tapestry needle in the first stitch of the back needle as if to knit *(drawing 4)*; draw the yarn through and leave the stitch on the knitting needle.

Step 3: Again insert the tapestry needle in the first stitch of the front needle, this time as if to knit *(drawing 5)*; slip the stitch off the knitting needle, drawing the yarn through *(drawing 6)*. Insert the tapestry needle into the next stitch on the front needle, as if to purl *(drawing 7)*; draw the yarn through but leave a stitch on the knitting needle.

Step 4: Again insert the tapestry needle in the first stitch of the back needle, this time as if to purl *(drawing 8)*; slip stitch off the knitting needle, drawing the yarn through. Insert the tapestry needle in the next stitch on the back needle as if to knit; draw the yarn through but leave a stitch on the knitting needle.

Repeat Steps 3 and 4 until all the stitches from both knitting needles have been woven together and slipped from the needles. Run the tapestry needle through several stitches in the toe to secure the yarn end; then cut it off.

FINISHING THE SOCK

Turn the sock wrong side out and weave all the loose ends of yarn into the work with a crochet hook, or by threading each through the tapestry needle and running it through

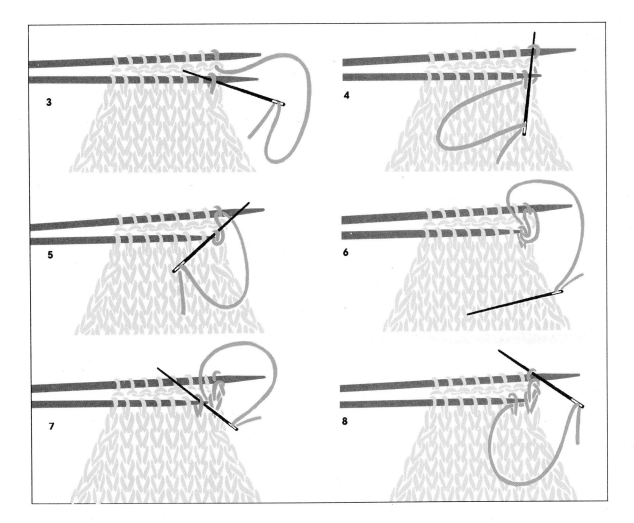

nearby stitches. Weave together the edges of the instep and sole. Make a duplicate sock for the other foot. Block both socks.

THE KNEE-LENGTH BARBER-POLE SOCKS

You will need eight ounces of sport-weight yarn—4 one-ounce skeins of color A (blue in the photograph on pages 140-141), 2 one-ounce skeins of color B (green) and 2 one-ounce skeins of color C (white).

Working the ribbing: Starting at the top of the sock and using one of the pair of Size 3 straight needles and color A yarn, loosely cast on 60 stitches. Be sure that you cast on loosely or the edge of the cuff will be too tight. Then using both needles knit 1 stitch and purl 1 stitch across the row. Continue to knit 1 stitch and purl 1 stitch until the ribbing measures 1 1/2 inches. Then purl 1 row, increasing 6 stitches at evenly spaced intervals across the row so you have 66 stitches in all. Break off color A.

Making the first pattern sequence: Using colors B and C yarn as well as color A, work the stripes in the stockinette stitch—knit 1 row and purl 1 row—by following the chart (opposite page).

Row 1: Beginning at the upper-right corner, follow the chart across the top row from right to left—that is, attach color B, and knit 20 stitches. Attach color C and knit 23 stitches. Attach color A and knit 22 stitches. Attach the second skein of color B and knit 1 stitch.

Row 2: Following the chart from left to right, purl 3 stitches with color B. Pick up color A and draw it loosely across the back of color B, and purl 23 stitches. (When changing from one color to another, always bring up the second color from underneath the first one. Be sure not to pull the yarn too tightly or the work will pucker.) Pick up color C from underneath and purl 22 stitches. Pick up the first thread of color B and purl 18 stitches.

Rows 3-30: Knit the third pattern row, beginning at the right of the chart and working toward the left. Then purl the fourth row, beginning at the left of the chart and working toward the right. Every subsequent odd-numbered row is a knit row and is worked from the chart from right to left. Every subsequent even-numbered row is a purl row and is worked from the chart from left to right.

Repeating the pattern: Rows 31-105: When you have worked 30 pattern rows, or one pattern sequence, begin it again, starting at the arrow to the right of the chart. Repeat the pattern sequence two and a half more times, using the arrangement of colors on the diagram (right), ending with the 15th row of the pattern. You will have completed 105 rows, ending with a knit row. Break off both color-C skeins.

Preparing to make the back of the heel: Using a double-pointed needle and color A, purl across 17 stitches, slip the next 32 stitches onto a stitch holder or a large safety pin to be worked later for the instep, and slip the remaining 17 stitches onto a second double-pointed needle. With the wrong side of the work facing you, bring the two 17-stitch sections around to the front so they are next to each other and can be worked as a single piece to form the heel. Transfer both sections of 17 stitches onto a straight nee-

dle, positioning the stitches on the needle so that you can knit the first row. With color A, knit across the row, decreasing 4 stitches at evenly spaced intervals. You will have 30 stitches left on the needle.

Working the foot: With the wrong side of the heel section facing you, follow the instructions for the checkerboard socks (page 144, column 1) for fashioning the back of the heel, turning the heel, shaping the gusset and knitting the sole.

Working the instep: Slip the 32 instep stitches from their holder back onto a needle. Purl across the row in pattern, picking up color B on the 18th stitch in from the left of the 16th pattern row on the chart. Work the 32 instep stitches

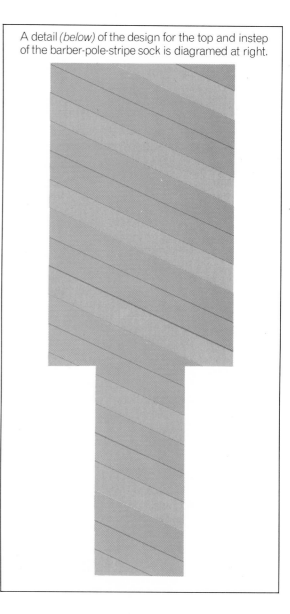

A detail (below) of the design for the top and instep of the barber-pole-stripe sock is diagramed at right.

in pattern beginning each row on the 18th stitch of the chart, using the color arrangement on the diagram *(left)*. Knit the instep piece in pattern to the same length as the sole piece; end with a purl row. It is not necessary to complete an entire pattern sequence at the end of the instep.

Shaping the toe: Follow the instructions for the checkerboard socks *(page 144, column 2)* for the toe of the sock, shaping the toe and weaving the toe.

Finishing the sock: Turn the sock wrong side out, and weave all the loose ends of yarn into the work with a crochet hook, or by threading each through the tapestry needle and running it through nearby stitches. Then weave together the edges of the instep and sole. Align the stripes at the back of the calf and weave the back seam. Make a duplicate sock for the other foot. Block both socks.

THE MID-CALF-LENGTH ARGYLE SOCKS

To make the socks, you will need ten ounces of sport-weight yarn—four ounces of color A (purple in the photograph on pages 140-141), two ounces of color B (light brown), two ounces of color C (light pink), one ounce of color D (deep pink) and one ounce of color E (deep red).

Working the ribbing: Starting at the top of the sock and using one of the pair of Size 3 straight needles and color A yarn, loosely cast on 60 stitches. Be sure that you cast on loosely or the edge of the cuff will be too tight. Then, using

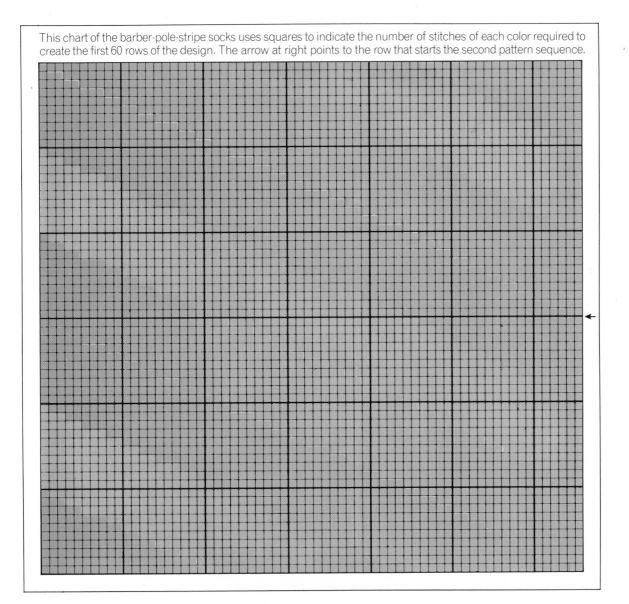

This chart of the barber-pole-stripe socks uses squares to indicate the number of stitches of each color required to create the first 60 rows of the design. The arrow at right points to the row that starts the second pattern sequence.

both needles, knit 1 stitch and purl 1 stitch across the row. Continue to knit 1 stitch and purl 1 stitch until the ribbing measures 1 1/2 inches. Then purl 1 row, increasing 8 stitches at evenly spaced intervals across the row so you have 68 stitches in all. Break off color A.

Making the first pattern sequence: Before you begin to knit the first pattern row, prepare two bobbins of each color yarn. To do this, wind as much yarn onto a yarn bobbin as the bobbin will hold. Then break off the yarn, leaving a 6-inch-long loose end. Using all five yarn colors, work the diamonds in the stockinette stitch—knit 1 row and purl 1 row—by following the chart *(opposite page)*.

Row 1: Beginning at the upper-right corner, follow the chart across the top row from right to left—that is, attach a bobbin of color E by joining the 6-inch-long loose end of the yarn and knit 1 stitch. Attach a bobbin of color B and knit 16 stitches. Attach a bobbin of color C and knit 16 stitches. Attach a bobbin of color D and knit 1 stitch. Attach the second bobbin of color E and knit 1 stitch. Draw the bobbin of color C loosely across the back of colors D and E and knit 16 stitches. Attach the second bobbin of color B and knit 16 stitches. Attach the second bobbin of color D and knit 1 stitch.

Row 2: Following the chart from left to right, purl 1 stitch with color B. Pick up color D from underneath, then draw it loosely across the back of color B and purl 1 stitch. (When you are changing from one color to another, always bring up the second color from underneath the first one.) Pick up color B from underneath and purl 14 stitches. Now attach a bobbin of color A yarn and purl 2 stitches. Pick up color C from underneath and purl 14 stitches. Pick up color E from underneath and purl 1 stitch. Pick up color C from underneath and purl 2 stitches. Pick up color D from underneath and purl 1 stitch. Pick up color C from underneath and purl 14 stitches. Then attach the second bobbin of color A and purl 2 stitches. Pick up color B from underneath and purl 14 stitches. Pick up color E from underneath and purl 1 stitch. Pick up color B from underneath and purl 1 stitch.

Rows 3-64: Knit the third pattern row, beginning at the right of the chart and working toward the left. Purl the fourth pattern row, beginning at the left of the chart and working to the right. Every subsequent odd-numbered row is a knit row and is worked from the chart from right to left. Every subsequent even-numbered row is a purl row and is worked from the chart from left to right. As you finish each block of color on the pattern, break off the bobbin. Refill the bobbins as the yarn is used up.

Repeating the pattern: When you have worked 64 pattern rows, or one pattern sequence, begin again at the top-right corner of the chart. Repeat half of the pattern sequence, or 32 rows, using the arrangement of colors that is shown on the diagram *(right)*. You will now have completed 96 pattern rows, ending with a purl row. Break off both bobbins of color C yarn.

Preparing to make the back of the heel: Slip the first 17 stitches onto a double-pointed needle, place the next 34 stitches onto a stitch holder or a large safety pin to be

worked later for the instep, and slip the remaining 17 stitches onto a second double-pointed needle. With the wrong side of the work facing you, bring the two 17-stitch sections around to the front so they are next to each other and can be worked as a single piece to form the heel. Transfer both sections of 17 stitches onto a straight needle, positioning the stitches on the needles so that you can knit the first row. With color A, knit across the row, decreasing 4 stitches at evenly spaced intervals. You will have 30 stitches left on the needle.

Working the foot: With the wrong side of the heel section facing you, follow the instructions for the checkerboard

The diagram below shows the completed design for the top and the instep sections of an Argyle sock.

socks *(page 144, column 1)* for fashioning the back of the heel, turning the heel, shaping the gusset, and knitting the sole.

Working the instep: Slip the 34 instep stitches from their holder back onto a needle. Knit across the row in pattern, beginning with color E on the 18th stitch in from the right on the 33rd pattern row, but following the arrangement of colors shown on the diagram *(left)*. Work the 34 instep stitches in pattern to the same length as the sole piece, ending with a purl row. On the final instep row, purl the first 2 stitches together, purl 30 stitches in pattern, purl 2 stitches together. It is not necessary to complete an entire pattern sequence at the end of the instep.

Shaping the toe: Follow the instructions for the checkerboard socks *(page 144, column 2)* for the toe of the sock, shaping the toe and weaving the toe.

Finishing the sock: Turn the sock wrong side out and weave all the loose ends of yarn into the work by weaving each of them with a crochet hook, or by threading each through the tapestry needle and running it through nearby stitches. Then weave together the edges of the instep and sole pieces. Match the diamonds at the back of the calf and weave the back seam. Make a duplicate sock for the other foot. Block both socks.

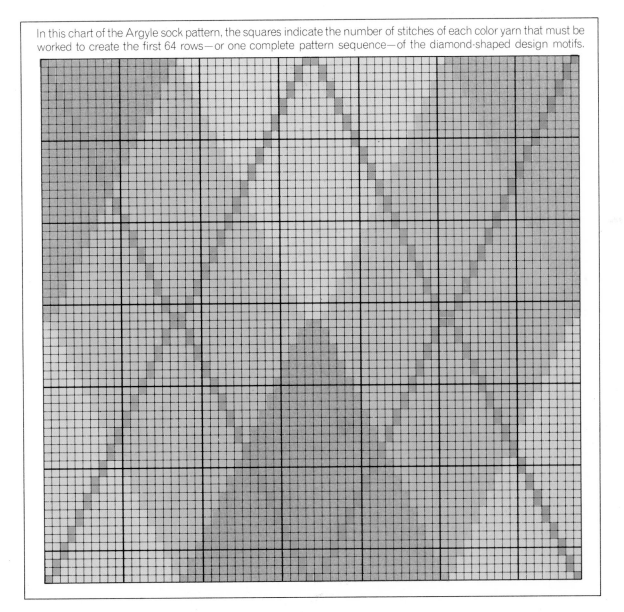

In this chart of the Argyle sock pattern, the squares indicate the number of stitches of each color yarn that must be worked to create the first 64 rows—or one complete pattern sequence—of the diamond-shaped design motifs.

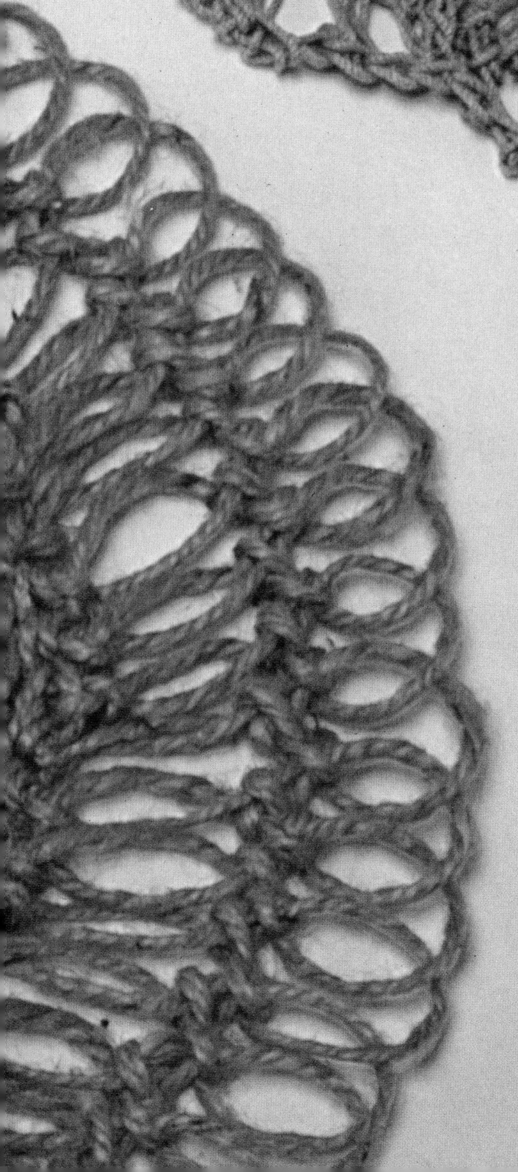

Lace from a loom

The handsome place mats shown here were fashioned with an age-old technique called hairpin lacemaking, which originally combined conventional crocheting with an unconventional tool—a slender hairpin —to produce a strip of delicate lace. The modern crocheter, however, can rapidly fashion bold, contemporary designs with the same technique by using the loom on page 137 and such everyday materials as wrapping twine or jute.

Old loom or new, the method for making hairpin lace strips is the same *(overleaf).* The working thread is wound around the loom's parallel prongs, forming a series of large loops, which are held together by a row of crochet stitches running down the center. The loops are then slipped from the loom and edged with more crochet stitches. Finally, the strips are joined in bands, circles or ovals to create the shape desired.

Instructions for making hairpin lace

Hairpin lace projects, such as the graceful place mats that are shown on pages 150-151 and described overleaf, begin as strips of crochet work created with a conventional crochet hook and one special device called a loom. The loom consists of two 12-inch-long metal rods, called prongs, around which the working thread or yarn is wrapped to form loops, and two bars that hold the prongs and set their spacing. Each of these bars has six holes 1/2 to 4 inches apart so the prongs can be inserted into the holes at whatever separation is required for the width of the work being done.

The lace is formed in strips by anchoring each loop, as it is wrapped around the loom, with a crochet stitch at the loop's center, midway between the two prongs. As the work progresses, the vertical row of stitches forms a spine running down the center of the loops.

Strips can be made any length desired by removing the bottom bar after the loom is filled and slipping off all but four loops from each prong. Then the bar is simply replaced and the work continued.

MAKING HAIRPIN LACE CROCHET

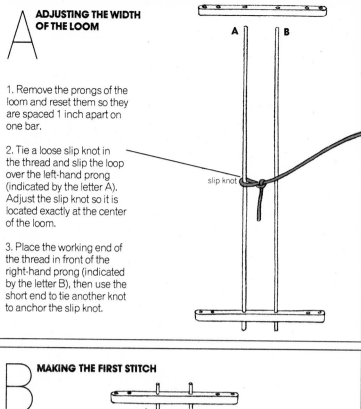

A ADJUSTING THE WIDTH OF THE LOOM

1. Remove the prongs of the loom and reset them so they are spaced 1 inch apart on one bar.

2. Tie a loose slip knot in the thread and slip the loop over the left-hand prong (indicated by the letter A). Adjust the slip knot so it is located exactly at the center of the loom.

3. Place the working end of the thread in front of the right-hand prong (indicated by the letter B), then use the short end to tie another knot to anchor the slip knot.

B MAKING THE FIRST STITCH

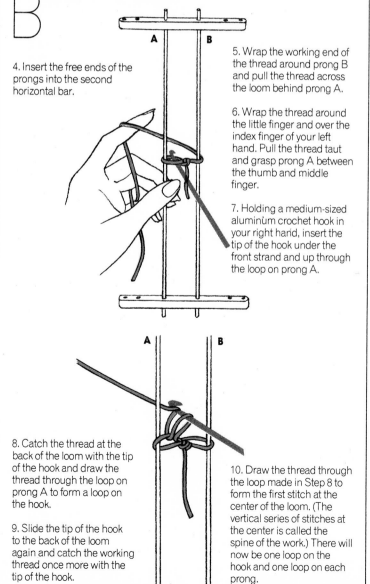

4. Insert the free ends of the prongs into the second horizontal bar.

5. Wrap the working end of the thread around prong B and pull the thread across the loom behind prong A.

6. Wrap the thread around the little finger and over the index finger of your left hand. Pull the thread taut and grasp prong A between the thumb and middle finger.

7. Holding a medium-sized aluminum crochet hook in your right hand, insert the tip of the hook under the front strand and up through the loop on prong A.

8. Catch the thread at the back of the loom with the tip of the hook and draw the thread through the loop on prong A to form a loop on the hook.

9. Slide the tip of the hook to the back of the loom again and catch the working thread once more with the tip of the hook.

10. Draw the thread through the loop made in Step 8 to form the first stitch at the center of the loom. (The vertical series of stitches at the center is called the spine of the work.) There will now be one loop on the hook and one loop on each prong.

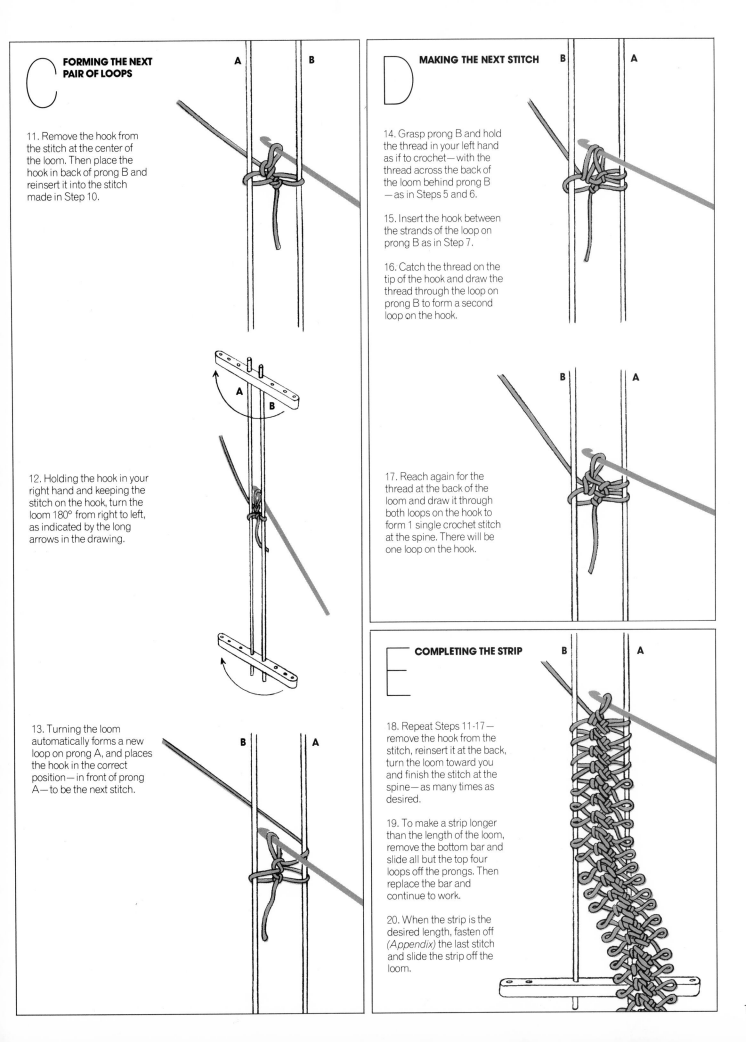

C FORMING THE NEXT PAIR OF LOOPS

A   B

11. Remove the hook from the stitch at the center of the loom. Then place the hook in back of prong B and reinsert it into the stitch made in Step 10.

12. Holding the hook in your right hand and keeping the stitch on the hook, turn the loom 180° from right to left, as indicated by the long arrows in the drawing.

A   B

13. Turning the loom automatically forms a new loop on prong A, and places the hook in the correct position—in front of prong A—to be the next stitch.

B   A

D MAKING THE NEXT STITCH

B   A

14. Grasp prong B and hold the thread in your left hand as if to crochet—with the thread across the back of the loom behind prong B —as in Steps 5 and 6.

15. Insert the hook between the strands of the loop on prong B as in Step 7.

16. Catch the thread on the tip of the hook and draw the thread through the loop on prong B to form a second loop on the hook.

B   A

17. Reach again for the thread at the back of the loom and draw it through both loops on the hook to form 1 single crochet stitch at the spine. There will be one loop on the hook.

E COMPLETING THE STRIP

B   A

18. Repeat Steps 11-17— remove the hook from the stitch, reinsert it at the back, turn the loom toward you and finish the stitch at the spine—as many times as desired.

19. To make a strip longer than the length of the loom, remove the bottom bar and slide all but the top four loops off the prongs. Then replace the bar and continue to work.

20. When the strip is the desired length, fasten off (Appendix) the last stitch and slide the strip off the loom.

Instructions for the hairpin lace place mats

The materials needed for the hairpin lace place mats *(pages 150-151)* depend on the shape. Each 11 1/2-by-16-inch rectangular and 17-inch round place mat requires one 150-yard ball of tightly twisted wrapping twine—medium-weight for the rectangular mat, lightweight for the round one.

Each oval place mat, which measures approximately 14 inches by 18 inches, requires 100 yards of 3-ply heavy jute wrapping twine.

For all three place mats you will need a tapestry needle and an adjustable hairpin lace loom. You will also need a Size G aluminum crochet hook for the rectangular mat, a Size F hook for the round mat, and a Size H hook for the oval mat.

The foundation for all three place mats is strips of hairpin lace crochet *(pages 152-153)* that are worked identically, except for length and width.

THE RECTANGULAR PLACE MAT

Adjust the hairpin lace loom to a 1-inch spacing. Using the Size G crochet hook, follow the instructions on pages 152-153 to make a lace strip with 56 loops on each side of the loom. To facilitate counting, place a marker on the 25th loop by tying a piece of contrasting color thread or yarn around the loop.

When you have made the last set of loops, fasten off. Remove the bottom bar on the loom, then carefully slide the strip off the loom. Make five more strips in exactly the same manner.

Edging the strips: Using one of the lace strips and working along one side edge, begin to make the edging stitches in the following manner: using the crochet hook and working from the bottom right-hand edge of the strip, attach the wrapping twine to the first loop.

Now insert the crochet hook from the back to the front through the first loop, then again from the back to the front through the second loop. Then bring the wrapping twine over the crochet hook and draw it through the first two loops. Complete a single crochet stitch by drawing the twine through the last two loops on the hook, thus forming a figure 8.

Chain 2, then work another single crochet stitch through the next two loops, making sure that you twist them in the same way as you twisted the first two loops. Continue in this manner—chain 2, work 1 single crochet stitch through the next two loops—all along the entire edge, ending with a single crochet stitch through the last two loops. Chain 1 and turn.

Work 1 single crochet stitch in each stitch of the previous row and 2 single crochet stitches in each space formed by the chain-2 stitches. Fasten off at the end of this row. Repeat the 2 rows of edging stitches along the other side of this strip.

Then edge three more strips on both sides in exactly the same way. These four strips will be used to form the central portion of the mat.

Now edge the two remaining lace strips on one side only. These strips will be used along the top and bottom of the mat.

Joining the strips: Arrange the strips in the correct order —the two unedged strips at the top and bottom with the unedged loops extending out, and the four double-edged strips in between. Using the tapestry needle, make overcast stitches *(Appendix)* in order to attach the bottom of the top strip to the top of the one that is directly beneath, sewing through both loops of each single crochet stitch at the edges of the strips. Then attach the bottom of the second strip to the top of the next one. Continue in this manner, ending with attaching the bottom of the fifth strip to the top of the bottom strip.

Finishing the place mat: Weave in all loose ends on each short side of the mat. Then work 2 rows of single crochet stitches along each of these edges.

Block the finished place mat, using a warm iron over a very damp pressing cloth.

THE ROUND SCALLOPED PLACE MAT

Using the hairpin lace loom, a Size F crochet hook and appropriate twine, use the technique on pages 152-153 to make four strips as follows:

The first strip: Adjust the loom to 1 1/2 inches. Make a hairpin lace strip that consists of 30 loops on each side of the loom. Fasten off. Remove the bottom bar, then carefully slide the strip off the loom.

Working on one side of the strip and using the Size F crochet hook, edge the strip in the following manner: insert the crochet hook into the first six loops, then work a single crochet stitch through the six loops. Continue now along the edge, working each successive set of six loops together with a single crochet stitch. Fasten off at the end of the row. This edge will form the center of the place mat.

Working on the other edge, make 1 single crochet stitch in each loop of this side, and at the same time increase 6 stitches evenly spaced on this row by working 2 single crochet stitches in each of the six loops where the increases occur. Fasten off at the end of the row. Shape this strip into a circle, then—using the tapestry needle—join the ends by sewing the first and last single crochet stitches made along the edges together at the top and bottom. Also sew the two ends of the spine—the slip knot at the beginning of the strip and the fastened-off stitch at the end —together.

The second strip: Keep the loom adjusted to 1 1/2 inches. Make a hairpin lace strip with 50 loops on each side of the loom.

Fasten off, then carefully slide the strip off the loom. Using the crochet hook, edge this strip by working 1 single crochet stitch in each loop along one long edge of the strip; on the other edge, work 2 single crochet stitches in the first loop, then 1 single crochet stitch in the next loop and repeat this sequence across the row. Fasten off.

Shape this strip into a circle and join the ends together as you did for the first strip.

Slip the first joined strip into the inner circle formed by the second joined strip. Ease the outer edge of the first strip around the inner edge of the second strip, then use a tapestry needle to sew the strips together with overcast stitches (Appendix), making the stitches through both outside loops of the single crochet stitches on the pieces.

The third strip: Adjust the loom to 2 1/2 inches. Make this hairpin lace strip with 84 loops on each side of the loom. Fasten off. Edge each side of this strip in the same way you edged the second strip, then join the short ends as before to form a circle.

Slip the joined first and second strip into the ring formed by the third strip, then join the inside edge of the third strip to the outside edge of the second strip as you did when joining the other two strips.

The fourth strip: Keep the loom adjusted to 2 1/2 inches. Make this hairpin lace strip with 126 loops on each side of the loom. Fasten off.

Edge one side only of this strip by making 1 single crochet stitch in each loop along that edge. Join the short ends

in the same manner as for the other strips, making sure the edged side is on the inside of the ring.

Ease this strip around the outside edge of the third strip, then sew the strips together as before.

Finishing the place mat: To make the scalloped edge around the outside of the place mat, start at any point and make 1 single crochet stitch in each of the first nine loops. Then work 1 triple crochet stitch into the joining seam between the third and fourth strip. Repeat the sequence—1 single crochet stitch in each of the next nine loops, 1 triple crochet stitch into the joining seam—around the piece. Fasten off.

THE OVAL PLACE MAT

Using the hairpin lace loom, a Size H crochet hook and the appropriate twine, use the technique that is shown on pages 152-153 to make hairpin lace strips for this place mat as follows:

The first strip: Adjust the loom to 1 1/2 inches. Make a hairpin lace strip that consists of 12 loops on each side of the loom. Fasten off, then carefully slide the strip off the loom. Using the crochet hook, edge this strip by working 1 single crochet stitch in each loop along one long side.

When you reach the end of this strip and have worked the last loop, chain 1. Then work 1 single crochet stitch into the end of the spine. Chain 1, then work 1 single crochet stitch in each loop along the opposite long side edge to the end.

After you have worked the last loop, chain 1, then work 1 single crochet stitch into that end of the spine. Chain 1, then join the loop on the crochet hook to the starting single crochet stitch with a slip stitch—first inserting the hook into the single crochet stitch, then bringing the yarn over the hook and drawing it through both the stitch and the loop on the hook. Fasten off.

The second strip: Adjust the loom to 2 1/2 inches. Make a hairpin lace strip that consists of 42 loops on each side of the loom. Now edge one side of the strip only by working 1 single crochet stitch in each loop along this edge. Fasten off. Pin the finished edge of this strip around the outside edge of the first strip, then use the tapestry needle to sew the edges together with overcast stitches (Appendix). Remove the pins as you sew. Sew the ends of the spine together.

Using the crochet hook, work an edging around the entire outside edge of the piece, making 2 single crochet stitches in each loop.

The third strip: Adjust the loom to 3 1/2 inches. Make this hairpin lace strip with 78 loops on each side of the loom. Fasten off, then carefully slide the strip off the loom. Edge this strip by working 1 single crochet stitch in each loop along only one long side edge of the strip. Sew the ends of the spine together.

Join the crocheted edge of this strip to the last crocheted edge of the piece—that is, the outside edge of the second strip—using overcast stitches and sewing through the outside loops of each set of stitches only.

Lace from a broomstick

Although the intricate and laborious art of true lacemaking is all but lost, lacy effects can still be obtained with two ingenious methods that are variants of crocheting: broomstick and hairpin lace. Hairpin lace, shown on pages 150-151, employs a small loom. The saucy brimmed hat and matching purse shown here are made by the second method, with an extra-large knitting needle—the "broomstick"—and a conventional crochet hook.

With these tools and a repeat of only two pattern rows, large shell-like designs are rapidly made from the two strands of thread that create the bicolored effect. On the first row, loops of thread are pulled up with the hook and slipped onto the needle; on the next row the loops are crocheted off to form the pattern.

Instructions for the broomstick lace purse and hat

The instructions that follow are for making the broomstick lace purse and hat on pages 156-157. The purse will measure 9 inches wide and 7 inches high, and the hat—because it is elastic—will fit all head sizes.

To make the purse, you will need four 100-yard balls of medium-weight cotton thread. (For a two-color effect like the one in the photograph, use two balls of each color.)

To work the purse you will need a broomstick lace pin in Size 35, a Size G aluminum crochet hook and a tapestry needle. To finish the purse, you will also need 1/4 yard of lining fabric, a snap fastener, a metal chain measuring approximately 22 inches long and an 8-inch-long strip of nylon boning,

sold by the yard, to support the top of the bag and keep it from sagging.

To make the hat, you will need six 100-yard balls of the same yarn used for the purse—for a two-color effect, three balls of each color—a Size 35 broomstick lace pin, a Size G aluminum crochet hook, a tapestry needle and about a yard of narrow, flexible flower-arranging wire to support the brim.

Both the purse and the hat are worked in the same shell-like broomstick lace pattern on a multiple of 6 stitches and to a gauge of one complete 2-row pattern sequence to 1 1/4 inches. All the crochet techniques and stitches are in the Appendix.

To practice the lace technique and to test the gauge, follow the instructions that begin below for working the broomstick lace pattern sequence for the purse, but work only on 18 stitches. Make at least three complete sequences. Measure the height of one complete shell. If it is more than 1 1/4 inches high, change to a smaller crochet hook; if less, use a larger hook.

THE BROOMSTICK LACE PURSE
THE BROOMSTICK LACE PATTERN SEQUENCE

Using two strands of thread—one each of color A and color B for a two-color purse—make a loose foundation chain of 36 stitches, 18 if you are making a practice swatch. Begin to work the broomstick lace pattern sequence in the following manner:

Row 1: Hold the lace pin in your left hand and the crochet hook in your right hand. Draw up on the hook the loop made when you formed the last chain stitch, then slide the loop onto the lace pin (drawing 1). Hold the thread now in

your left hand as you would for regular crocheting. Insert the hook through the next chain stitch after the drawn-up

loop and catch the double strand (drawing 2) then draw the strands through the chain stitch to form another loop.

Draw up this loop on the hook as you did for the previous chain stitch loop and place it on the pin *(drawing 3)*. Leave

3

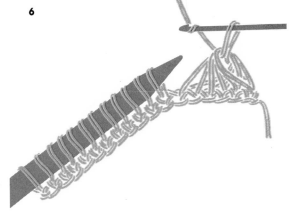

the loop loose enough to slide easily. Repeat this sequence — insert the hook through the next chain stitch, catch a double strand, draw it through the chain stitch and place the loop on the pin—across the row until all the chain stitches of the foundation chain have been worked and there are 36 loops (18 if you are making a swatch) on the pin *(drawing 4)*. Do not turn at the end of the row. Note: for

4

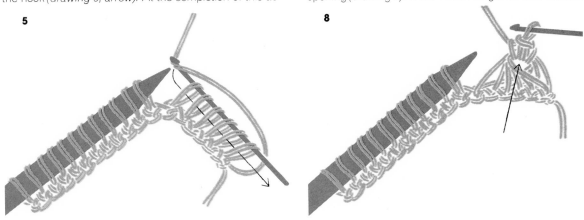

each piece of broomstick lace, row 1 is worked only once to pick up the loops from the original foundation chain.
Row 2: Insert the hook from right to left through the first six loops on the pin. Then slide the loops off the pin onto the hook and catch the double strands over the tip of the hook *(drawing 5)*. Draw the thread through all six of the loops on the hook *(drawing 5, arrow)*. At the completion of this ac-

5

tion one loop will have been made on the hook. Now bring the thread over the hook once more *(drawing 6)* and draw

6

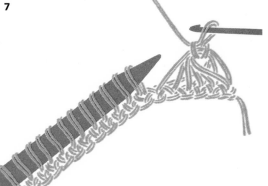

the thread through the loop on the hook; this will form a chain stitch at the top of the six large loops *(drawing 7)*.

7

The chain stitch will hold the six large loops together. Turn the cluster of large loops slightly so you can clearly see the opening at the center *(drawing 8, arrow)*. Insert the hook in the opening, then work 1 single crochet stitch through the opening *(drawing 8)*. Work 4 more single crochet stitches

8

through the opening—a total of 5 single crochet stitches in all—to form the first shell-like pattern *(drawing 9)*. Insert the hook from right to left through the next six loops on the

9

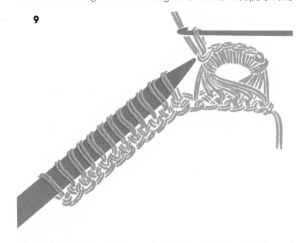

pin and slide these loops onto the hook. Bring the thread over the hook and draw it through the six loops, as illustrated in drawing 5. With two loops—but four strands because you are working with double strands—now on the hook, bring the thread over the hook. Draw the thread through the two loops on the hook *(drawing 10, arrow)* to form a single crochet stitch and to hold the loops together at the top. Turn the loops so you can see the opening at the

10

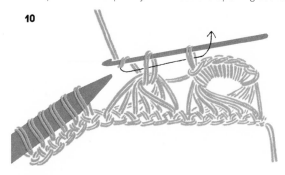

center, as illustrated in drawing 8, arrow. Insert the hook through the opening, then work 5 more single crochet stitches—6 single crochet stitches in all—through the opening. Repeat this sequence—slide the next six loops onto the hook, thread over and draw it through the loops, thread over and draw it through the two loops on the hook —then work 5 more single crochet stitches through the center of the large loops to complete another shell pattern. Continue across the row until all the stitches have been worked and there are six complete shell-like broomstick lace patterns—three for the swatch—on the row. At the end of the row, do not turn.

Row 3: Draw up the double-strand loop remaining from the previous row after you completed the last single crochet stitch. Place the loop on the pin. With the work extending

to the right of the tip of the pin, insert the hook through the first single crochet stitch of the previous row (four loops on the hook, because of the double strands). Bring the thread over the hook, then draw it through the stitch *(drawing 11)* to form one loop on the hook. Draw up this loop and place it on the pin *(drawing 11, arrow)*. Repeat this sequence

11

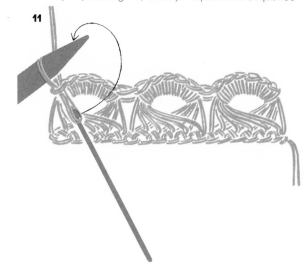

across the row—insert the hook in the next single crochet stitch, thread over and draw it through, draw up the loop formed and place it on the pin—until all the single crochet stitches have been worked and there are a total of 36 loops on the pin (18 loops if you are only making a swatch). At the end of the row do not turn. Repeat rows 2 and 3, which together form the pattern, until 18 shell patterns have been worked. As you are making the last pattern sequence, end with row 2. Fasten off. This piece will form the body of the purse.

Making the lining: Place the lining fabric on a flat surface, then lay the piece for the body of the purse over it. Cut out the lining, allowing 1/4 inch extra all around the edges of the purse for seam allowances on the lining. Turn under the seam allowances of the lining to the wrong side and press them flat. Then place the piece of broomstick lace on a flat surface, wrong side up, and position the lining on top of it, right side up. Using slip stitches *(Appendix)*, attach the lining to the piece of broomstick lace around all four sides. Turn the work so that the broomstick lace is facing up, and shape the purse as follows: to form the bottom fold of the purse, count up seven complete shell patterns from the bottom edge of the work and fold the piece under at this point, lining sides together. Baste or pin to hold the two layers together. To form the flap, turn the folded work over and fold down the single layer at the top. There will be seven complete bands of shell patterns in the front and back of the body of the purse and four complete bands of shell patterns in the flap.

Edging the purse: Continuing to use two strands of thread —one in each color for a two-color purse—and with the outside of the work facing you, start at one top corner of the flap, the extended single layer of the work, and attach the strands. Work one row of single crochet stitches down along the edge of the flap to the point where the double thickness of the work, created by the bottom fold, begins. Working now through the double thickness of the front and the back, continue to make single crochet stitches through both layers in order to join them together. Now work across the bottom fold and up the other side of the bag to the flap, joining together the double thickness of front and back on that side as well. Continue to make single crochet stitches through the single thickness to the second top corner of the flap. Chain 1 and turn, then work a second row of single crochet stitches all around the purse, making these stitches through the stitches of the previous row. Fasten off.

FINISHING THE PURSE

Making the closure: Sew the ball portion of the snap fastener to the wrong side of the flap at the center of the flap and near the top edge. Then sew the socket portion of the snap fastener to the top edge of the front of the bag. Be sure that you position the socket so that it meets the ball portion exactly.

Crocheting the flower decoration: Again using two strands together, begin the flower by making a foundation chain of 6 chain stitches. To form a ring, join the ends with a slip stitch by inserting the hook into the first chain stitch (*drawing 12, arrow*), bringing the thread over the hook and draw-

12

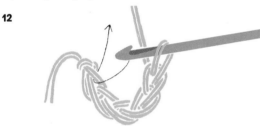

ing it through both the first stitch in the chain and the loop on the hook made by the last stitch in the chain. Chain 4, then bring the thread over the hook (*drawing 13*), and insert the hook into the center of the ring (*drawing 13, arrow*).

13

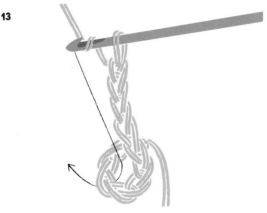

Work 1 double crochet stitch into the center of the ring (*drawing 14*). Chain 2 and work another double crochet

14

stitch into the center of the ring. Repeat this sequence — chain 2, work 1 double crochet stitch into the center of the ring — three more times to form six spokes radiating outward from the center of the ring. At the end of the round, chain 2 (*drawing 15*), then insert the hook into the second stitch of the chain-4 sequence made at the beginning of the round (*drawing 15, arrow*). Join the loop on the

15

hook to the chain stitch with a slip stitch, working this stitch in the same way as the one used to join the original chain-6 sequence into a ring *(drawing 16)*.

16

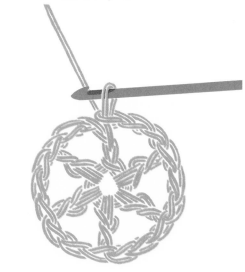

On the next round, work 1 single crochet, 1 double crochet, 1 triple crochet, 1 double crochet and 1 single crochet — 5 complete stitches in all — into the first large hole (called a chain-loop space) between the spaces formed in the previous round *(drawing 17)*. Then insert the hook into the next double crochet stitch of the previous round *(drawing 17, arrow)* and work a slip stitch in order to complete the first

17

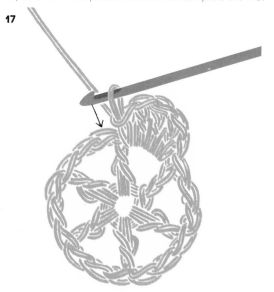

petal of the flower. Repeat this sequence of 5 complete stitches — 1 single crochet stitch, 1 double crochet stitch, 1 triple crochet stitch, 1 double crochet stitch and 1 single crochet stitch, then 1 slip stitch into the next double crochet stitch — in each of the five remaining chain-loop spaces. At the end of this round, make a slip stitch into the first stitch of the previous round. Fasten off. Sew the flower into place on the outside of the flap, centering it over the snap fastener.

Making the handle: Sew the two ends of the metal chain into place at either end of the top fold, attaching the ends to the lining on the underside of the fold, at the point where the lining is double thick because of the seam allowance.

Inserting the boning: Measure the width of the purse and cut a strip of nylon boning 1/4 inch shorter than the width measurement. To form a casing for the boning, cut out a strip of lining fabric large enough to cover the boning strip, plus 1/4 inch extra on all four sides for seam allowances. Then turn under the seam allowances of the lining strip and press them flat. Open up the bag to expose the lining. Place the lining strip wrong side down just below the fold line of the flap. By hand, stitch the two long edges and one end of the lining strip to the purse lining, using tiny hemming stitches *(Appendix)*. Slip the nylon boning into the open end of the casing strip and then stitch the end closed.

THE BROOMSTICK LACE HAT

Using two strands of thread — one in each color for a two-color hat — make a loose foundation chain of 24 stitches. Work the first 3 rows of the broomstick lace pattern sequence, following the directions for making the broomstick lace purse *(pages 158-160)*. There will be four complete shell-like patterns in the work at the conclusion of these 3 initial rows.

THE CROWN

Continuing in the pattern sequence — repeating rows 2 and 3 as instructed — complete row 2. On the next row (row 3 of the pattern sequence) begin to shape the crown by increasing in the following manner. Insert the hook into the first stitch of the previous row. Bring the thread over the hook, draw up a loop — because you are working with double strands of thread the loop will actually consist of two strands — and place the loop loosely on the lace pin. Then draw up a double strand from the second stitch in the same manner. Now insert the hook in the back loop of the same second stitch, bring the thread over and draw it through this loop. Draw up the new loop and place it on the pin, thus forming a new stitch. Continue to repeat this sequence of drawing up two loops in every other single crochet stitch across the row. At the end of this row you will have 36 stitches, or loops, on the pin. On the next row, continuing in the pattern sequence, complete row 2, working off the loops in the established manner. At the end of this row you will have worked six complete shell-like patterns — two more than you had at the conclusion of the pattern sequence.

On the next row, row 3 of the pattern, increase 12 more stitches, just as you increased on the previous row 3, but this time make the increases in every third stitch of the row. At the end of this row, you will have 48 stitches. Continuing in the pattern sequence, work row 2 in the established manner. At the end of this row, you will have worked eight complete shell-like patterns—again an increase of two over the previous pattern sequence. Continue alternating the 2 rows of the pattern sequence, increasing 12 stitches on every row 3, having 1 stitch more between each point of increase on each successive row 3 and two more complete shell-like patterns on each successive row 2, until you have 84 stitches on the pin when you have completed row 3, then 16 shell-like patterns upon completing row 2.

Working now on 84 stitches and 16 patterns, work even for two more double-row pattern sequences. End with row 2. On the next row put aside the broomstick lace pin and work in regular crochet in the following manner: turn the work, then begin the row by making 2 chain stitches. Now work 1 single crochet stitch in each of the 2 stitches at the center of the first pattern, then chain 4. Repeat this sequence—1 single crochet stitch in each of the 2 center stitches of the next pattern, then chain 4—across the row. End the row by making 2 chain stitches, then chain 1 to turn. On the next row, work 1 single crochet stitch in each of the first 2 chain stitches. Then work 1 single crochet stitch through the back loops only of the first 2 single crochet stitches made in the center stitches on the previous row, then work 4 single crochet stitches in each of the chain-4 stitches that follow. Repeat this sequence—1 single crochet stitch through the back loops of the 2 single crochet stitches, 1 single crochet stitch in each chain stitch —across the row. End the row by working 1 single crochet stitch in each of the last chain-2 stitches. At the completion of the row, the work will contain a total of 84 single crochet stitches. Chain 1 stitch and turn at the end of the row. This completes the crown section.

THE BRIM

Continuing to work in single crochet, start to increase now to shape the brim. On the next row, work 1 single crochet stitch in each of the first 5 stitches. Then work 2 single crochet stitches in the next stitch to increase 1 stitch. Repeat the sequence—5 single crochet stitches, then 2 single crochet stitches in the next stitch—across the row, increasing 1 stitch in every sixth stitch. At the completion of the row, it will contain a total of 98 single crochet stitches. Chain 1 stitch and turn at the end of the row.

On the next row, work 2 single crochet stitches in the first single crochet stitch of the previous row, 1 single crochet stitch in each of the next 5 single crochet stitches, then 2 single crochet stitches in the next stitch and 1 single crochet in each of the next 6 single crochet stitches. Repeat the sequence—2 single crochet stitches in the next stitch, then 1 single crochet stitch in each of the next 6 stitches—across the row, stopping within the last 7 stitches. End the row by working 2 stitches in the next stitch, 1 stitch in each of the next 5 stitches, then 2 stitches in the

last stitch. At the completion of the row there will be a total of 114 single crochet stitches.

Begin making the broomstick lace pattern sequence again with row 3, pulling up the loops in the 114 stitches of the work and placing them on the lace pin. Then work row 2 to work off the loops and form the shell-like patterns. There will be 19 complete patterns on the work. On the next row (row 3 of the pattern sequence), increase 36 stitches on the row, making these increases just as you did for enlarging the size of the crown (opposite page), but spacing the increases as directed here. Begin the row by drawing up the loops of the first 6 stitches (the first pattern) in the usual way and without increasing. Work the first 2 stitches of the next pattern even (without increasing). Then increase 1 stitch in the established manner in the next 2 stitches (the 2 center stitches of the pattern). Work the last 2 stitches of the pattern even. Repeat this sequence—work the first 2 stitches even, make an increase in the next 2 stitches, work the last 2 stitches even—in each successive pattern across the row. At the end of the row, there will be 150 stitches on the work. On the next row (row 2 of the pattern sequence), work off the loops in the usual way to form 25 complete shell-like patterns. On the next row, begin by drawing up the loops—without increasing—of the first 4 stitches. Then draw up a loop in the fifth stitch and another loop in the back loop of the same fifth stitch to make an increase of 1 stitch. Repeat the sequence—draw up loops in the next 4 stitches, increase 1 stitch in the fifth stitch —across the row. At the end of this row, you will have a total of 180 loops on the lace pin. On the final pattern row, work off the loops in the manner previously established to form 30 complete shell-like patterns along the outside edge of the brim. Fasten off.

FINISHING THE HAT

Attaching the wire: Place the work on a flat surface. Coil the flexible flower-arranging wire around the bottom edge of the brim. Cut off a length of wire equal to the brim's outer circumference plus an additional 2 inches for working the wire into the crochet stitches. Hold one end of the wire securely to the edge of the brim. Using the crochet hook and two strands of thread, work 1 single crochet stitch into each of the first 5 stitches along the edge of the brim, making the stitches directly over the wire. Then work 1 slip stitch —by inserting the hook in the next stitch, bringing the thread over the hook and drawing the thread through the stitch and the loop on the hook—into the next stitch, still making the stitches over the wire. Repeat the sequence —5 single crochet stitches, then 1 slip stitch—across the row, thus covering the wire with stitches and simultaneously attaching it to the edge of the brim. Fasten off.

Completing the hat: Starting at the crown, weave together the back seam. When you reach the bottom edge of the brim, twist the ends of the wire together to hold the hat together securely at that point. Trim off any excess wire, and tuck the twisted section into the stitches of the outer brim. Then block the hat on a hat mold, using a warm iron over a damp pressing cloth.

GLOSSARY

BASTE: To make long, loose stitches by hand or machine to join pieces of fabric temporarily or indicate pattern markings on both sides of a piece of fabric. A line of basting is usually ended with a fastening or backstitch.

BEADING HOOK: A slender instrument used for attaching beads to fabric.

BEADING NEEDLE: An extra-slender and long needle used to attach beads.

BIAS: A line diagonal to the threads in a woven fabric. A 45° bias is called a true bias.

BIAS BINDING: Double-fold bias tape that will stretch smoothly to cover curved and straight edges.

BIAS STRIPS: Strips of fabric obtained by first folding fabric diagonally on the bias so that one selvage edge is perpendicular to the other selvage edge and then cutting, one layer at a time, parallel to the fold.

BLOCK: To set the final shape of finished knitting or crocheting by pressing it with a warm iron through a damp cloth.

CUTTING LINE: A long, unbroken line marked on a pattern to indicate where it must be cut.

DART: A stitched fold, tapering to a point at one or both ends, to shape fabric around curves.

DRESSMAKER'S CARBON: Heavyweight white or colored carbon paper that is used with a tracing wheel to transfer pattern markings to fabric.

EASE: An even distribution of fullness in fabric, without perceptible gathers or tucks, that enables one section of a garment to be smoothly joined to another slightly smaller section—as in the seam joining a sleeve to its armhole.

FACING: A piece of fabric that is sewed along the raw edge of an opening, such as a neckline, and then turned to the inside to give the edge a smooth finish.

FUSIBLE WEB: A lightweight nonwoven material that forms a flexible, durable bond between layers of fabric. The bond is sealed by pressing the fabric with a dry or steam iron, depending on the product used.

GAUGE: The number of stitches and rows to the inch in a piece of knitted or crocheted material.

GRADE: To trim each seam allowance within a multilayer seam to a different width so as to reduce bulk and make the seam lie flat.

GRAIN: In woven fabric, grain is the direction of the threads: the warp (the threads running from one cut end to the other) forms the lengthwise grain; the woof, or weft (the threads running across the lengthwise grain from one finished edge to the other), forms the crosswise grain.

GRAIN-LINE ARROW: The double-ended arrow that is marked on a pattern piece to indicate how the piece should be aligned with the grains of the fabric.

HOOP: A pair of circular frames, one adjustable to fit snugly around the other, that holds fabric taut for embroidering or rug hooking.

INTERFACING: A special firm fabric or fusible nonwoven material attached between two layers of garment fabric to stiffen or strengthen parts of the garment.

LEATHER NEEDLE: A wedge-pointed needle used for sewing leather.

LINING: Fabric covering the inside of part or all of a garment.

MIRROR-IMAGE DUPLICATE PATTERN PIECE: A copy of a printed pattern piece used for cutting fabrics that should not be folded, or for making a continuous pattern for two identical, adjacent garment sections. The duplicate is made by cutting paper to the shape of the pattern piece, pinning the pieces together, placing dressmaker's carbon under them carbon side up and transferring all pattern markings to the paper. The duplicate is then labeled with the same number as the original and used marked side up. (If the original was to be laid out on a fold the duplicate is taped to the original before cutting.)

MITER: A diagonal fold at a corner.

NAP: On the surface of fabric or leather, the short fibers that are pulled and brushed in one direction. Pattern pieces for fabrics with nap are usually laid out and cut in one direction—with the nap.

NOTCH: A V- or diamond-shaped marking made on the edge of a garment piece as an alignment guide.

PASSEMENTERIE BRAID: Any decorative tubular braid that can be coiled into loops and arabesques and stitched to fabric.

PIVOT: A technique for machine stitching around angular corners by stopping the machine with the needle down at the apex of a corner, raising the presser foot, turning the fabric and then lowering the presser foot before continuing.

PRESHRINKING: The process of treating fabric to shrink it to an irreducible size before cutting. Washable fabric can be preshrunk simply by washing it as directed by the manufacturer.

PRESSER FOOT: The part of a sewing machine that holds down fabric while it is being stitched. A general-purpose foot has two prongs of equal length and is used for most stitching. A two-pronged even-feed foot, for use on machines that do zigzag stitching, has teeth on the bottom to move two or more layers of fuzzy, slippery or heavy fabric at the same speed. A zipper foot has only one prong and is used to stitch close to zippers and thick areas such as beaded pattern pieces and welting.

RUNNING STITCH: A hand-sewing stitch made by weaving a needle in and out of fabric at evenly spaced intervals, usually about 1/8 inch. A line of running stitches is usually ended with a fastening stitch.

SEAM ALLOWANCE: The extra fabric, usually 5/8 inch, that extends outside a seam line.

SEAM LINE (also called stitching line): The long broken line marked on a pattern to indicate where a seam must be stitched.

SEAM TAPE: A narrow flat tape of finishing fabric —usually 1/2 to 5/8 inch wide—used to reinforce seams or finish hems.

SELVAGE: The lengthwise finished edge in woven fabric.

SHIRRING: Decorative gathering of fabric, used primarily to control fullness.

STRAIGHTENING FABRIC: Woven fabrics that are not glazed or permanently treated are straightened crosswise by snipping into the selvage, pulling a crosswise thread and cutting along the pulled thread. (For certain projects, such as smocking, fabrics may also be straightened lengthwise by pulling and cutting along lengthwise threads.) To make sure the grain is straight, the fabric is then folded in half crosswise. If the edges do not align they are pinned together evenly and the fabric is steam-pressed toward the fold to straighten the grain, or the fabric is pulled at a diagonal from opposite selvage edges until the grain is straight.

TACKING STITCH: Several stitches made in the same place to hold pieces of fabric permanently in position.

TRACING WHEEL: A small revolving disk attached to a handle and used with dressmaker's carbon to transfer pattern markings to fabric.

TWILL TAPE: A thin, extrastrong tape of twilled cotton or polyester, usually 1/2 to 5/8 inch wide, used to reinforce seams.

WELTING: Fabric-covered cording with exposed seam allowances that can be sewed into seams for decoration and to reinforce edges.

BASIC STITCHES

The diagrams below and on the following pages demonstrate how to make the elementary hand-sewing, knitting and crocheting stitches referred to in this volume.

THE FASTENING STITCH

To end a row with a fastening stitch, insert the needle back 1/4 inch and bring it out at the point at which the thread last emerged. Make another stitch through these same points for extra firmness. To begin a row with a fastening stitch, leave a 4-inch loose end and make the initial stitch the same way as an ending stitch.

THE DIAGONAL BASTING STITCH

Anchor the basting with a fastening stitch *(above)* through all fabric layers. Keeping the thread to the right of the needle, make a 3/8-inch stitch from right to left, 1 inch directly below the fastening stitch. Continue making diagonal stitches, ending with a backstitch if the basting is to be left in, or a 4-inch-long loose end if the basting is to be removed.

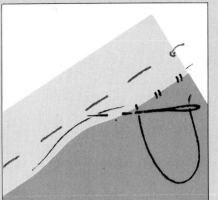

THE SLIP STITCH

Fold under the hem edge and anchor the first stitch with a knot inside the fold. Point the needle to the left. Pick up one or two threads of the garment fabric close to the hem edge, directly below the first stitch, and slide the needle horizontally through the folded edge of the hem 1/8 inch to the left of the previous stitch. Continue across in the same manner and end with a fastening stitch.

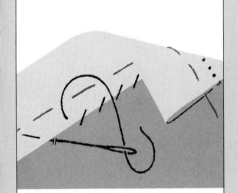

THE HEMMING STITCH

Anchor the first stitch with a knot inside the hem; then, pointing the needle up and to the left, pick up one or two threads of the garment fabric close to the hem. Push the needle up through the hem 1/8 inch above the edge; pull the thread through. Continue picking up one or two threads and making 1/8-inch stitches in the hem at intervals of 1/4 inch. End with a fastening stitch.

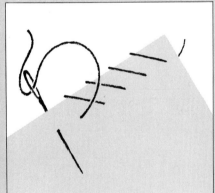

THE OVERCAST STITCH

Draw the needle, with knotted thread, through from the wrong side of the fabric 1/8 to 1/4 inch down from the top edge. With the thread to the right, insert the needle under the fabric from the wrong side 1/8 to 1/4 inch to the left of the first stitch. Continue to make evenly spaced stitches over the fabric edge and end with a fastening stitch.

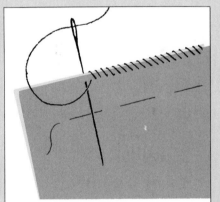

THE WHIPSTITCH

Using a knotted thread, draw the needle up from the bottom layer of fabric about 1/16 inch from the edge. Reinsert the needle, again from the bottom layer of fabric, about 1/16 inch to the left of the point from which the thread emerged, making sure the needle is at a right angle to the edge. Continue to make tiny, slanted, even stitches over the fabric edge. End with a fastening stitch.

KNITTING

CASTING ON STITCHES
1. Form a slipknot in the yarn, leaving a free end long enough for the number of stitches to be cast on (allow about 1 inch per stitch).

2. Slide a needle through the slipknot and hold the needle in your right hand. Loop the yarn attached to the ball over your right index finger and loop the free end of the yarn around your left thumb.

3. Insert the tip of the needle through the loop on your left thumb and bring the yarn attached to the ball under and over the needle from left to right.

4. Draw the tip of the needle back through the loop on your thumb, then slip the loop off your thumb. Pull the short end of the yarn down to tighten the loop, which is now a stitch. Repeat Steps 3 and 4 for the required number of stitches.

THE KNIT STITCH
1. Insert the right needle in the front of the stitch closest to the tip of the left needle, as shown. Bring the yarn under and over the right needle.

2. Pull the right needle back through the stitch, bringing with it the loop of yarn. Slide this loop—which is now a stitch—off the left needle and onto the right. Repeat Steps 1 and 2 for each knit stitch.

THE PURL STITCH
1. Insert the right needle into the stitch closest to the tip of the left needle, as shown. Bring the yarn around and under the right needle.

2. Push the needle back through the stitch, bringing with it the loop of yarn —which is now a stitch. Transfer this new stitch to the right needle, letting it slip off the left needle as you do so. Repeat Steps 1 and 2 for each purl stitch.

DECREASING STITCHES
1. Insert the right needle into two stitches instead of one, either from front to back as shown, for a knit stitch, or from back to front as for a purl stitch. Proceed as though you were knitting or purling one stitch at a time.

INCREASING STITCHES
1. On a knit row, insert the right needle through the back of a stitch. Knit the stitch, but do not drop it off the left needle.

2. Knit the same stitch in the ordinary way, and transfer the two stitches to the right needle.

1. On a purl row, insert the right needle from right to left through the horizontal loop at the bottom of a stitch. Make a purl stitch but do not let it slide off the left needle.

2. Now insert the right needle into the vertical loop above the horizontal one. Purl the stitch in the ordinary way, and slide both loops onto the right needle.

BINDING OFF STITCHES
1. Knit (or purl) two stitches. Then insert the left needle through the front of the second stitch from the tip of the right needle.

  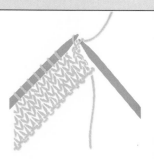

2. With the left needle, lift the second stitch on the right needle over the first stitch and let it drop.

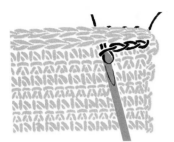

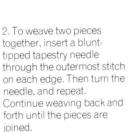

JOINING KNITTED AND CROCHETED PIECES

1. Knitted and crocheted garments can be seamed by crocheting, weaving or sewing. For all three, place the edges together, wrong sides out, and align the stitches and rows. To crochet pieces together, insert a crochet hook through the first stitch on each edge, and draw a loop of new yarn through both stitches. Repeat on each pair of stitches, drawing the new loop through the loop on the hook.

2. To weave two pieces together, insert a blunt-tipped tapestry needle through the outermost stitch on each edge. Then turn the needle, and repeat. Continue weaving back and forth until the pieces are joined.

3. To sew two pieces together, insert a blunt-tipped tapestry needle through both pieces 1/4 inch below the aligned edges. Leaving a long end of yarn, insert the needle 1/4 inch to the right of the first stitch, and bring it out, from back to front, 1/4 inch to the left of the first stitch. Continue making stitches in this manner along the edges.

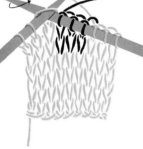
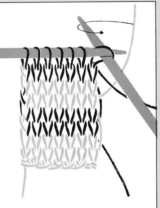

PICKING UP A DROPPED COLOR

1. On a knit row, reach under and behind the second color that you have been working to pick up the first color that you dropped earlier. Bring the strand of the first color forward and under the second color, and proceed to knit.

2. On a purl row, reach over and behind the first color and pick up the second color. Bring the strand under the first color and forward, and proceed to purl.

3. To carry a color from row to row, pick up the first color from where it was dropped on an earlier row in the same way you would in the middle of the row—from underneath, if you are beginning a knit row, as shown; or from over and behind if you are beginning a purl row.

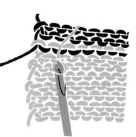
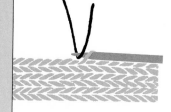

JOINING YARN
1. Wrap the new yarn around the working needle, leaving a long end. Use the new yarn to knit the next stitch. Break off the previous color if your instructions so indicate, leaving a long end.

2. After knitting two or three rows with the new yarn, use a crochet hook to weave the loose ends of yarn through nearby stitches on the wrong side of the work.

PICKING UP STITCHES AT AN EDGE
1. To pick up stitches along a finished edge, as when you intend to add ribbing, start by inserting the needle into the first stitch to be picked up. Then wrap another strand of yarn around the needle; draw the yarn through the stitch.

2. Continue in this manner along the edge, drawing the yarn through each successive stitch to be picked up.

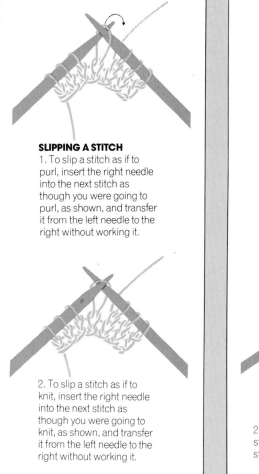

SLIPPING A STITCH
1. To slip a stitch as if to purl, insert the right needle into the next stitch as though you were going to purl, as shown, and transfer it from the left needle to the right without working it.

2. To slip a stitch as if to knit, insert the right needle into the next stitch as though you were going to knit, as shown, and transfer it from the left needle to the right without working it.

PASSING A SLIPPED STITCH OVER
1. To pass a slipped stitch over one or more stitches knitted or purled in the ordinary way, start by inserting the left needle into the stitch that was slipped onto the right needle.

2. Then bring the slipped stitch over the stitch—or stitches—behind it.

3. Drop the slipped stitch off the right needle.

CROCHETING

THE CHAIN STITCH

1. Form a loose slipknot around the crochet hook, about 1 inch from the end of the yarn. Grasp the yarn attached to the ball with the tip of the hook and pull the yarn through the slipknot with the tip of the hook, as shown.

2. Hold the hook in your right hand much like a pencil. Place the yarn from the ball around the left little finger, then up and over the left index finger. Grasp the free end of the yarn between the thumb and middle finger of the left hand.

3. With your left index finger, bring the yarn from the back to the front of the hook and catch it under the tip of the hook.

4. Pull the tip of the hook through the loop in the hook, bringing the yarn with it to create the first chain stitch in the foundation chain. Repeat Steps 3 and 4 to form a chain of the desired length.

THE SINGLE CROCHET STITCH

1. To single crochet the first row after a foundation chain, insert the hook through the second chain stitch from the hook (arrow)—do not count the loop on the hook.

2. With two loops now on the hook, bring the yarn over the hook from back to front and catch it under the tip as shown. Then draw the yarn caught under the tip through the loop closest to the tip.

3. Bring the yarn over the hook again and draw it through both of the loops that were on the hook; there is now only a single loop on the hook. Insert the crochet hook into the next chain stitch and repeat Step 2. At the end of each row, chain 1 stitch if the next row is to be worked in single crochet, 2 stitches for a double crochet pattern and 3 stitches for a triple crochet pattern.

4. Turn the work to crochet back across the previous row. Insert the hook through both loops of the second stitch from the edge, as shown, and all subsequent stitches on this and all rows after the foundation chain.

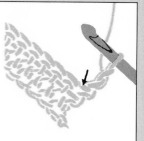

THE DOUBLE CROCHET STITCH

1. To double crochet the first row of stitches after a foundation chain, chain 2 and count back to the third chain stitch from the hook (*arrow*)—do not count the loop on the hook. Swing the yarn over the hook from back to front, then insert the hook through this third chain stitch.

2. Bring the yarn over the hook again and draw it through the loop closest to the tip. Bring the yarn over the hook again and draw it through the two loops closest to the tip.

3. Bring the yarn over the tip again and draw it through the remaining two loops on the hook. At the end of each row, chain one stitch if the next row is to be worked in single crochet, two stitches for double crochet and three stitches for triple crochet.

4. Turn the work to crochet back across the previous row. Bring the yarn over the hook and insert the hook through both loops of the first stitch from the edge (*arrow*) on this and all rows after the first.

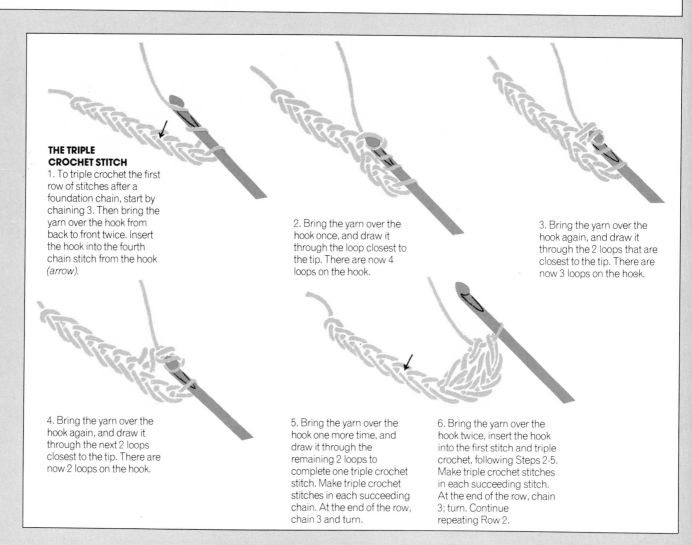

THE TRIPLE CROCHET STITCH

1. To triple crochet the first row of stitches after a foundation chain, start by chaining 3. Then bring the yarn over the hook from back to front twice. Insert the hook into the fourth chain stitch from the hook (*arrow*).

2. Bring the yarn over the hook once, and draw it through the loop closest to the tip. There are now 4 loops on the hook.

3. Bring the yarn over the hook again, and draw it through the 2 loops that are closest to the tip. There are now 3 loops on the hook.

4. Bring the yarn over the hook again, and draw it through the next 2 loops closest to the tip. There are now 2 loops on the hook.

5. Bring the yarn over the hook one more time, and draw it through the remaining 2 loops to complete one triple crochet stitch. Make triple crochet stitches in each succeeding chain. At the end of the row, chain 3 and turn.

6. Bring the yarn over the hook twice, insert the hook into the first stitch and triple crochet, following Steps 2-5. Make triple crochet stitches in each succeeding stitch. At the end of the row, chain 3; turn. Continue repeating Row 2.

JOINING YARN

1. Join a new ball of yarn at the beginning of a row by drawing it through the first loop; leave a 1-inch-long end. Join a new color at the end of a row, working the last two loops on the hook with the new yarn.

2. When you have crocheted two or three rows, weave the loose ends of the yarn through nearby stitches with the crochet hook.

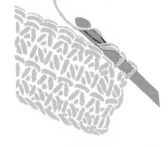

DECREASING STITCHES, SINGLE CROCHET

1. To decrease in a row of single crochet stitches, insert the hook into both loops of a stitch. Bring the yarn over the hook and draw it through the two loops closest to the tip; this leaves two loops on the hook.

2. Insert the hook through both loops of the next stitch. Bring the yarn over the hook and draw it through the two loops closest to the tip. Bring the yarn over the hook again and draw it through the three remaining loops on the hook.

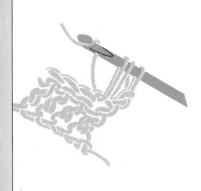

DECREASING STITCHES, DOUBLE CROCHET

1. To decrease in a row of double crochet stitches, bring the yarn over the hook and insert it through both loops of a stitch. Bring the yarn over the hook again, as shown, and draw it through the two loops closest to the tip. Then bring the yarn over the hook again and insert it through both loops of the next stitch.

2. Again bring the yarn over the hook and draw it through the two loops closest to the tip, as shown; there are now five loops on the hook. Bring the yarn over the hook again and draw it through the two loops now closest to the tip. Repeat the process until there are three loops remaining on the hook. Then pull the yarn through the three remaining loops.

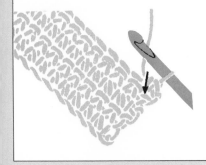

INCREASING STITCHES

To increase stitches, work one stitch—either a single, double or triple crochet, as called for in the instructions —then insert the crochet hook back into the same loop or loops (*arrow*) and repeat the stitch.

FASTENING OFF

Cut the yarn from the ball, leaving a 2-inch-long end. Pull this end through the loop on the hook to secure it and weave it through one or two nearby stitches.

TRANSFERRING DESIGNS

TRACING A DESIGN

1. Tape the drawing, print or photograph to be traced to a table top or board. Center a sheet of tracing paper over the design and tape it at the top.

2. Trace the design with a fine-tipped black pen.

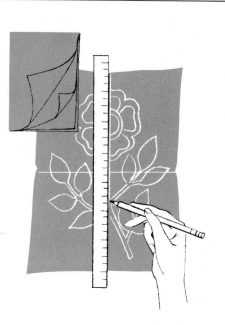

3. Remove the tracing and fold it into quarters.

4. Unfold it and lightly mark the fold lines with a ruler and pencil.

ENLARGING OR REDUCING A DESIGN

1. Trace the design onto a square piece of paper—it must be square to preserve proportions in rectangular designs—and fold the tracing in half across its width, then across its length. Unfold and fold it in quarters and eighths across its width and length to make a grid with eight squares on each side. (For an elaborate design, the paper may be folded into a 16-square grid.) With a ruler and pencil draw lines along the fold marks.

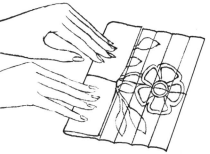

2. Identify horizontal and vertical coordinates as on a map, by penciling letters (A to H) along the top and numbers (1 to 8) down the side.

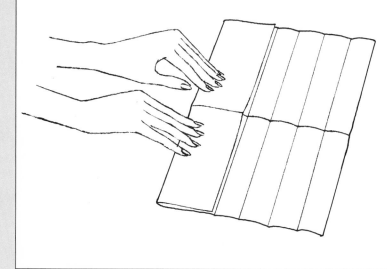

3. Cut a sheet of drawing paper into a square about the size you want the design to be.

4. Fold it just as you folded the original and pencil in the same lines and coordinates.

5. Using the coordinates to locate matching squares, copy the design freehand, square by square.

6. Transfer the enlarged or reduced design as shown opposite.

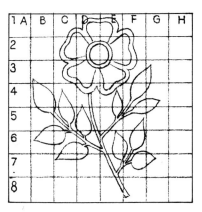

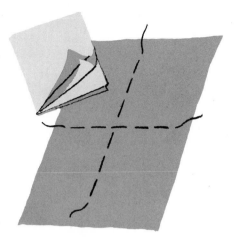

TRANSFERRING A DESIGN TO FABRIC

1. Fold the fabric into quarters and crease the fold lines with your fingers or an iron.

2. Unfold the fabric and baste along the creases, taking long stitches on the visible side for easily followed guide lines.

3. Tape the fabric, wrong side down, to the work surface.

4. Lay the paper tracing over the fabric, aligning its center fold lines with the basting on the fabric, and tape the tracing down along the top. At the bottom corners, put tabs of tape that can easily be lifted as you work.

5. Insert dressmaker's carbon paper, carbon side down, between the tracing or enlarged or reduced drawing and the fabric. (If the carbon paper is smaller than the design, move it as you work.)

6. Trace the design with a dull pencil, pressing hard. From time to time lift the paper and check that the design is coming through distinctly on the fabric. Avoid smudging by working from top to bottom. Remove the fabric and baste around the edges to prevent fraying.

TRACING A DESIGN ONTO CANVAS

1. Cut a piece of canvas at least 2 or 3 inches larger than your design on each side. Fold it in quarters; then unfold it and mark the fold lines with a pencil.

2. Place the tracing under the canvas and align the marked center fold lines on the design with the fold lines made on the canvas in Step 1. Tape the tracing and the canvas in place with masking tape.

3. Trace the design directly onto the canvas with a fine-tipped pen and indelible ink, which will not rub off or stain the finished work. (You may want to use several colors of indelible ink as a helpful stitching guide.) Minor details may be drawn on the canvas freehand or be stitched in at will. Draw a border limiting the area of the design.

4. Remove the canvas from the design and attach masking tape to the edges to prevent the canvas from unraveling as you work.

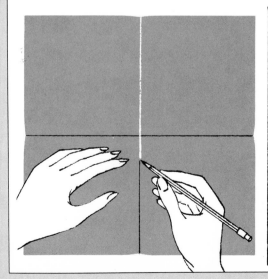

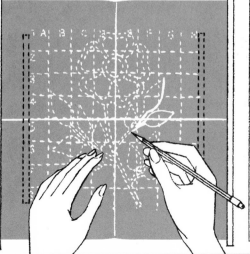

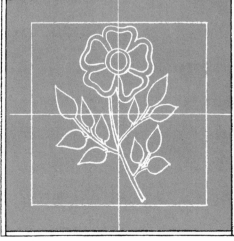

CREDITS

Sources for illustrations and fashions in this book are shown below. Credits from left to right are separated by semicolons, from top to bottom by dashes.

ILLUSTRATIONS: Cover—Fabric by Corhan Fabrics, Inc. 6,7—Ryszard Horowitz. 11—Henry Groskinsky; Sherman Hines. 12,13—Norman Mosallem. 14 through 17—Ryszard Horowitz. 18,19—Susan Wood. 22—Susan Wood. 23 through 31—Drawings by Raymond Skibinski. 32—Susan Wood. 33 through 39—Drawings by Raymond Skibinski. 40—Susan Wood. 41 through 45—Drawings by Raymond Skibinski. 46—Susan Wood. 47 through 53—Drawings by John Sagan. 54—Susan Wood. 55 through 63—Drawings by John Sagan. 64 through 69—Norman Mosallem. 70 through 75—Drawings by John Sagan. 76,77—Norman Mosallem. 78 through 83—Drawings by John Sagan. 84,85—Norman Mosallem. 86 through 89—Drawings by John Sagan. 90 through 95—Richard Jeffery. 96 through 101—Drawings by John Sagan. 102,103—Richard Jeffery. 104,105—Drawings by Raymond Skibinski. 107—Design, copyright O. Oehlenschläger's Eftr. Copenhagen. 108,109—Richard Jeffery. 110 through 125—Drawings by Raymond Skibinski. 126,127—Richard Jeffery. 128 through 135—Drawings by Raymond Skibinski. 136 through 141—Susan Wood. 143 through 149—Drawings by Jean Held. 150,151—Susan Wood. 152,153—Drawings by Raymond Skibinski. 156,157—Susan Wood. 158 through 162—Drawings by Jean Held. 165,166—Drawings by John Sagan. 167—Drawings by John Sagan—Drawings by Carolyn Mazzello. 168—Drawings by John Sagan—Drawings by Carolyn Mazzello. 169 through 171—Drawings by John Sagan. 172—Drawings by Raymond Skibinski—Drawings by John Sagan. 173—Drawings by Raymond Skibinski—Drawings by John Sagan.

FASHIONS: 6,7—Passementerie by the Gelberg Braid Co., Inc.—cathedral-window patchwork fabric by Frederica Siegelbaum. 12,13—Hooked rug designed by Steve DiFranza, made by Happy DiFranza; beaded vest designed by Oria Douglas-Hamilton, made in the Ol'Oria Workshop, Naivasha, Kenya; pillow from Moon Over the Mountain at Patch Works; hairpin-lace place mat from Suttles and Seawinds; spoon from Fortunoff Fine Jewelry and Silverware, Inc.; glassware from Crystal Clear. 14,15—Pillow from The Gazebo; purse made by Shirley Botsford. 16,17—Shawl from Cherchez; pillow from La Provence de Pierre Deux; napkin courtesy Pauline Fischer Needlework Collection; napkin ring from La Provence de Pierre Deux. 22—Hat made by Toni Scott. 32—Patchwork technique and vest created by Toni Scott—glassware from Crystal Clear. Reverse appliqué designed and made by Shirley Botsford. 65—Needlepoint band courtesy Pauline Fischer Needlework Collection. 68,69—Chamois vest by Melissa Greenberg at Namas de Leather; red vest by Pat Sukhaprayura, passementerie by the Gelberg Braid Co., Inc. Black dress from Jax New York, Inc. 76—Beaded purse by Rose Gambino at Barbara Matera, Ltd. 84,85—Scarf top designed and made by Nancy Kotkin of Nani's Nowhere Else, scarves from Baar & Beards, Inc. 90,91—Lampshade frames from Whitehall-Hoffman. 94,95—Bench cover and rug design by Steve DiFranza. Bench cover made by Happy DiFranza; rug by Susanna Cuyler. Bench from Dalmar A. Tifft. 102,103—Embroidery by Marianne Papaj, design copyright O. Oehlenschläger's Eftr. Copenhagen, basket from Clipper Industries, Inc. 108,109—Pillows made by Delta Upholsterers, Inc., fabric from La Provence de Pierre Deux. 126,127—Pleated lampshade from Fabrications; smocked lampshade made by Toni Scott, fabric from Patch Works. 140,141—Socks knitted by Annette Feldman. 150,151—Place mats crocheted by Annette Feldman; glassware from Crystal Clear. 156,157—Lace purse and hat made by Annette Feldman.

ACKNOWLEDGMENTS

Special consultants for this book were: Henrietta Blau, Delta Upholsterers (pillows); Shirley Botsford (appliqué); Susanna Cuyler (latch hooking); Happy and Steve DiFranza (rug hooking); Gelberg Braid Co., Inc. (fringe and passementerie); Judith Glassman (beading); Julia Hammelcourt (beading); Grace Hoeven, Whitehall-Hoffman (lampshades); Barbara Matera, Ltd. (beading); Marianne Papaj (embroidery); Norma E. Pelletier (rug hooking); Toni Scott (piecing and smocking).

For their help in the preparation of this book the editors would like to thank the following individuals: *in Bridgeport, Connecticut:* Joe Rifkin, Flecto Products; *in Charleston, West Virginia:* Sharon Percy Rockefeller; *in Eastville, Virginia:* Mittie Moore; *in New Germany, Nova Scotia:* Vicki Lynn Crowe, Suttles and Seawinds; *in New York City:* Lou Bogner, Joanna Western Mills Company; Harry Dennis, New York State Craftsmen, Inc.; Rose Gambino; Ginetta Giaccio; Nancy Kotkin; John Kraus, Shade Magic; Ursula Kraus, Spinnerin Yarn Co., Inc.; Jill Losson; Renny Malfatti; Vicki Mileti, Simplicity Pattern Co., Inc.; Lois Moran, American Crafts Council; Mary Palu; Territa Percelay, Craft Yarns of Rhode Island; Franklin Rizzo, Gelberg Braid Co., Inc.; Dnorah Ronero; Christine Roth; Hilda Sachs, Window Shade Manufacturers Association; Julie Schafler, Julie: Artisans' Gallery; Melpo Theodoro; Elizabeth Tobin, Museum of American Folk Art; Cecelia K. Toth; Ruth Vitow; Hilde Walborg Weinberg, Walborg Handbag Import Corporation.

The editors would also like to thank the following organizations: *in Chicago, Illinois:* The Boye Needle Co.; *in New York City:* American Indian Arts Center; Butterick Fashion Marketing Company; Fabrications; The Gazebo; M & J Trimming Co.; New York Exchange for Women's Work; Threadbare Unlimited.

INDEX
Numerals in italics indicate an illustration of the subject mentioned.